SUBJECT CATALOGING DIVISION
PROCESSING SERVICES
LIBRARY OF CONGRESS

CLASSIFICATION

CLASS B

SUBCLASSES BL, BM, BP, BQ

Religion:
Religions, Hinduism, Judaism, Islam, Buddhism

THIRD EDITION

LIBRARY OF CONGRESS
WASHINGTON 1984

The additions and changes in Class B, Subclasses BL, BM, BP, BQ adopted while this work was in press will be cumulated and printed in List 218 of LC Classification—Additions and Changes

Library of Congress Cataloging in Publication Data

Library of Congress. Subject Cataloging Division.
Classification class B, subclasses BL, BM, BP, BQ, religion.

Includes index.
Supt. of Docs. no.: LC 26.9:B/985
1. Classification—Books—Religion. 2. Classification—Books—Religions. 3. Classification—Books—Theology. 4. Classification, Library of Congress.
I. Title.
Z696.U5B2 1984 025.4'62 84-600334
ISBN 0-8444-0489-6

For sale by the Cataloging Distribution Service,
Library of Congress, Washington, D.C. 20541

PREFACE

The first edition of the schedule for religion (Class B, Part II: BL–BX) was published in 1927, after application to some 105,000 volumes over a 10-year period. The second edition was published in 1962, including all additions and changes adopted through March 1960.

The increase in the size of the schedule, especially with the development of BQ, Buddhism, required that this third edition be published in three volumes. These are: *BL–BQ, Religion: Religions, Hinduism, Judaism, Islam, Buddhism; BR–BV, Religion: Christianity, Bible;* and *BX, Religion: Christian denominations.* It is expected that BX will be published in 1986, followed by BR–BV. These three volumes will take the place of the previous single volume.

This edition represents a cumulated edition, incorporating the additions and changes made since 1960. The BQ subclass for Buddhism was developed by Kenneth Tanaka and printed in *Additions and Changes* List 168, 1972, where names of sacred texts were accompanied by the handwritten Chinese characters. The expanded and redesigned development for Hinduism (BL1100–1295) was prepared by Kio Kanda, subject cataloger. Other changes from the previous edition are editorial in nature and include the deletion of many parenthesized numbers, the updating of terminology, and the arranging of notes and references to conform to current practice.

The editorial work for this edition was done by Elizabeth Blomeyer, assistant editor of classification and Lawrence Buzard, editor of classification.

Mary K. D. Pietris, Chief
Subject Cataloging Division

Henriette D. Avram, Assistant
Librarian for Processing Service

SYNOPSIS

BL RELIGIONS. MYTHOLOGY. RATIONALISM

BM JUDAISM

BP ISLAM. BAHAISM. THEOSOPHY, ETC.

BQ BUDDHISM

OUTLINE

BL — RELIGIONS. MYTHOLOGY. RATIONALISM

1-50	Religion (General)
51-65	Religion in relation to special subjects
70-71	Sacred books (General)
71.5-72	Biography
74-98	Religions of the world
175-290	Natural theology
175-190	General
200	Theism
205-215	Nature and attributes of Deity
217	Polytheism
218	Dualism
220	Pantheism
221	Monotheism
224-226	Creation. Theory of the earth
239-265	Religion and science
270	Unity and plurality
290	The soul
300-325	The myth. Comparative mythology
350-385	Classification of religions
410	Religions in relation to one another
425-490	Religious doctrines (General)
430	Origins of religion
435-457	Nature worship
458	Women in comparative religion
460	Sex worship. Phallicism
465-470	Worship of human beings
473-490	Other
500-547	Eschatology
550-619	Worship. Cultus
624-627	Religious life
630-632.5	Religious organization
660-2670	History and principles of religions
660	Indo-European. Aryan
685	Ural-Altaic
687	Mediterranean region
690-980	European. Occidental
700-820	Classical (Etruscan, Greek, Roman)
830-875	Germanic and Norse
900-980	Other European

BL RELIGIONS. MYTHOLOGY. RATIONALISM

OUTLINE

BM	JUDAISM
534-538	Relation of Judaism to special subject fields
534-536	Religions
545-582	Principles of Judaism (General)
585-585.2	Controversial works against the Jews
590-591	Jewish works against Christianity and Islam
600-645	Dogmatic Judaism
646	Heresy, heresies
648	Apologetics
650-747	Practical Judaism
651-652.7	Priests, rabbis, etc.
653-653.7	Congregations. Synagogues
654-655.6	The tabernacle. The temple
656-657	Forms of worship
660-679	Liturgy and ritual
690-695	Festivals and fasts
700-720	Rites and customs
723-729	Jewish way of life. Spiritual life. Personal religion
730-747	Preaching. Homiletics
750-755	Biography
900-990	Samaritans

BP	ISLAM. BAHAISM. THEOSOPHY, ETC.
1-253	Islam
1-68	General
42-48	Study and teaching
50-68	History
70-80	Biography
75-77.75	Muḥammad, d. 632
87-89	Islamic literature
100-137.5	Sacred books
100-134	Koran
128.15-129.83	Special parts and chapters
130-134	Works about the Koran
135-136.9	Hadith literature. Traditions. Sunna
137-137.5	Koranic and other Islamic legends

BP — ISLAM. BAHAISM. THEOSOPHY, ETC.

	Islam - Continued
160-165	General works on Islam
165.5	Dogma ('Agā'id)
166-166.94	Theology (Kalam)
167.5	Heresy, heresies
168	Apostasy from Islam
169	Works against Islam and the Koran
170	Works in defense of Islam. Islamic apologetics
170.2	Benevolent work. Social work. Welfare work, etc.
170.3-170.5	Missionary work of Islam
171-173	Relation of Islam to other religions
173.25-173.45	Islamic sociology
174-190	The practice of Islam
176-181	The five duties of a Moslem
182	Jihad (Holy War)
184-184.9	Religious ceremonies, rites, etc.
186-186.97	Special days and seasons, fasts, feasts, festivals, etc.
187-187.9	Shrines, sacred places, etc.
188-190	Islamic religious life
188.2-188.3	Devotional literature
188.45-189.65	Sufism. Mysticism. Dervishes
189.68-189.7	Monasticism
191-253	Branches, sects, etc.
192-194.9	Shiites
221-223	Black Muslims
231-233	Moorish Science Temple of America
251-253	Nurculuk
300-395	Bahaism
500-585	Theosophy
595-597	Anthroposophy
600-610	Other beliefs and movements

BQ — BUDDHISM

1-10	Periodicals. Yearbooks (General)
12-93	Societies, councils, associations, clubs, etc.
96-99	Financial institutions. Trusts
100-102	Congresses. Conferences (General)
104-105	Directories (General)

BQ	BUDDHISM
107-109	Museums. Exhibitions
115-126	General collections. Collected works
128	Encyclopedias (General)
130	Dictionaries (General)
133	Terminology
135	Questions and answers. Maxims (General)
141-209	Religious education (General)
210-219	Research
221-249	Antiquities. Archaeology
240-244	Literary discoveries
246-249	Inscriptions, etc.
257-799	History
800-829	Persecutions
	Biography
840-858	Collective
	Individual
860-939	Gautama Buddha
940-999	Other
1001-1045	Buddhist literature
1100-3340	Tripiṭaka (Canonical literature)
4000-4060	General works. Treatises
4061-4570	Doctrinal and systematic Buddhism
4180-4565	Special doctrines
4570	Special topics and relations to special subjects
4600-4610	Relations to other religious and philosophical systems
4620-4905	Buddhist pantheon
4911-5720	Practice of Buddhism. Forms of worship
4965-5030	Ceremonies and rites. Ceremonial rules
5035-5065	Hymns. Chants. Recitations
5070-5075	Altar, liturgical objects, ornaments, memorials, etc.
5080-5085	Vestments, altar cloths, etc.
5090-5095	Liturgical functions
5100-5125	Symbols and symbolism
5130-5137	Temple. Temple organization
5140-5355	Buddhist ministry. Priesthood. Organization
5251-5305	Education and training
5310-5350	Preaching

BQ	BUDDHISM
	Practice of Buddhism. Forms of worship - Cont.
5360-5680	Religious life
5485-5530	Precepts for laymen
5535-5594	Devotional literature. Meditations. Prayers
5595-5633	Devotion. Meditation. Prayer
5635-5675	Mysticism. Enlightenment. Perfection
5700-5720	Festivals. Days and seasons
5725-5845	Folklore of Buddhism
5821-5845	Miracle literature
5851-5899	Benevolent work, social work, welfare work, etc.
5901-5975	Missionary work
6001-6160	Monasticism and monastic life. Saṃgha (Order)
6200-6240	Asceticism. Hermits. Wayfaring life
6300-6388	Monasteries. Temples. Shrines. Sites
6400-6495	Pilgrims and pilgrimages
7001-9800	Modifications, schools, etc.
7100-7285	Theravāda (Hinayāna) Buddhism
7300-7524	Mahāyāna Buddhism
7530-7950	Lamaism
7960-7989	Bonpo (Sect)
8000-9800	Special modifications, sects, etc.
8500-8769	Pure Land Buddhism
8900-9099	Tantric Buddhism
9250-9519	Zen Buddhism

RELIGION

	Periodicals. Serials
1.A1A-Z	International or polyglot
.A2-Z	English and American
2	Dutch
3	French
4	German
5	Italian
6	Scandinavian
7	Spanish and Portuguese
9	Other languages, A-Z
10	Yearbooks
11-19	Societies Subarranged like BL1-9
21	Congresses
	Collected works Including monographs, papers, essays, etc.
25	Several authors
27	Individual authors
29	Selections
31	Dictionaries. Encyclopedias
35	Directories
41	Study of comparative religion. Historiography. Methodology
	Religious education
42	General works
.5	By region or country, A-Z
43	Biography of students and historians, A-Z
	Museums. Exhibitions
45	General works
46	Individual, A-Z Subarranged by place or name
48	General works
50	Addresses, essays, lectures
51	Philosophy of religion. Philosophy and religion Cf. BD573, Philosophy and religion
	Psychology of religion. Religious experience Cf. BP175, Islam BR110, Christianity HQ61, Religious emotion and eroticism
53.A1	Periodicals. Societies. Serials
.A2-Z	General works
54	Glossolalia. Gift of tongues Cf. BT122.5, Glossolalia or tongues as one of the gifts of the Holy Spirit

Religion - Continued
55 Religion and civilization
Religion and ethics, see BJ47
Religion and literature, see PN49; PN1077; PR145; PR830.R5; etc.
Religion and science, see BL239+
60 Religion and sociology
65 Religion in relation to other subjects, A-Z
Cf. BR115+, Christianity in relation to other subjects
.A4 Aesthetics
Art, see N72.R4
.A85 Atomic warfare
.C58 Civil rights
The comic, see .L3
.C7 Crime. Criminals
Cf. HV8865+, Provision for religious and moral instruction of prisoners (Administrative aspects)
.C8 Culture

.D7 Drugs. Hallucinogenic drugs
Economics, see HB72
.G4 Geography
Hallucionogenic drugs, see .D7
Health, see .M4

.H5 History
.H8 Humanities (General)
Cf. N72.R4, Religion and visual art
PN49, Religion and literature
Humor, see .L3
Hygiene, see .M4

.H9 Hypnotism
.I55 International affairs
.J87 Justice
.L2 Language

.L3 Laughter. The comic. Wit and humor
.L33 Law
.M2 Magic
.M4 Medicine. Health. Hygiene

.N3 Nationalism
Cf. BV629+, Church and state
.N35 Nature
Cf. BL435+, Nature worship
GF80, Religious aspects of human ecology

Religion

65 Religion in relation to other subjects, A-Z - Continued

.P3 Parapsychology

.P4 Peace

.P7 Politics

.R3 Race

Science, see BL239+

.S4 Sex

.S8 The state

.S85 Suffering

Technology, see BL265.T4

.U5 Underdeveloped areas

Utopias, see HX807

.W2 War

Wit and humor, see .L3

Sacred books (General)

Cf. BL1010, Ancient oriental religions

70 Collected works

71 History and criticism

e. g. Leblois' Les bibles

Biography

.5 History and criticism

72 Collective

Religions of the world

Including historical and comparative works

74 Collected works

e. g. Fontes historiae religionum

Cf. BL70, Sacred books

General works

75 Early through 1800

80 1801-1950

.2 1951-

82 Handbooks, manuals, etc.

85 General special

87 Addresses, essays, lectures

90 Pictorial works

92 Juvenile works

95 Outlines, syllabi, etc.

History (By period)

Cf. GN470+, Religion of primitive peoples

For early works, see BL75

For Christianity, see BR

Origins of religion, see BL430

96 Ancient

97 Medieval

98 Modern

Religion - Continued
100 Religion and the supernatural
Cf. BT960+, Invisible world
Natural theology
175 Collected works
e. g. Bridgewater treatises
.B7 Collected. By date
.B81-88 Miscellaneous volumes. By number and date
General works
180 Early through 1800
181 1801-1950
182 1951-

185 Juvenile works
190 Insufficiency of natural theology
200 Theism
Including belief in God apart from revelation
Cf. BL51, Philosophy of religion
BL2700+, Rationalism, deism, etc.
BT98+, Christian doctrine of God

Nature and attributes of Deity
Cf. BT98+, Doctrinal theology
205 General works
210 Analogies and correspondences
215 Anthropomorphism
217 Polytheism
218 Dualism
220 Pantheism
221 Monotheism
Cf. BT98+, Doctrinal theology
Creation. Theory of the earth
Cf. BD493+, Cosmology
BL263, Evolution
BS651, Genesis and science
BT695+, Doctrinal theology
General works
224 Early through 1800
225 1801-1950
226 1951-

Providence
Cf. BT135, Doctrinal theology
230 General works
235 Fatalism. Destiny
237 Religion and the intellectual

Religion
Natural theology - Continued
Religion and science
Cf. BT1095+, Apologetics
General works
239 Early through 1800
240 1801-1950
.2 1951-

241 Addresses, essays, lectures
243 Juvenile works
245 Conflict of science and religion
Special sciences
250 Archaeology
Astronomy
253 General works
254 Astronautics

256 Ethnology. Anthropology
259 Geology
Natural history
262 General works
263 Evolution
Cf. BS659, Bible and evolution
GN281+, Human evolution
QH361+, General biology

265 Other, A-Z
.C4 Chemistry
.E6 Electricity
.L5 Light

.M3 Mathematics
Medicine, see BL65.M4
.P4 Physics
.T4 Technology

270 Unity and plurality
Good and evil, see BJ1400+
Evil, see BJ1406+
Prayer, adoration, see BL560

Sacrifice, see BL570
290 The soul
Cf. BD419+, Philosophy
BT740+, Doctrinal theology
Future life, see BL535+

Religion - Continued

The myth. Comparative mythology

Cf. GR, Folklore

300 Periodicals. Societies. Serials
301 Congresses
303 Dictionaries

304 Myth. The nature of myth

General works

305 Early through 1800
310 1801-1950
311 1951-

313 General special
315 Addresses, essays, lectures
320 Study and teaching

325 Topics in comparative mythology, A-Z

.A35 Agriculture
.A6 Animals
.B45 Bisexuality. Androgyny. Hermaphroditism
.B5 Blood
.C7 Creation
Darkness, see .L47
.D33 Days of the week
.D35 The dead

.D4 Deluge
.E3 Eagle
.E35 Eclipses
.E4 Edens

Evil, see .G58
.E93 Eye
.F3 Fall of man
.F35 Fathers
.F4 Female deities. Nymphs. Fairies, etc.
Cf. BL325.L5, Lilith

.F5 Fire
.F6 Fleeing
.G5 Giants
.G58 Good and evil

.G6 Gorgons
Great mother of the gods, see BL820.C8
.G7 Griffins
.H23 Hand

Religion
The myth. Comparative mythology
325 Topics in comparative mythology, A-Z - Continued
.H25 Head
.H3 Headless gods
.H4 Healing deities
Hermaphroditism, see .B45
.H46 Heroes
Cf. GR515, Heroes in folklore
.I5 Incubation
.K5 Kings and rulers
Cf. GR520, Kings in folklore

.L3 Labyrinths
.L4 Leadership
.L47 Light and darkness
.L5 Lilith

.M3 Matriarchy
.M35 Mensuration
.M4 Metamorphosis
.M5 Mice

.M56 The moon
Cf. BL438, Moon worship
.M6 Mother-goddesses
.M63 Mountains

.N35 Navel
.N5 Night
.O4 Oedipus
.O74 Order

.P45 Phoenix
Cf. GR830.P4, Folklore
.P6 Plants
.P7 Polarity. Opposites

.R2 Rainbow
.R6 Rome
.S3 Samson
.S5 Sky-gods

.S7 Spirals
.S8 The sun
Cf. BL438, Sun worship
.T45 Thirteen (The number)

Religion
The myth. Comparative mythology
325 Topics in comparative mythology, A-Z - Continued
.T8 Twins
Cf. BL820.C2, Castor and Pollux

.V5 Virgin birth
.V55 Virginity
.W45 Wheels

Classification of religions
350 General works
355 Polytheistic
360 Monotheistic
365 Revealed
Preliterate peoples (General), see GN470+

380 Ethnic
385 National

390 Proposed, universal, or world religions
410 Religions in relation to one another
For Christianity in relation to other religions, see BR127+

Religious doctrines (General)
425 General works
430 Origins of religion
Cf. GN470.5, Preliterate peoples

Nature worship
Including religious interpretations of nature
435 General works
438 Celestial bodies. Sun, moon, stars
Cf. BL325.M56, The moon in comparative mythology
BL325.S8, The sun in comparative mythology
.2 Earth
Animals
Cf. GR820+, Mythical animals
439 General works
440 Crocodile
441 Serpent
442 Birds

Religion
Religious doctrines (General)
Nature worship
Animals - Continued
443 Other, A-Z
e. g. .B4 Bears
.B8 Bulls
.C3 Cats

.H6 Horses
.L6 Llamas
444 Plants. Trees
Cf. BL583, Sacred wood and field cults
447 Mountains
450 Water
453 Fire

457 Other, A-Z
e. g. .C3 Caduceus
.C6 Corn
.E3 Earthquakes
.H3 Hawthorn

.M4 Metals
.S7 Stones (Sacred)
.S75 Storms
.W5 Wine

458 Woman in comparative religion
Cf. BL325.F4, Female deities, etc., in comparative religion
460 Sex worship. Phallicism
Cf. BL65.S4, Sex in religion
BL441, Serpent worship
BL444, Tree worship

Worship of human beings. Apotheosis. Superman
465 General works
Cult of the Roman emperors, see DG124

467 Ancestor worship
470 Worship of the dead. Fear of the dead
473 Gods
Cf. GR500+, Supernatural beings (Folklore)

.5 Goddesses
474 Trinities

Religion
Religious doctrines (General) - Continued
475 Saviors. Messiahs
.5 Revelation
476 Redemption. Salvation
.5 Reconciliation
477 Angels. Good spirits
Cf. BT965+, Doctrinal theology
478 Cherubim
480 Demons. Evil spirits. Devil worship
For individual religions, see BL1456.7; BP166.89; BT975; etc.
Cf. BF1501+, Demonology
BL1595, Yezidis
GR525+, Demonology (Folkore)

482 Spirit possession
485 Idolatry. Image worship
487 Miracles
490 Superstitions in relation to religion
Cf. BR135+, Christian superstitions

Eschatology
Cf. BT819+, Christian eschatology
500 General works
501 Apocalypticism. Apocalyptic literature
503 End of the world
.5 Ascension
504 Death
505 Resurrection
510 Incarnation
Reincarnation. Metamorphoses. Transmigration
515 General works
518 Addresses, essays, lectures
Biography
519 Collective
520 Individual, A-Z
530 Immortality
Future life
535 General works
540 Other worlds. Paradise, etc.
Cf. BD655, Plurality of worlds, life on other planets
545 Infernal regions
547 Judgment of the dead

Worship. Cultus
For classical cults, see DE-DG
550 General works
560 Prayer. Prayers. Hymns, etc.
570 Sacrifice. Offerings. Vows

Religion
Worship. Cultus - Continued
Sacred places
Cf. GR505, Sacred places in folklore
580 General works
583 Groves. Rivers
Including wood and field cults
Cf. BL444, Plant and tree worship
584 Underground areas. Grottoes
586 Temples. Pagodas, etc.

Sacred times, seasons, days
590 General works

595 Special, A-Z
.S9 Sunday
Rites and ceremonies. Ritual, cult, symbolism
600 General works
602 Altar
Symbols. Emblems
603 General works
604 Special, A-Z
.B64 Body, Human
.C5 Circle
.C7 Cross
Cf. BV160, Christian art and symbolism
.D6 Dove
.D7 Drinking vessels

.H6 Horns
Human body, see .B64
.S4 Serpent
.S8 Swastika
.S85 Sword

.T7 Triangle
.V2 V symbol
.W3 Walls
.W4 Wheel

.W7 Wreaths
.Y2 Y symbol
.Y5 Yin Yang symbol

605 Music. Dances
610 Mysteries
613 Divination. Oracles, etc.
Cf. BF1745+, Occult sciences

615 Initiations
617 Covenants

Religion
Worship. Cultus
Rites and ceremonies. Ritual, cult, symbolism - Continued
619 Other, A-Z
.C3 Castration
.C57 Circumcision
.C6 Confession
.E9 Eye

.H4 Headgear
.L8 Lustration
.N7 Nocturnal ceremonies
.O6 Ordure (Use)

.O7 Orientation
.P3 Paper (Use)
.P5 Pilgrims and pilgrimages

.S3 Sacraments
.S5 Silence (Use)
.W3 Water

Religious life
624 General works
625 Asceticism. Mysticism
626 Ecstasy
.5 Martyrdom
627 Meditation
Cf. BF637.M4, Applied psychology
BF637.T68, Transcendental Meditation
Prayer, see BL560

Religious organization
630 General works
631 Monasticism and religious orders
Cf. BP189.2+, Islam
BV4518, Christianity (General)
BX385+, Orthodox Eastern Church
BX580+, Russian Church
BX2400+, Roman Catholic Church
BX5183+, Church of England
BX5970+, Protestant Episcopal Church

Communities and institutions
632 General works
.5 By region or country, A-Z
633 Prophets and prophecy
635 Priests and priestcraft
637 Missionary activities
Cf. BM729.P7, Judaism
BV2000+, Christianity

Religion - Continued
639 Conversion. Converts
640 Religious liberty

History and principles of religions
660 Indo-European. Aryan
Celtic, see BL900+

Hamitic, see BL2410
Semitic, see BL1600+
Slavic, see BL930+

685 Ural-Altaic
For special divisions, see BL690+
687 Mediterranean region
European. Occidental
690 General works
Classical religion and mythology
Cf. DE-DG, Classical history and antiquities
N7760, Art
PZ8.1, Juvenile literature
For cultural studies, see DE-DG
700 Periodicals. Societies. Serials
710 Collections
715 Dictionaries
Cf. DE5, Classical dictionaries
717 Historiography. Methodology

General works
720 Early through 1800
721 1801-1950
722 1951-

725 Elementary works
727 General special
730 Addresses, essays, lectures

735 Future life. Elysium. Hades
Etruscan
740 General works
745 General special

750 Addresses, essays, lectures
760 Special topics, A-Z
e. g. .V6 Votive offerings
Cf. DG223.7.V67, Etruscan antiquities

Religion
History and principles of religions
European. Occidental
Classical religion and mythology - Continued
Greek
Cf. PA4037, Homeric mythology
General works
780 Early through 1800
781 1801-1950
782 1951-

785 General special
788 Ritual
790 Addresses, essays, lectures

793 Local, A-Z
e. g. .A7 Arcadia
.C6 Corinth
.C7 Crete
Cf. BL793.M8, Mycenae

.C75 Crimea
.C8 Cumae
.C85 Cyrenaica

.D4 Delphi
.L2 Laconia
.L4 Lemnos

.M8 Mycenae
Cf. BL793.C7, Crete
.P3 Patrae
.P4 Pergamon

.S3 Samothrace
.S5 Sicily
.T4 Thera

.T43 Thessaly
.T7 Troy

795 Special topics, A-Z
.A54 Animals
.A7 Aromatic plants
.C6 Contests
.C7 Crime and criminals

Religion
History and principles of religions
European. Occidental
Classical religion and mythology
Greek
795 Special topics, A-Z - Continued
.D35 Dancing
Darkness, see .L54
.D4 Death
Delphian oracle, see DF261.D35

.D5 Demons
.D6 Dolphin
.D7 Dragons

.E5 Eleusinian mysteries
.E6 Elysium
.E7 Eschatology
.E8 Europa
.F55 Fire
.F6 Foot
.F8 Future life

.G6 God
.H6 Homosexuality
.H85 Hunting

.I5 Immortality
.L3 Landscapes
Including gardens, meadows, etc.
.L54 Light and darkness
.M4 Mental illness
.M65 Monsters
.M9 Mysteries
.N3 Navel
.O7 Orpheus
.P6 Prayer
.P7 Priests and priestesses

.S23 Sacred meals
.S62 Soul
.S63 Sphere
.S65 Springs

Stars, etc., see GR625
.T54 Thesmophoria
.T8 Tree worship
.T85 Trials
Trojan War, see BL793.T7
.V6 Votive offerings
.W28 War
.W3 Water
.Z63 Zodiac

Religion
History and principles of religions
European. Occidental
Classical religion and mythology - Continued
Roman
General works
800 Early through 1800
801 1801-1950
802 1951-

805 General special
808 Ritual
810 Addresses, essays, lectures

813 Local, A-Z
e. g. .A3 Africa (North)
.A7 Aricia

.C3 Campania
.E8 Etruria
.O7 Ostia

.P6 Pompeii
.S3 Sabine territory

815 Special topics, A-Z
.C74 Crime and criminals
.E8 Evocation
.F8 Future life
.H47 Heroes
.I4 Immortality

.L3 Laurel
.L8 Lupercalia
.M6 Monotheism

.M8 Mysticism
.P68 Prayer
.P7 Priests

.R4 Regifugium
.S15 Sacred meals
.S3 Sacrifice (Human)

.S8 Sun worship
.T3 Tanaquil legend
.T35 Taurobolium

.T45 Terminus
.V3 Ver sacrum
.V4 Vestals
.W6 Women

Religion
History and principles of religions
European. Occidental
Classical religion and mythology - Continued
820 Special deities and characters of classical mythology, A-Z
Including cults
.A25 Adonis
.A3 Aeacus
.A34 Aeneas

.A4 Aesculapius
.A46 Agamemnon
.A6 Amazons
Aphrodite, see .V5
.A7 Apollo
Ares, see .M2
.A8 Argonauts

.A83 Ariadne
Artemis, see .D5
Athene, see .M6

.A84 Attis
.B28 Baucis and Philemon
.B2 Bacchus. Dionysus

.C13 Cadmus
.C127 Cacus
.C18 Cassandra
.C2 Castor and Pollux. The Dioscuri
Cf. BL325.T8, Twin myths

.C4 Cerberus
.C5 Ceres. Demeter
.C55 Charon

.C6 Circe
.C65 Cupid. Eros
.C7 Curetes

.C8 Cybele. Rhea Cybele
Including Great mother of the gods
.C85 Cyrene (nymph)
.D25 Daedalus
.D3 Danaids

Demeter, see .C5
.D5 Diana. Artemis
Dionysus, see .B2
Dioscuri, see .C2

Religion
History and principles of religions
European. Occidental
Classical religion and mythology

820 Special deities and characters of classical mythology, A-Z - Cont.

.E5 Eileithyia
.E7 Epaphus
.E8 Erichthonius

Erinyes, see .F8
Eros, see .C65
Eumenides, see .F8

.F7 Fortuna. Tyche
.F8 Furies. Erinyes
.G5 Giants

.G7 Gorgons
.G8 The graces
Hephaestus, see .V8

.H45 Helen of Troy
Hera, see .J6
.H5 Hercules. Heracles

Hermes, see .M5
.H7 Horatii
.H9 Hyacinthus

Ino, see .M3
.I8 Itys
.J2 Janus
Jason, see .A8
.J6 Juno. Hera
Cf. BL820.E5, Eileithyia
.J8 Jupiter. Zeus

.L3 Lares
Leucothea, see .M3
.M2 Mars. Ares

.M26 Marsyas
.M3 Matuta. Leucothea. Ino
.M37 Medea
.M4 Memnon

.M45 Mens
.M5 Mercury. Hermes
.M55 Midas
.M6 Minerva. Athene (Athena)

Religion
History and principles of religions
European. Occidental
Classical religion and mythology
820 Special deities and characters of classical mythology, A-Z - Cont.

.M65 Mother goddesses
.M8 Muses
.N5 Neptune. Poseidon

.O3 Odysseus. Ulysses
.O43 Oedipus
.O6 Ops

.O7 Orpheus
.P2 Pan
.P4 Pegasus

.P45 Penelope
Persephone, see .P7
.P5 Perseus

Philemon and Baucis, see .B28
Poseidon, see .N5
.P68 Prometheus

.P7 Proserpina. Proserpine. Persephone
.P8 Psyche

.P9 Pyrrus. Pyrros
Rhea, see .C8
.R65 Roma

.S29 Saturn
.S3 Satyrs
.S5 Sirens
.T5 Theseus.

.T6 Tiber River. Tiberinus
.T63 Titans
Tyche, see .F7

Ulysses, see .O3
.V5 Venus. Aphrodite
.V55 Vesta

.V6 Victory
.V8 Vulcan. Hephaestus
Zeus, see .J8

Religion
History and principles of religions
European. Occidental - Continued
Germanic and Norse mythology

830 Periodicals. Societies. Serials
Collected works
840 Several authors
845 Individual authors

850 Dictionaries
855 Sources
Cf. PT, Literature
860 General works
863 General special

865 Addresses, essays, lectures
870 Special topics, A-Z
Including individual gods
.B3 Balder
.D7 Drinks and drinking

.F3 Fate and fatalism
.F5 Freyr
.F6 Frigg

.F7 Funeral rites and ceremonies
.F8 Future life
.H4 Heimdallr

.I6 Immortality
.L6 Loki
.M3 Mannus

.M5 Miogarosormr
.M8 Muspilli
.N4 Nerthus

.O3 Odin
.R4 Reincarnation
.S2 Sacrifice

.S5 Skadi
.S8 Sun worship
.S87 Symbolism

.T4 Temples
.T5 Þórr (Thor)
.U4 Ull
.V3 Valkyries

Religion
History and principles of religions
European. Occidental
Germanic and Norse mythology - Continued
875 Individual countries (except Germany and Scandinavia), A-Z
e. g. .F5 Finland
.F8 France or Gaul (Germanic only)
Cf. BL980.F8, Non-Christian religions (except Germanic and Norse) in France

Other primitive European religions
By ethnic group
900 Celtic
910 Druids
Individual countries (except for Druids), see BL980
915 Individual deities, A-Z
e. g. .N4 Nehalennia
.T4 Teutates

Slavic
930 General works
935 Special topics, A-Z
Including individual gods
.S6 Slovak mythology
.S94 Svarog
.W4 Wendic cultus

945 Baltic
Including the Latvians, Lithuanians, Yatvyags, and Prussians (Baltic tribe)
Ural-Altaic
Cf. BL2370, Other Asian religions
960 General works
Special, see BL980
975 Other, A-Z
e. g. .B3 Basque
.C4 Celtiberi
.F8 Finno-Ugrian

.G5 Getae (Zalmoxis cult)
.M6 Mordvinians
.T5 Thracians
.U34 Udmurts

Religion
History and principles of religions
European. Occidental - Continued
980 By region or country, A-Z

e. g. .F8 France or Gaul

.G7 Great Britain. England

.H8 Hungary. The Magyars

.I7 Ireland

.L3 Lapland

.N5 Netherlands. Holland

.S3 Scotland

.S6 Serbia. Yugoslavia

Asian. Oriental
1000 Periodicals. Societies. Serials
1105 Dictionaries. Encyclopedias
Collections
Several authors
1010 Ancient. Sacred books

e. g. Müller's Sacred books of the East

1015 Modern
1020 Individual authors

General works
1030 Early through 1800
1031 1801-1950
1032 1951-

1035 Addresses, essays, lectures

By region
1050 Northern and Central Asia
1055 Southern and Eastern Asia
1060 Southwestern Asia. Asia Minor. Levant
Cf. BL1600+, Semitic religions

Religion
History and principles of religions
Asian. Oriental - Continued
By religion
Hinduism
1100 Periodicals. Yearbooks
Societies. Councils. Associations. Clubs
Class here international and Indian national organizations. For other national or local organizations, see BL1153.7+. For works limited to a sect or independent religious organization, see BL1272+
1101 General works. History
.3 Individual, A-Z

.5 Congresses. Conferences (General)
For works limited to a sect, see the sect in BL1272+
.7 Directories (General)
Museums. Exhibitions
1102.3 General works. India
.5 Local, India, A-Z, or individual A-Z if location is unnamed
Under each locality:
.x General works
.x2 Individual, A-Z

.7 Other regions or countries, A-Z
Under each country:
.x General works
.x2 Local, A-Z

1105 Encyclopedias. Dictionaries. Terminology
General collections. Collected works
For sacred books, see BL1111+
For collections limited to a particular country except India, see Bl1154.2+
For sectarian collections, see BL1272+
Several authors
1107 Comprehensive volumes
.3 Minor collections. Collected essays. Festschriften
.5 Individual authors
For works by founders and most important leaders of sects, see BL1272+

Religion
History and principles of religions
Asian. Oriental
By religion
Hinduism - Continued
Religious education. Study and teaching
For works limited to a sect, see the sect in BL1272+. For works dealing with ministerial education, see BL1241.64. For works dealing with general education managed by Hindu institutions, see LC951

1108.2 General works
By region or country
India
General works, see BL1108.2
.5 Local, A-Z
.7 Other regions or countries, A-Z
Under each country:
.x General works
.x2 Local, A-Z

Antiquities. Archaeology. Inscriptions, etc.
Class here works limited to religious points of view only; for descriptive or philological works, see DS, PK, or PL
1109.2 General works
.3 General special

By region or country
India
General works, see BL1109.2
.5 Local, A-Z
Under each:
.x General works
.x2 Individual
.7 Other regions or countries, A-Z
Under each country:
.x General
.x2 Local, A-Z

Religion
History and principles of religions
Asian. Oriental
By religion
Hinduism - Continued
Sacred books. Sources

Tables to be used as indicated

Table I

	Comprehensive collections
(0)	Original. By date
(2)	Translations. By language, A-Z, and date
	Selections, anthologies, etc.
(3)	Original. By date
(4)	Translations. By language, A-Z, and date
(5)	Adaptations and paraphrases. By adaptor, A-Z
(6)	General works, commentaries, criticism, etc.
(7)	Special topics (not A-Z)
(9)	Dictionaries, terminology, indexes, concordances

Table II

	Complete texts
(0)	Original. By date
(2)	Translations. By language, A-Z, and date
	Partial editions, selections, anthologies, etc.
	Original
(3)	General. By date
(32)	Individual chapter, book, section, etc. By title, A-Z, and date
	Translations
(4)	General. By language, A-Z, and date
(42)	Individual chapter, book, section, etc. By title, A-Z, language, A-Z, and date
(5)	Adaptations and paraphrases. By adaptor, A-Z
(6)	General works, commentaries, criticism, etc.
(7)	Special topics (not A-Z)
(9)	Dictionaries, terminology, indexes, concordances

Religion
History and principles of religions
Asian. Oriental
By religion
Hinduism
Sacred books. Sources

Tables to be used as indicated - Continued

Table III

	Complete texts
.x	Original. By date
.x2	Translations. By language, A-Z, and date
	Partial editions, selections, anthologies, etc.
	Original
.x3	General. By date
.x32	Individual chapter, book, section, etc. By title, A-Z, and date
	Translations
.x4	General. By language, A-Z, and date
.x42	Individual chapter, book, section, etc. By title, A-Z, and date
.x5	Adaptations and paraphrases. By adaptor, A-Z, and date
.x6	General works, commentaries, criticism, etc.
.x7	Special topics (not A-Z)
.x9	Dictionaries, terminology, indexes, concordances

	Collections
	Original
1111	Comprehensive Class here comprehensive collections of two or more major groups of sacred books
.2	Selections. Anthologies Class here selections from two or more major groups of sacred books
	Translations
.3	Comprehensive. By language, A-Z
.32	Selections. Anthologies. By language, A-Z
.4	General works. History and criticism
.5	General special

Religion
History and principles of religions
Asian. Oriental
By religion
Hinduism
Sacred books. Sources - Continued
1111.6 Dictionaries
Including terminology, indexes, concordances, etc.
Biography. Characters of two or more sacred books
Cf. BL1112.3+, Characters of Vedic texts
BL1138.3+, Characters of the Mahabharata
BL1139.4+, Characters of the Ramayana
.7 General works
.72 Special groups of characters, A-Z
.R57 Rishis
.8 Special topics, A-Z
1112.2-29 Vedic texts (Table I)
Class here comprehensive collections of or works about two or more Vedas not limited to samhitas
Biography. Characters in Vedic texts
.3 Collective
.35 Individual, A-Z
.4-49 Samhitas (Table I)
Class here collections of or works about samhitas of two or more Vedas

.5-59 Rgveda samhita (Table II)
Class here also collections of or works about Rgveda texts including Brahmanas, Upanisads, etc.
.6-69 Yajurveda samhitas (Table I)
Class here also collections of or works about Yajurveda texts including Brahmanas, Upanisads, etc.
Individual recensions (Table II)
.7-79 Kathakasamhita
.8-89 Kapisthalakathasamhita
1113.3-39 Maitrayanasamhita
.4-49 Taittriyasamhita
.6-69 Vajasaneyisamhita (White Yajurveda samhita)
.7-79 Kanvasamhita

Religion
History and principles of religions
Asian. Oriental
By religion
Hinduism
Sacred books. Sources
Vedic texts (Table I)
Saṃhitās (Table I) - Continued

1114.2-29 Sāmaveda saṃhitās (Table I)
Class here also collections of or works about Sāmaveda texts including Brāhmaṇas, Upaniṣads, etc.
Individual recensions (Table II)
.3-39 Jaiminīyasaṃhitā
.4-49 Kauthumarāṇāyaṇīyasaṃhitā

.6-69 Atharvaveda saṃhitās (Table I)
Class here also collections of works about Atharvaveda texts including Brāhmaṇas, Upaniṣads, etc.
Individual recensions (Table II)
.7-79 Paippilāda
.8-89 Śaunaka

1116.2-29 Brāhmaṇas (Table I)
.3-39 Ṛgveda Brāhmaṇas (Table I)
Individual texts (Table II)
.4-49 Aitareyabrāhmaṇa
.6-69 Kausītakibrahmaṇa
.7-79 Śāṅkhāyanabrāhmaṇa

1118.2-29 Yajurveda Brāhmaṇas (Table I)
Individual texts (Table II)
.3-39 Kathabrāhmaṇa (Kāṭhakabrāhmaṇa)
.4-49 Taittirīyabrāhmaṇa
.5-59 Śatapathabrāhmaṇa

1121.2-29 Sāmaveda Brāhmaṇas (Table I)
.3 Individual texts. By title, A-Z (Table III)
.A78-789 Ārṣeyabrāhmaṇa
.D35-359 Daivatabrāhmaṇa (Devatādhyāyabrāhmaṇa)
.J35-359 Jaiminīyabrāhmaṇa

.J36-369 Jaiminīyārṣeyabrāhmaṇa
.J37-379 Jaiminīyopaniṣadbrāhmaṇa
.S34-349 Ṣaḍviṃśabrāhmaṇa

Religion
History and principles of religions
Asian. Oriental
By religion
Hinduism
Sacred books. Sources
Vedic texts (Table I)
Brāhmaṇas (Table I)
Sāmaveda Brāhmaṇas (Table I)

1121.3 Individual texts. By title, A-Z (Table III) - Continued
.S35-359 Sāmavidhānabrāhmaṇa
.S36-369 Saṃhitopaniṣadbrāhmaṇa

.T35-359 Tāṇḍyabrāhmaṇa
.U63-639 Upaniṣadbrāhmaṇa (Chāndogyabrāhmaṇa. Mantrabrāhmaṇa)
.V36-369 Vaṃśabrāhmaṇa

.7-79 Atharvaveda Brāhmaṇa (Table II)
e. g. Gopathabrāhmaṇa

1122.2-29 Āranyakas (Table I)
.3-39 Ṛgveda Āraṇyaka (Table I)
Individual texts (Table II)
.4-49 Aitareyāraṇyaka
.5-59 Śāṅkhāyanāraṇyaka

1123.2-29 Yajurveda Āraṇyaka (Table I)
Individual texts (Table II)
.3-39 Kathāranyaka
.4-49 Taittirīyaraṇyaka
.5-59 Śatapathāraṇyaka (Bṛhadāraṇyaka)

.7-79 Sāmaveda Āraṇyakas (Table I)
Individual texts (Table II)
.8-89 Talavakārāraṇyaka (Jaiminīyopaniṣadbrāhmaṇa)

1124.5-59 Upaniṣads (Table I)
.7 Individual Upaniṣads. By title, A-Z (Table III)
.A45-459 Adhyātmopaniṣad
.A58-589 Aitareyopaniṣad
.A65-659 Akṣyupaniṣad (Akṣikopaniṣad)

.A75-759 Ātmapūjopaniṣad
.A88-889 Avyaktapaniṣad
.B53-539 Bhāvanopaniṣad

Religion
History and principles of religions
Asian. Oriental
By religion
<u>Hinduism</u>
Sacred books. Sources
Vedic texts (Table I)
Upanisads (Table I)

1124.7 Individual Upanisads. By title, A-Z (Table III) - Continued

.B75-759 Bṛhadāraṇyakopaniṣad
.C53-539 Chāndogyopaniṣad
.D35-359 Dakṣiṇāmūrtyupaniṣad

.D37-379 Darśanopaniṣad
.D48-489 Devyupaniṣad
.G36-369 Gaṇapatyatharvaśīrṣopaniṣad

.G37-379 Garbhopaniṣad
.G66-669 Gopālatāpanīyopaniṣad
.I76-769 Īśopaniṣad

.K35-359 Kaivalyopaniṣad
.K38-389 Kaṭhopaniṣad
.K39-399 Kauṣītakibrāhmaṇopaniṣad

.K46-469 Kenopaniṣad
.M34-349 Mahānārāyaṇopaniṣad
.M35-359 Maitrāyanīyopaniṣad

.M36-369 Maṇḍalabrāhmaṇopaniṣad
.M37-379 Māṇḍūkyopaniṣad
.M86-869 Muṇḍakopaniṣad

.P73-739 Praśnopaniṣad
.R36-369 Rāmatāpanīyopaniṣad
.S84-849 Śvetāśvataropaniṣad
.T35-359 Taittirīyopaniṣad

1126.2-29 Kalpasūtras (Vedic rituals sūtras) (Table I)
For other Vedaṅga texts, e. g. Prātiśākhyasūtras, Anukuramaṇīs, etc., <u>see</u> the corresponding saṃhitās

.3 Individual Kalpasūtras. By title, A-Z, (Table III)

.A63-639 Āpastambakalpasūtra
.A77-779 Ārṣeyakalpasūtra

	Religion
	History and principles of religions
	Asian. Oriental
	By religion
	Hinduism
	Sacred books. Sources
	Vedic texts (Table I)
	Kalpasūtras (Vedic ritual sūtras) (Table I) - Continued
1126.4-49	Śrautasūtras (Table I)
.6-69	Ṛgvedic Śrautasūtras (Table I)
	Individual Śrautasūtras (Table II)
.7-79	Āśvalāyanaśrautasūtra
.8-89	Āśvalāyanaśrautapariśiṣṭa
1127.2-29	Śāṅkhāyanaśrautasūtra
.4-49	Yajurvedic Śrautasūtras (Table I)
	Individual Śrautasūtras (Table II)
.5-59	Kāṭhakaśrautasūtra
.7-79	Mānavaśrautasūtra
.8-89	Vārāhaśrautasūtra
1128.2-29	Baudhāyanaśrautasūtra
.3-39	Vādhūlaśrautasūtra
.4-49	Bhāradvājaśrautasūtra
.6-69	Āpastambaśrautasūtra
.7-79	Hiraṇyakeśinśrautasūtra
.8-89	Vaikhānasaśrautasūtra
1129.2-29	Sāmavedic Śrautasūtras (Table I)
	Individual Śrautasūtras (Table II)
.3-39	Lāṭyāyanaśrautasūtra
.4-49	Drāhyāyaṇaśrautasūtra
.6-69	Jaiminīyaśrautasūtra
.7-79	Atharvavedic Śrautasūtra (Table II)
	e. g. Vaitānaśrautasūtra
1131.2-29	Gṛhyasūtras (Table I)
.3-39	Ṛgvedic gṛhyasūtras (Table I)
	Individual Gṛhyasūtras (Table II)
.5-59	Āśvalāyanagṛhyasūtra
.6-69	Āśvalāyanagṛhyapariśiṣṭa
.7-79	Śāṅkhāyanagṛhyasūtra

Religion
History and principles of religions
Asian. Oriental
By religion
Hinduism
Sacred books. Sources
Vedic texts (Table I)
Kalpasūtras (Vedic rituals sūtras) (Table I)
Gṛhyasūtras (Table I) - Cont.

1131.9-99 Yajurvedic Gṛhyasūtras (Table I)
Individual texts (Table II)
1133.2-29 Kāthakagṛhyasūtra (Laugākṣigṛhyasūtra)
.3-39 Mānavagṛhyasūtra (Maitrāyaṇīyagṛhyasūtra)

.4-49 Vārāhagṛhyasūtra
.6-69 Baudhāyanagṛhyasūtra
.7-79 Bhāradvājagṛhyasūtra

.8-89 Āpastambagṛhyasūtra
.9-99 Hiraṇyakeśingṛhyasūtra
1134.2-29 Vādhūlagṛhyasūtra

.3-39 Agniveśyagṛhyasūtra
.4-49 Vaikhānasagṛhyasūtra
.5-59 Pāraskaragṛhyasūtra (Kātīyagṛhyasūtra)

.8-89 Sāmavedic Grhyasūtras (Table I)
Individual texts (Table II)
.9-99 Gobhilagrhyasūtra
1136.2-29 Khādiragṛhyasūtra (Drāhyāyaṇagṛhyasūtra)
.3-39 Jaiminīyagṛhyasūtra

Dharmasūtras (including Code of Manu), see Class K
1136.7-79 Śulbasūtras (Table I)
.8 Individual Śulbasūtras. By title, A-Z (Table III)
.A63-639 Āpastambaśulbasūtra
.B38-389 Baudhāyanaśulbasūtra

1137.2-29 Pitrmedhasūtras (Table I)
.3 Individual Pitṛmedhasūtras. By title, A-Z (Table III)
.B38-389 Baudhāyanapitṛmedhasūtra
.B53-539 Bhāradvājapitṛmedhasūtra
.H57-579 Hiraniyakeśipitṛmedhasūtra

Religion
History and principles of religions
Asian. Oriental
By religion
Hinduism
Sacred books. Sources
Vedic texts (Table I) - Continued

1137.5 Other individual Vedic ritual sutras. By title, A-Z (Table III)

Prātiśākhya, etc., see the corresponding saṃhitās

1138.2-29 Mahābhārata (Table II)
Class here the Mahābhārata alone or the Mahābhārata and Rāmāyana combined. For the Rāmāyana alone, see BL1139.2+

Biography. Characters of the Mahābhārata
.3 Collective
.4 Individual, A-Z
.6-69 Bhagavadgīta (Table II)

1139.2-29 Rāmāyana (Table II)
Class here the Rāmayana alone. For the Mahābharata and Rāmāyana combined, see BL1138.2+
Biography. Characters of the Rāmāyana
.4 Collective
.5 Individual, A-Z

1140.2-29 Purāna (Table I)
.4 Individual Purāṇas. By title, A-Z (Table III)

.A46-469 Agnipurāṇa (Āgneyapurāṇa)
.B43-439 Bhāgavatapurāṇa
.B44-449 Bhaviṣyapurāṇa

.B45-459 Bhaviṣyottarapurāṇa
.B73-739 Brahmaṇḍapurāṇa
.B74-749 Brahmapurāṇa (Ādipurāṇa)

.B75-759 Brahmavaivartapurāṇa (Brahmāvaivasvata)
.B76-769 Bṛhaddharmapurāṇa
.B77-779 Bṛhannāradīyapurāṇa

.D47-479 Devībhāgavatapurāṇa
.D48-489 Devīpurāṇa
.D53-539 Dharmaranyapurāṇa

Religion
History and principles of religions
Asian. Oriental
By religion
Hinduism
Sacred books. Sources
Purānas (Table I)

1140.4 Individual Purānas. By title, A-Z (Table III) - Continued

.G36-369 Gaṇeśapurāṇa
.G38-389 Garuḍapurāṇa
.K34-349 Kālikāpurāṇa

.K35-359 Kalkipurāṇa
.K36-369 Kapilapurāṇa
.K87-879 Kūrmapurāṇa

.L56-569 Liṅgapurāṇa
.M35-359 Mallapurāṇa
.M37-379 Mārkaṇḍeyapurāṇa

.M38-389 Matsyapurāṇa
.M84-849 Mudgalapurāṇa
.N37-379 Nāradapurāṇa (Nāradīyapurāṇa)

.N55-559 Nīlamatapurāṇa
.P34-349 Padmapurāṇa
.S27-279 Śaurapurāṇa
.S48-489 Sivapurāṇa (Vāyavīyapurāṇa)

.S53-539 Skandapurāṇa
.V35-359 Vāmanapurāṇa
.V37-379 Varāhapurāṇa
.V3793-37939 Vāsukipurāṇa
.V38-389 Vāyapurāṇa
.V56-569 Viṣṇudharmaottarapurāṇa

.V57-579 Viṣṇupurāṇa
.V75-759 Vṛhannāradīyapurāṇa

Dharmaśāstras, see Class K

1141.2-29 Tantric texts. Śaiva Agamas. Vaiṣṇava saṃhitās (Table I)

.4-49 Āgamas (Table I)

.5 Individual Āgamas. By title, A-Z (Table III)

.K35-359 Kāmikāgama
.K57-579 Kiraṇāgama
.L35-359 Lalitāgama

.M38-389 Mataṅgaparameśvarāgama
.V38-389 Vātulāgama

Religion
History and principles of religions
Asian. Oriental
By religion
Hinduism
Sacred books. Sources
Tantric texts. Śaiva Āgamas.
Vaiṣṇava saṃhitās (Table I) - Cont.

1141.7-79 Pāñcarātra (Table I)
.8 Individual saṃhitās. By title, A-Z (Table III)

.A55-559 Ahirbudhynasaṃhitā
.B53-539 Brahmasaṃhitā
.J38-389 Jayākhyasaṃhitā

.L35-359 Lakṣmītantra
.N37-379 Nāradapañcarātra
.N38-389 Nāradīyasaṃhitā

.P34-349 Pādmasaṃhitā
.P37-379 Paramasaṃhitā
.P38-389 Pārameśvarasaṃhitā

.S36-369 Sanatkumārasaṃhitā
.S47-479 Śeṣasaṃhitā
.S75-759 Śrīpraśnasaṃhitā

.S76-769 Śrīśrībramnsamhitā
.V57-579 Viṣvaksenasaṃhitā

1142.2-29 Vaikhānasa (Table I)
.3 Individual saṃhitās. By title, A-Z (Table III)
.A87-879 Atrisaṃhitā

.M36-369 Mantrasaṃhitā
.M37-379 Marīcisṃhitā

.5-59 Tantric texts (Table I)
.6 Individual tantras. By title, A-Z (Table III)
.A55-559 Annadākalpatantra
.B48-489 Bhūtaḍāmaratantra
.C56-569 Cīnācārasāratantra

.D38-389 Dattātreyatantra
.G87-879 Guptasādhanatantra

.G88-889 Gurutantra
.J53-539 Jñānārnavatantra

Religion
History and principles of religions
Asian. Oriental
By religion
Hinduism
Sacred books. Sources
Tantric texts. Śaiva Āgamas.
Vaiṣṇava saṃhitās (Table 1)
Tantric texts (Table I)

1142.6 Individual tantras. By title, A-Z (Table III) - Continued

.J54-549	Jñānasankalinītantra
.K34-349	Kālītantra
.K35-359	Kāṃadhenutantra
.K3592-35929	Kāmākhyātantra
.K36-369	Kaṅkālamālinītantra
.K82-829	Kubjikātantra
.K84-849	Kulaprakāśatantra
.K85-859	Kulārṇava
.M35-359	Mahānirvaṇa
.M37-379	Mātṛkābhedatantra
.M47-479	Merutantra
.M75-759	Mṛgendra
.M86-869	Muṇḍamālātantra
.N55-559	Nīlatantra
.N5595-55959	Niruttaratantra
.N56-569	Nirvāṇatantra
.N57-579	Nityāṣoḍaśikārṇava
.P73-739	Prapañcasāratantra
.R84-849	Rudrayāmalatantra
.S35-359	Śaktisanganatantra
.S36-369	Sammohanatantra
.S37-379	Śāṅkhyāyanatantra
.S38-389	Sāradātilaka
.S39-399	Sarasvatītantra
.T35-359	Tantrarāja
.T64-649	Toḍalatantra
.U44-449	Uḍḍīśatantra
.Y65-659	Yoginīhṛdayatantra
.Y66-669	Yoginītantra
.Y68-689	Yonitantra

1143.2 Other sacred books, and sources. By title, A-Z (Table III)

Religion
History and principles of religions
Asian. Oriental
By religion
Hinduism - Continued
Hindu literature. Hindu authors
Including devotional or theologico-philosophical works of Hindu authors not limited specifically by subject
For works on specific subjects, regardless of authorship, see the appropriate subject
For works by founders of special sects or movements, see BL1245+
Cf. B130+, B5130+, Philosophy of India

Sacred books, see BL1110+
Biography, see BL1170+

Collections of several authors
1145 Two or more volumes
.5 Single volumes
1146 Individual authors
Including individual anonymous works, subarranged like separate works in table below
Under each (using two or five successive Cutter numbers):

		Collected works
(1) .A1	(1)	Original texts. By date
(1) .A2	(2)	Partial editions, selections, etc. By editor or date
(1) .A3	(3)	Translations. By language, A-Z
(1) .A4-Z	(4)	Separate works, A-Z
(2)	(5)	General works. Criticism, interpretation, etc.
		Biography, see BL1170+

1147 History and criticism
History
1149 Collections. Collected works. Sources

Religion
History and principles of religions
Asian. Oriental
By religion
Hinduism - Continued
1150 General works. India
For local of India, see BL1153.7

1151.3 General special
.5 Addresses, essays, lectures
By period
1152.3 Early and medieval
.5 Origins. Early
.7 Rise and development of Hindu sects ca. 200 B.C. to 11th century A.D.

1153.2 11th century to 18th century
.5 Modern period
By region or country
South Asia
General, see BL1150
Special countries

India
General, see BL1150
.7 Local, A-Z

Bangladesh
1154.2 Periodicals. Societies. Collections. Sources
.3 General works. History
.5 General special
.7 Biography (Collective)
.8 Local, A-Z

Nepal
1156.2 Periodicals. Societies. Collections. Sources
.3 General works. History
.5 General special
.7 Biography (Collective)
.8 Local, A-Z

Pakistan
1158.2 Periodicals. Societies. Collections. Sources
.3 General works. History
.5 General special
.7 Biography (Collective)
.8 Local, A-Z

Religion
History and principles of religions
Asian. Oriental
By religion
Hinduism
History
By region or country
South Asia
Special countries - Continued

Sikkim
1159.2 Periodicals. Societies. Collections. Sources
.3 General works. History
.5 General special
.7 Biography (Collective)
.8 Local, A-Z

Sri Lanka
1160.2 Periodicals. Societies. Collections. Sources
.3 General works
.5 General special
.7 Biography (Collective)
.8 Local, A-Z

1161 Other South Asia regions and countries, A-Z
Under each country:

.x Periodicals. Societies. Collections. Sources
.x2 General works. History
.x3 General special
.x4 Biography (Collective)
.x5 Local, A-Z

.H56 Himalaya region
.K37 Kashmir
.L34 Ladakh

Southeast Asia
1162.2 Periodicals. Societies. Collections. Sources
.3 General works. History
.5 General special
.7 Biography (Collective)

Religion
History and principles of religions
Asian. Oriental
By religion
Hinduism
History
By region or country
Southeast Asia - Continued
Special countries

Indonesia
1163.2 Periodicals. Societies. Collections. Sources
.3 General works. History
.5 General special
.7 Biography (Collective)
.8 Local, A-Z
Malaysia. Malaya
1164.2 Periodicals. Societies. Collections. Sources
.3 General works. History
.5 General special
.7 Biography (Collective)
.8 Local, A-Z
1165 Other Southeast Asia regions and countries, A-Z
Divide like BL1161
1168 Other regions or countries, A-Z
Divide like BL1161
.A37 Africa, East
.U53 United States
Biography
Cf. BL1112.3+, Characters of Vedic texts
BL1138.3+, Characters of Mahābhārata
BL1139.4+, Characters of Rāmāyana
1170 Collective (General and India)
For sectarian collective biography, see the sect
1171 Saints. Gurus. Leaders, etc.
1175 Individual, A-Z (Table IV) 1/
For works limited to founders and most important leaders of individual sects, see the sect in BL1272+
General works
1200 Early through 1800
1201 1801-1946
1202 1947-

1/ For tables, see p. 64

Religion
History and principles of religions
Asian. Oriental
By religion
Hinduism - Continued
1203 Juvenile works
1205 General special
1210 Addresses, essays, lectures
1211 Controversial works against Hinduism
For works limited to a sect, see the sect in BL1272+

.5 Apologetic works
For works limited to a sect, see the sect in BL1272+
Doctrines. Theology
For works limited to a sect, see the sect in BL1272+
1212.32 Periodicals. Societies
.34 Collected works. Festschriften
History
For works limited to a particular country except India, see the country in BL1154+
.36 General works
.38 General special
By period
.52 Early Vedic period (Brahmanism) to 2nd century B.C.
Cf. B130+, Ancient Hindu philosophy
.54 2nd century B.C. to 1800 A.D.
.56 Modern period

.72 General works. Introductions
.74 General special
.76 Addresses, essays, lectures
Special doctrines
1213.32 God (Concept). Istadeva
For works dealing with attributes, cults, etc., of deities, see BL1216+
.34 Trimurti
.36 Avatars
Cf. BL1219, Vishnu avatāra
.38 Pantheism

.52 Dharma
Cf. B132.D5, Dharma (Philosophy)

.54 Man. Puruṣa
Cf. B132.M27, Man (Philosophy)
.56 Ātman-Brahman. Soul. Self. Atman. Jīva
Cf. B132.A8, Atman. Anātman

Religion
History and principles of religions
Asian. Oriental
By religion
Hinduism
Doctrines. Theology
Special doctrines - Continued

1213.58 Moksa. Mukti. Deliverance
.72 Salvation
.74 Truth
Religious life, Theoretical
For works dealing with practice, see BL1225.2+
1214.22 General works
.24 General special
.26 Addresses, essays, lectures
.32 Special topics, A-Z

Ahimsā, see BJ123.A45

Āśramas. Four stages, see BL1237.75

.A85 Atonement
.B53 Bhakti

.D88 Duty
.G87 Guru worship
Cf. BL1241.48, Guruship
.P68 Poverty, Life of

.S72 Śraddhā. Faith

.V45 Vegetarianism
.V56 Violence and non-violence
Yoga, see B132.Y6, BL1238.52+

.34 Śakti
Cf. BL1282.2+, Saktism
.36 Kāma
.38 Māya
Eschatology
.56 General works
.58 Future life
.72 Death
.74 Transmigration. Rebirth. Samsara
.76 Heaven
.78 Hell

Religion
History and principles of religions
Asian. Oriental
By religion
Hinduism
Doctrines. Theology - Continued
1215 Other special topics and relations to special subjects, A-Z
Altars, see BL1236.76.A48
Amrta, see .I66
Amulets, see BL1236.76.A49
Ancestor worship, see BL1239.5.A52
.A56 Animism
Asceticism, see BL1239.5.A82
Atonement, see BL1214.32.A85
Avatars, see BL1213.36
Bhakti, see BL1214.32.B53
Brahmans, see DS432.B7 for works dealing with Brahmans as a caste; see BL1241.55 for works about Brahman priesthood
.C3 Caste
Celibacy, see BL1237.82.C46
.C45 Chakras (Cakra)
.C53 Clairvoyance
.C6 Cosmogony
.C7 Cows. Cattle
.C76 Culture
.D3 Dawn
Death, see BL1214.72
.D45 Deluge
.D8 Dualism
Cf. B132.D8, Dvaita
.E27 Economics
.E3 Ecstasy
.E5 Endogamy and exogamy
Fasting, see BL1237.75
.F66 Food
Future life, see BL1214.58
Gurus, see BL1241.48

Religion
History and principles of religions
Asian. Oriental
By religion
Hinduism
Doctrines. Theology
1215 Other special topics and relations to special subjects, A-Z - Continued

Hair. Haircutting, see BL1239.5.H35
Hell, see BL1214.78
.H57 History. Yuga concept

.H86 Humanism
.I66 Immortality. Amrta
.J3 Jatakarma

.K56 Kings and rulers
Kuṇḍalinī, see BL1238.56.K86
.L54 Life, Meaning of

Man, see BL1213.54
Meditation, see BL1238.32
.M48 Metaphor

.M57 Miracles
.M87 Music
.M9 Mysticism

.N3 Names
.P3 Parables
.P4 Peace

.P65 Politics
Prayer, see BL1237.77
Priests, see BL1241.55

.P77 Prophecies
.P8 Psychology
.R34 Race

.R4 Revelation
Rishis, see BL1241.52
.R5 Rivers

Rulers, see .K56
Sacrifices, see BL1236.76.S23
Saktism, see BL1282.2

Salvation, see BL1213.72
Sannyasi, see BL1241.54
.S36 Science

Religion
History and principles of religions
Asian. Oriental
By religion
Hinduism
Doctrines. Theology
1215 Other special topics and relations to special subjects, A-Z - Continued

Serpent worship, see BL1239.5.S37
.S64 Sociology
Soma, see BL1236.76.S66
Soul, see BL1213.56

Śraddhā, see BL1214.32.S72
.S83 State
Class here works dealing with theoretical aspects of Hinduism and state; for works dealing with history, see BL1149+

.S87 Superstition
.T4 Tēr
Tree planting, see BL1239.5.T74

Vrata, see BL1237.78
Yakshas, see BL1225.Y29
Yuga, see .H57

Relation of Hinduism to other religious and philosophical systems
Including comparative studies of Hinduism and other religious and philosophical systems
For works limited to a sect, see the sect in BL1272+
.3 General works
.5 General special
.7 Special, A-Z

Buddhism, see BQ4610.H6
Christianity, see BR128.H5

Islam, see BP173.H5
Jainism, see BL1358.2

Judaism, see BM536.H5

Religion
History and principles of religions
Asian. Oriental
By religion
Hinduism - Continued
Hindu pantheon. Deities. Mythical characters
1216 General works. History
.2 General special
By region or country
India
General works, see BL1216
.4 Local, A-Z
.6 Other regions or countries, A-Z
Under each country:
.x General works
.x2 By local, A-Z
Individual deities
For deities adopted in Buddhist pantheon, see BQ1718+
Brahmā
1217 General works
.2 Cult. Liturgy. Prayers
By region or country
India
General works, see BL1217
.3 Local, A-Z
.4 Other regions or countries, A-Z
Under each country:
.x General works
.x2 Local, A-Z
1218 Siva (Shiva)
Cf. BL1280.5+, Saivism
Subarranged like BL1217-1217.4
1219 Vishnu
Cf. BL1284.5+, Vaishnavism
Subarranged like BL1217-1217.4
1220 Krishna (Kṛṣna)
Subarranged like BL1217-1217.4

1225 Other individual deities, A-Z
Under each deity:
.x General works. India
.x2 Cult. Liturgy. Prayers
.x3 Local, India, A-Z
.x4 Other regions or countries, A-Z
.A37 Aatim
.A4 Aditi
.A443 Ādityas

Religion
History and principles of religions
Asian. Oriental
By religion
Hinduism
Hindu pantheon. Deities. Mythical characters
Individual deities
1225 Other individual deities, A-Z - Continued

.A45 Agni
.A57 Aiyanār
.A64 Annapūrnā

.A65 Apsarases
.A7 Aśvins
.A9 Ayyappan

.B3 Bagalāmukhī
.B345 Balarāma
.B35 Bargabhima

.B37 Bāṭa Ṭhākurānī
.B47 Bhādū
.B49 Bhagavati

.B494 Bhairava
.B5 Bhavānī
.B58 Bhūvaneśvarī

.B65 Bōre Dēvaru
Brahmā, see BL1217
.B7 Bṛhaspati (Brihaspati)

.C24 Cāmuṇḍā (Cāmuṇḍī)
.C25 Caṇḍī (Caṇḍikā, Caṇḍā)
.D3 Dattātreya

.D48 Devanārāyana
.D8 Durgā
.G3 Gandharvas

.G34 Ganeśa
.G35 Gaṅgā
.G37 Gaurī

.G38 Gāyatrī
.G67 Gosānī
.G8 Guruvayurappan

Religion
History and principles of religions
Asian. Oriental
By religion
Hinduism
Hindu pantheon. Deities. Mythical characters
Individual deities
1225 Other individual deities, A-Z - Continued

.H3 Hanumān
.H34 Hayagriva (Hayaśiras)

.H35 Hayavadana
.I6 Indra
.J3 Jagannātha

.J96 Jyotibā
.K3 Kālī
.K35 Kalki

.K36 Kāma
.K37 Kaṇṇaki
.K377 Kanyakāparamēśvari

.K38 Kārttikeya
.K39 Karumari
.K48 Khamlāmba

.K5 Khandobā
.K56 Khoḍiyāra Mātā
Krishna (Kṛṣna), see BL1220

.L3 Lakshmī
.L345 Lakṣmaṇa
.M3 Manasā

.M48 Mīnākṣī
.M5 Mitra
.M8 Murugan
Cf. BL1225.K38, Kārttikeya

.N33 Nabagraha
.P23 Paccaināyaki
.P25 Panthoibi

.P27 Paraśurāma
.P3 Pārvatī
.P34 Pattini
.P8 Pūsan

Religion
History and principles of religions
Asian. Oriental
By religion
Hinduism
Hindu pantheon. Deities. Mythical characters
Individual deities

1225 Other individual deities, A-Z - Continued

.R24 Rādhā
.R3 Rāma (Rāmacandra)
.R344 Raṇachoḍarāya

.R345 Raṅganātha
.R47 Revanta
.R5 Ribhus

.R8 Ṛudra
.S18 Śakti
Cf. BL1214.34, Śakti concept
BL1282.2+, Śaktism
.S19 Sampatkumāra

.S22 Sani
.S23 Santoshī Mātā
.S25 Sarasvatī

.S28 Satyā-nārāyan
.S3 Sāvitrī
.S48 Shambulinga

.S5 Shamlaji
.S57 Sītā
.S59 Śītalā

Śiva (Shiva), see BL1218
.S63 Soma
Cf. BL1236.76.S66, Soma (Liturgical object)
BL1226.82.V3, Vajapeya
.S65 Sonārāya

.S7 Śri Venkateśvara
.S8 Sūrya (Savitar)
.T3 Tārā (Tārākā)

.T45 Tejāji
.T7 Tripurā Bhairavī
.T73 Tripurasundarī

Religion
History and principles of religions
Asian. Oriental
By religion
Hinduism
Hindu pantheon. Deities. Mythical characters
Individual deities
1225 Other individual deities, A-Z - Continued
.T83 Tulasī
.T86 Tushu
.V3 Varuṇa

.V38 Vāyu
.V48 Vīrabhadra

Vishnu (Viṣṇu), see BL1219
.V49 Viśvakarman

.V5 Viṭhobā
.Y27 Yakshas

.Y3 Yama

Practice. Forms of worship. Religious life
1225.2 Collections. Collected works
.3 Encyclopedias. Dictionaries
.5 History
1226 General works
.12 General special
.13 Addresses, essays, lectures
By region or country
India
History, see BL1225.5
.15 Local, A-Z
.17 Other regions or countries, A-Z
Under each country:
.x General works
.x2 Local, A-Z
Liturgy. Rites and ceremonies
For works limited to a sect, see the sect in BL 1272+
For ritual texts of antiquities, e. g. Brāhmaṇas, Śrautasūtras, Gṛhyasūtras, etc., see BL1116+, BL1126+

.18 Collections. Collected works
.2 General works
.72 General special
.74 Service books. Liturgical books

Religion
History and principles of religions
Asian. Oriental
By religion
Hinduism
Practice. Forms of worship. Religious life
Liturgy. Rites and ceremonies - Continued
1226.82 Special rites and ceremonies, A-Z
For pūjas and rituals of an individual deity, see the individual deity in BL1217+

.A33 Agnicayana
.A35 Agnihotra
.A85 Atonement
Cf. BL1214.32.A85, Atonement doctrine
.B38 Bathing (Snāna)
.B48 Bhasma
.C66 Confession

.D66 Domestic rites
Cf. BL1131+, Gṛhyasūtras
.F5 Fire rite (General)
Cf. BL1226.82.A33, Agnicayana
BL1226.82.A35, Agnihotra

.F6 Foot worship rite
.F86 Funeral rites
.I54 Initiation rites (General)
Cf. BL1226.82.S2, Sacred thread ceremony

.M27 Mahāpradosa
.M3 Marriage rites
.R75 Ṛshipañcamī

.S2 Sacred thread ceremony. Upanayana
.S24 Samskāras. Sacraments
.S25 Sandhyā

.S3 Self-worship
Śoma sacrifices, see .V3
.S73 Śrāddhā
.T5 Timiti
Upanayana, see .S2
.V3 Vājapeya (Soma sacrifices)
.V52 Vibhūti (Ash rite)

Religion
History and principles of religions
Asian. Oriental
By religion
Hinduism
Practice. Forms of worship. Religious life
Liturgy. Rites and ceremonies - Continued
Prayers. Hymns. Mantras. Chants. Recitations
For works limited to a sect, see the sect in BL1272+; for hymns with music, see M2145; for Vedic hymns, see BL1112.4+; for prayers, hymns, etc. for an individual deity, see the deity in BL1217+

1236.22 Collections of prayers, hymns, mantras, etc.
.34 Dictionaries
.36 General works. History and criticism
.38 General special
.52 Special prayers and hymns, A-Z

.M67 Morning prayer

.R35 Rain-wishing prayer

.54 Individual texts of prayers, hymns, mantras
Liturgical objects and functions. Altars, etc.
.72 General works
.74 General special
.76 Special topics, A-Z

.A48 Altars
.A49 Amulets

.B45 Bells
.F66 Food offering

.M84 Mudrās
.S23 Sacrifices

.S66 Soma
Cf. BL1225.S63, Soma (Hindu deity)
BL1226.82.V3, Vājapeya (Soma sacrifices)
.Y36 Yantra

Religion
History and principles of religions
Asian. Oriental
By religion
Hinduism
Practice. Forms of worship. Religious life - Continued
Religious life. Spiritual life.
Discipline
For doctrinal works, see BL1214.22+; for works limited to a sect, see the sect in BL1272+

1237.32 General works
.34 General special
.36 Addresses, essays, lectures
Religious life of special groups
Cf. BL1241.44+, Priesthood. Holymen
.42 Aged
.44 Men
.46 Women
.48 Parents
.52 Youth. Students
.54 Children
.58 Other groups, A-Z

.S65 Soldiers

Special observances. Duties
.75 Āśramas. Four stages
Cf. BL1238.72, Ashram life general
BL1243.72+, Modern institutional ashrams
BL1272+, Individual modern sectarian ashrams

.76 Fasting
Cf. BL1239.82.F37, Fasts and feasts
.77 Prayer
Cf. BL1236.22+, Prayers, etc.
.78 Vratas (Bratas)
.82 Other topics, A-Z

.C46 Celibacy
Cf. BL1241.44, Priesthood. Holymen

Religion
History and principles of religions
Asian. Oriental
By religion
Hinduism - Continued
Practice. Forms of worship. Religious life
Religious life. Spiritual life.
Discipline - Continued
Meditation. Spiritual exercises
For works limited to a sect, see the sect in BL1272+; for doctrinal works, see BL1214.22+

1238.32 General works
.34 General special
.36 Addresses, essays, lectures

Yoga
Class here works dealing with yoga as religious and spiritual discipline; for works dealing with yoga for health and therapeutic purposes, see RA781.7, RM727.Y64; for works dealing with yoga philosophy, see B132.Y6

.52 General works
.54 General special
.56 Special yoga, A-Z

.B53 Bhakti yoga
Cf. BL1214.32.B53, Bhakti doctrine

.H38 Haṭha yoga
Cf. RA781.7, Exercise
RM727.Y64, Therapeutics

.K37 Karma yoga
.K74 Kriya yoga
.K86 Kuṇḍalīnī yoga

.L38 Laya yoga

.R35 Rāja yoga

.S53 Siddha yoga

Religion
History and principles of religions
Asian. Oriental
By religion
Hinduism
Practice. Forms of worship. Religious life
Religious life. Spiritual life. Discipline
Meditation. Spiritual exercises - Continued
1238.58 Special topics, A-Z

.P67 Posture (Asana)
.P73 Prāṇāyāma
Cf. RA782, Breathing exercises
.S24 Sādhanā
For individual deity sādhanā, see BL1217+
.S26 Samādhi

Monasticism and monastic life. Ashram life
For works limited to a sect, see the sect in BL1272+
.72 General works. History
.74 General special
.76 Monastic discipline. Rules
By region or country
India
General works, see BL1238.72
.78 Local, A-Z
.82 Other regions or countries, A-Z
Under each country
.x General works
.x2 Local, A-Z
Pilgrims and pilgrimages
1239.32 General works
.34 General special
By region or country
India
General works, see BL1239.32
.36 Local, A-Z
.38 Other regions or countries, A-Z
Under each country:
.x General works
.x2 Local, A-Z

Religion
History and principles of religions
Asian. Oriental
By religion
Hinduism
Practice. Forms of worship. Religious life
Religious life. Spiritual life. Discipline - Continued

1239.5 Other special religious practice, A-Z

.A52 Ancestor worship
.A82 Asceticism

.G58 Giving
.H35 Hair. Haircutting

.H47 Hermitage life
Cf. BL1237.75, Āśramas

.S37 Serpent worship
.T74 Tree planting

.W38 Wayfaring life

Festivals. Days and seasons
Cf. GT4876, India
For works limited to a sect, see the sect in BL1272+

.72 General works
.74 General special
By region or country
India
General works, see BL1239.72
.76 Local, A-Z
.78 Other regions or countries
Under each country:
.x General works
.x2 Local, A-Z

.82 Special, A-Z

.D58 Dīvālī (Dīpāvalī)
.F37 Fasts and feasts
Cf. BL1237.75, Fasting
.H65 Holī
.K85 Kumbha Melā

Religion
History and principles of religions
Asian. Oriental
By religion
Hinduism
Practice. Forms of worship. Religious life - Continued
Temple organization. Institution.
Ministry. Priesthood. Government
Cf. BL1243.52, Monasteries, temples, etc.
For work limited to a sect, see the sect in BL1272+

1241.32 General works
.34 General special
By region or country
India
General works, see BL1241.32
.36 Local, A-Z
.38 Other regions or countries, A-Z
Under each country:
.x General works
.x2 Local, A-Z
.42 Offices
.44 Priesthood. Leadership. Sainthood. Holymen
Cf. BL1171, Biography of saints, gurus, leaders, etc.
Special groups
.46 Brahmans
.48 Guruship
.52 Rishis
.54 Sannyasins
.56 Siddhas
.58 Membership
.62 Finance
.64 Education and training for the ministry and leadership
Preaching
.72 General works
.74 General special

Sermons
For sermons on a particular subject, see the subject
Collections
.76 Several authors
.78 Individual authors

Religion
History and principles of religions
Asian. Oriental
By religion
Hinduism
Practice. Forms of worship. Religious life
Temple organization. Institution. Ministry. Priesthood. Government - Continued
Missionary works
1243.32 General works
.34 General special
.36 By region or country, A-Z
Under each country:
.x General
.x2 Local, A-Z
Benevolent work. Social work. Welfare work, etc.
.52 General works
.54 General special
.56 Work with special groups, A-Z
By region or country
India
General works, see BL1243.52
.57 Local, A-Z
.58 Other regions or countries, A-Z
Under each country:
.x General works
.x2 Local, A-Z
Monasteries. Temples. Shrines. Ashrams. Sacred sites, etc.
For works limited to a sect, see the sect in BL1272+
.72 Directories. India
.74 General works
By region or country
India
General works, see BL1243.74
.76 Local, A-Z
Under each:
.x General works. Directories
.x2 Individual, A-Z
.78 Other regions or countries, A-Z
Under each country:
.A1A-Z General works. Directories
.A3-Z Local, or by name if non-urban, A-Z
Under each city
.x General
.x2 Individual

Religion
History and principles of religions
Asian. Oriental
By religion
Hinduism - Continued
Modifications. Sects. Movements. Cults

1271.2 General works. India
.3 General special
Local, India, see BL1153.7
Other regions and countries, see BL1154.2+

Individual sects, movements, cults (Table V) 1/

1272.2-292 Akhilananda
.5-592 Alokhiyas (Alakhgīrs)
.8-892 Anand Marg
1273.2-292 Anuvrati Sangh

.5-592 Arya Samaj
Biography
.59 Collective
.592 Founders and most important leaders, A-Z (Table IV) 1/

.D38 Dayananda Sarvasti, Swami, 1824-1883

1273.8-892 Aurobindo Ashram
Biography
.89 Collective
.892 Founders and most important leaders, A-Z (Table IV)

.G56 Ghose, Aurobindo, 1872-1950

Bauls, see BL1284.8+
Bhāgavatas, see BL1285.2+
1274.2-292 Brahmakumari
Brahmanism, see BL1152.5, BL1212.52
1274.5-592 Brahma Samaj (Brahmo Samaj)
Biography
.59 Collective
.592 Founders and most important leaders, A-Z (Table IV) 1/

.R36 Rammohun Roy, Raja, 1772?-1833

.S35 Sen, Keshab Chandra, 1838-1884

1/ For tables, see pp. 64-65

Religion
History and principles of religions
Asian. Oriental
By religion
Hinduism
Modifications. Sects. Movements.
Cults
Individual sects, movements, cults (Table V) 1/ - Continued

	Buddhism, see BQ
	Chaitanya, see BL1285.3+
	Dādūpanthīs, see BL1285.5+
1275.2-292	Daśnāmīs
.5-592	Dattatreya
.8-892	Deva Samaj
1276.2-292	Dharmaṭhākura
.3-392	Divine Life Society
	Goraknāthīs, see BL1278.8+
1276.5-592	Gusains
	International Society of Krishna, see BL1285.8+
	Jainism, see BL1300+
	Kabirpanthīs, see BL2020.K3
.8-892	Karthābhajā
1277.2-292	Kaulas
.5-592	Krama
	Mādhvas, see BL1286.2
.8-892	Mahānubhāva
1278.2-292	Nagesh
.5-592	Nāthas
	Biography
.59	Collective
.592	Founders and most important leaders, A-Z (Table IV) 1/
	.M38 Matsyendra
.8-892	Kanphatas (Gorakhnāthīs, Kanaphāṭās)
	Biography
.89	Collective
.892	Founders and most important leaders, A-Z (Table IV) 1/
	.G67 Gorakhnāth (Goraksa)
	Nīmbārka, see BL1286.5+
1279.2-292	Palatu
	Biography
.29	Collective
.292	Founders and most important leaders, (Table IV) 1/
	.P35 Palatū Sāhiba, fl. 1800

1/ For tables, see pp. 64-65

Religion
History and principles of religions
Asian. Oriental
By religion
Hinduism
Modifications. Sects. Movements. Cults
Individual sects, movements, cults (Table V) 1/ - Continued
Pañcarātra, see BL1286.8+
1279.5-592 Prāthanā Samāj
Biography
.59 Collective
.592 Founders and most important leaders, A-Z (Table IV) 1/

.A84 Atma Ram Pandurang
Rādhā Vallabhīs, see BL1287.2+
.8-892 Ram Sanehīs
Biography
.89 Collective
.892 Founders and most important leaders, A-Z (Table IV) 1/

.D37 Dāsa, Rāma Ratana, 1908-1964
1280.2-292 Ramakrishna Mission
Biography
.29 Collective
.292 Founders and most important leaders, A-Z (Table IV) 1/

.R36 Ramakrishna, 1836-1886
.V58 Vivekananda, 1863-1902
Rāmānandīs, see BL1287.5+
Rāmānuja, see BL1288.2+
Sahajīya, see BL1287.8+
.5-592 Saivism
Cf. BL1218, Siva (Hindu deity)
.8-892 Kāpālikas
1281.2-292 Lingayats (Vīraśaivas)
Biography
.29 Collective
.292 Founders and most important leaders, A-Z (Table IV) 1/
.B37 Bāsava, fl. 1160 (Vasava)
.5-592 Pāśupatas
.8-892 Saiva Siddhānta
1282.2-292 Saktism
Cf. BL1214.34, Sakti concept

1/ For tables, see pp. 64-65

Religion
History and principles of religions
Asian. Oriental
By religion
Hinduism
Modifications. Sects. Movements. Cults
Individual sects, movements, cults
(Table V) 1/ - Continued

1282.5-592 Samarasa Suddha Sanmarga Sathia Sangam
Biography
.59 Collective
.592 Founders and most important leaders, A-Z (Table IV) 1/
.R36 Ramalinga, 1823-1874
.8-892 Samartha Sampradaya
Sanaka, see BL1286.5+
1283.2-292 Saktviśistādvaitavedanta
Sikhism, see BL2017+
.5-592 Siva Narayanis (Srīnārāyanīs)
Srīvaisnavas, see BL1288.2+
Swami-Narayanis, see BL1289.2+
.8-892 Tantrism
Tenkalais, see BL1288.8+
Vadakalais, see BL1288.5+
1284.5-592 Vaishnavism
.8-892 Bauls
1285.2-292 Bhagavatas
.3-392 Chaitanya
Biography
.39 Collective
.392 Founders and most important leaders, A-Z (Table IV) 1/
.C53 Chaitanya, 1486-1534
.5-592 Dādūpanthīs
Biography
.59 Collective
.592 Founders and most important leaders, A-Z (Table IV) 1/
.D34 Dādūdayāla, 1544-1603 (Dadu)
.8-892 International Society of Krishna Consciousness
Biography
.89 Collective
.892 Founders and most important leaders, A-Z (Table IV) 1/
.A28 A.C. Bhaktivedanta Swami, Prabhupada, 1896-1977

1/ For tables, see pp. 64-65

Religion
History and principles of religions
Asian. Oriental
By religion
Hinduism
Modifications. Sects. Movements. Cults
Individual sects, movements, cults (Table V) 1/
Vaishnavism - Continued

1286.2-292 Mādhvas
Biography
.29 Collective
.292 Founders and most important leaders, A-Z (Table IV) 1/

.M34 Madhva, 13th cent.

1286.5-592 Nimbārka (Nīmāvats, Nīmānandins, Sanaka)
Biography
.59 Collective
.592 Founders and most important leaders, A-Z (Table IV) 1/

.N55 Nimbarka

.8-892 Pañcarātra
Biography
.89 Collective
.892 Founders and most important leaders, A-Z (Table IV) 1/

.S36 Sāndilya

1287.2-292 Rādhā Vallabhīs
Biography
.29 Collective
.292 Founders and most important leaders, A-Z (Table IV) 1/

.H58 Hita Harivamsa Gosvāmī, 1502-1552

.3-392 Rām Sanehīs
Biography
.39 Collective
.392 Founders and most important leaders, A-Z (Table IV) 1/
.R36 Rāmacaraṇa, Swami, 1719-1798

1/ For tables, see pp. 64-65

Religion
History and principles of religions
Asian. Oriental
By religion
Hinduism
Modifications. Sects. Movements. Cults
Individual sects, movements, cults (Table V) 1/
Vaishnavism - Continued

1287.5-592 Rāmānandīs (Rāmavats, Rāmānandins)
Biography
.59 Collective
.592 Founders and most important leaders, A-Z (Table IV) 1/
.R56 Rāmananda
Rāmānuja, see BL1288.2+
.8-892 Sahajīya
1288.2-292 Srīvaisnavas (Rāmānuja sect)
Biography
.29 Collective
.292 Founders and most important leaders, A-Z (Table IV) 1/
.M35 Manavāla Māmuni, 1370-1444
.R36 Rāmānuja

.5-592 Vadakalais (Vadagalais, Northern Sect)
Biography
.59 Collective
.592 Founders and most important leaders, A-Z (Table IV) 1/
.V46 Veṅkatanātha, 1268-1369 (Deśika)
.8-892 Tenkalais (Tengalais, Southern sect)
1289.2-292 Swami-Narayanis (Svāmīnārāyaṇa)
Biography
.29 Collective
.292 Founders and most important leaders, A-Z (Table IV) 1/
.S25 Sashajānda, Swami, 1781-1830 (Swami Narayana)
.5-592 Vallabha sect (Vallabhācaryas)
Biography
.59 Collective
.592 Founders and most important leaders, A-Z (Table IV) 1/
.V35 Vallabhācarya, 1479-1531?
Vedism, see BL1152.3+, BL1212.52
1295 Other sects, movements, etc., A-Z (Table VI) 1/

1/ For tables, see pp. 64-65

Religion
History and principles of religions
Asia. Oriental
By religion
Hinduism - Continued

Tables of subdivisions

Biography

Table IV

	Collected works
.xA2	Original texts. By date
.xA25	Partial editions. Selections. Quotations, etc. By date
.xA26-269	Translations. By date
.xA27-279	Separate works
	Biography, criticism, etc.
.xA28-289	Periodicals. Societies. Congresses. Exhibitions
.xA29-299	Dictionaries. Indexes. Concordances, etc.
.xA3-39	Autobiography. Diaries, etc. By title
.xA4	Letters. By date
.xA6-Z	General works

Religion
History and principles of religions
Asian. Oriental
By religion
Hinduism

Tables of subdivisions - Continued

Modifications. Sects, etc.

Table V	Table VI	
(0)	.x	Periodicals. Societies. Directories. Congresses
(2)	.x2	Dictionaries. Encyclopedias
(22)	.x22	General collections. Collected works
		Including selections sacred to particular sect
(23)	.x23	Religious education. Study and teaching
		History
(3)	.x3	General works
		By region or country
		India
		General works, see (3); .x3
(32)	.x32	Local, A-Z
(35)	.x35	Other regions or countries, A-Z
		Under each country
		.x General works. History
		.x2 Local, A-Z
(4)	.x4	General works
(42)	.x42	General special
		Doctrines
(45)	.x45	General
(47)	.x47	General special. Special topics (not A-Z)
(5)	.x5	Relations to other religious and philosophical systems and to other branches of Hinduism, A-Z
		Practice. Forms of worship. Religious life
(52)	.x52	General works
(55)	.x55	Liturgy. Rituals. Meditation. Devotion
(6)	.x6	Devotional literature. Prayers. Meditations. Hymns
(7)	.x7	Organization. Government. Ministry
(73)	.x73	Monasteries. Temples. Shrines. Sacred sites
		For local or individual temples, etc., see BL1243.76+
		Biography
(9)	.x9	Collective
(92)	.x92	Founders and most important leaders, A-Z (Table IV)
		Other individuals, see BL1175

Religion
History and principles of religions
Asian. Oriental
By religion - Continued
Jainism

1300 Periodicals. Societies. Serials
1301 Congresses

1303 Dictionaries. Encyclopedias

1305 Collections (nonserial)
Museums. Exhibitions

1306 General works
1307 By region or country, A-Z
Each region or country subarranged by author

Sacred books. Sources. Āgama (Siddhānta) literature
Collections
Original
1310 Comprehensive
.2 Selections. Anthologies

Translations
.3 Comprehensive. By language, A-Z
.32 Selections. Anthologies. By language, A-Z

Religion
History and principles of religions
Asian. Oriental
By religion
Jainism
Sacred books. Sources. Āgama (Siddhānta) literature - Continued

1310.4 General works. History and criticism
.5 General special
.6 Dictionaries
Including terminology, indexes, concordances, etc.

Biography. Characters in the Āgamas (Collective)
.7 General works
.72 Special groups of characters, A-Z

.8 Special topics, A-Z
Special divisions and individual texts
1312.2-29 Angas (Table I) 1/

.3 Individual texts. By title, A-Z (Table III) 1/
.A58-589 Antagaḍadasāo (Antakṛtadaśā)
.A59-599 Anuttarovavāiyadasāo (Anuttaraupapātikadaśā)

.A93-939 Āyāranga (Acāra)
.B53-539 Bhagavaī (Bhagavatī)
.D58-589 Diṭṭhivāya (Dṛṣṭivāda)

.N39-399 Nāyādhammakahāo (Jñātādharmakathā)
.P35-359 Panhāvāgarana (Praśnavyākaranā)

.S35-359 Samavāyanga
.S88-889 Sūyagaḍa (Sūtrakṛta)
.T53-539 Ṭhāṇānga (Sthāna)

.U83-839 Uvāsagadasāo (Upāsakadaśā)
.V58-589 Vivāgasuya (Vipāka)

1/ For tables, see pp. 25-26

Religion
History and principles of religions
Asian. Oriental
By religion
Jainism
Sacred books. Sources. Āgama (Siddhānta) literature
Special divisions and individual texts - Continued

1312.5-59 Uvangas (Upāṅgas) (Table I) 1/
.6 Individual texts. By title, A-Z (Table III) 1/
.C35-359 Candapannatti (Candraprajñapti)
.J35-359 Jambuddīvapannatti (Jambūdvīpaprajñapti)
.J58-589 Jīvābhigama
.K36-369 Kappāvadamsiāo (Kalpāvatamsikā)
.N57-579 Nirayāvaliyāo (Kalpikā)
.P35-359 Pannavanā (Prajñāpanā)
.P85-859 Pupphacūliāo (Puṣpacūlikā)
.P87-879 Pupphiāo (Puṣikā)
.R38-389 Rāyapasenaijja (Rājapraśnīya)
.S87-879 Sūrapannatti (Sūriyapannatti)
.U83-839 Uvavāiya (Aupapātika)
.V35-359 Vaṇhidsāo (Vṛṣṇidaśā)

1312.8-89 Paiṇṇas (Prakīrnas) (Table I) 1/
.9 Individual texts. By title, A-Z (Table III) 1/
.A56-569 Angavijjā
.C35-359 Candāvejjhaya
.T35-359 Tandulaveyāliya (Tandulavaicārika)

1/ For tables, see pp. 25-26

Religion
History and principles of religions
Asian. Oriental
By religion
Jainism
Sacred books. Sources. Āgama (Siddhānta) literature
Special divisions and individual texts - Continued

1313.2-29 Cheyasuttas (Chedasūtras) (Table I) 1/
.3 Individual texts. By title, A-Z (Table III) 1/
.A83-839 Āyāradasāo (Acāradaśā)
.K36-369 Kappa (Bṛhatkalpa)

.N58-589 Nisīha (Niśītha)
.V38-389 Vavahāra (Vyavahāra)

.5 Cūlikasuttas (Table I) 1/
.6 Individual texts. By title, A-Z (Table III) 1/
.A58-589 Anuogadāra (Anuyogadvāra)
.N34-349 Nadīsutta (Nadīsūtra)
.8-89 Mūlasuttas (Mūlasūtras (Table I) 1/
.9 Individual texts. By title, A-Z (Table III) 1/
.A83-839 Āvassaya (Avaśyaka)
.D38-389 Dasaveāliya (Daśavaikālika)

.O53-539 Ohanijjutti (Oghaniryukti)
.U77-779 Uttarajjhayana (Uttarādhyayana)

1314.2 Other individual texts. By title, A-Z (Table III) 1/
.T38-389 Tattvārthadhigamasūtra

Jain literature. Jain authors
Including devotional or theologic-philosophical works of Jain authors not limited specifically by subject. For works on specific subjects, regardless of authorship, see the subject
For sacred books, see BL1310+
Collections of several authors
1315 Two or more volumes
.5 Single volumes

1/ For tables, see pp. 25-26

Religion
History and principles of religions
Asian. Oriental
By religion
Jainism
Jain literature. Jain authors - Cont.

1316 Individual authors, A-Z
Including individual anonymous works, subarranged like separate works in table below
Under each (using two or five successive Cutter numbers):

2 nos.	5 nos	
		Collected works
.xA1	.x	Original texts. By date
.xA2	.x2	Partial editions, selections, etc. By editor or date
.xA3	.x3A-Z	Translations. By language, A-Z
.xA4-Z	.x4A-Z	Separate works, A-Z Subarranged: x Original texts. By date x12-19 Translations x3-39 Criticism and interpretation
.x2A-Z	.x5A-Z	General works. Criticism, interpretation, etc.
		Biography, see BL1360+

Mahāvīra, see BL1370+

1317 History and criticism

1318 Study and teaching

1320 History

By region or country
India
General works, see BL1320

1324 By region or state, A-Z

1325.9 Local, A-Z

1327 Other regions or countries, A-Z

General works

1350 Through 1800

1351 1801-1950

.2 1951-

1353 General special

1355 Addresses, essays, lectures

Fasts and feasts

.5 General works

.6 Special, A-Z

Religion
History and principles of religions
Asian. Oriental
By religion
Jainism - Continued
Doctrine
1356 General works
1357 Special doctrines, A-Z

Philosophy, see B162.5
Relation to other religions, etc.
1358 General works
Special
Budhism, see BQ4610.J3
.2 Hinduism

Biography
1360 Collective
Individual
Māhāvīra
1370 Works
1371 Biography, criticism, etc.
1373 Other, A-Z

1375 Special topics, A-Z
.A35 Ahimsa
.A8 Atonement
.C3 Caste

.C6 Cosmogony. Cosmology
.D53 Dietary laws
.D73 Dreams
.F35 Family
.G58 Giving
.P4 Penance
.S26 Sallekhanā
.S3 Salvation

.S4 Self
.S43 Self-realization
.S65 Soul

.Y63 Yoga

Forms of worship. Jain practice
1376 General works
Ceremonies and rituals
1377 General works
.3 Hymns
.5 Sermons

Religion
History and principles of religions
Asian. Oriental
By religion
Jainism
Forms of worship. Jain practice - Cont.
Monasticism and monasteries
1378 General works
By region or country
India
General works, see BL1378
.2 By region or state, A-Z
.23 Local, A-Z

.3 Other regions or countries, A-Z
Under each country:
.x General works
.x2 Special. By city, A-Z

Temples and shrines
.4 General works
.45 By region or country, A-Z
Under each country:
.x General works
.x2 Special. By city, A-Z

.6 Devotion. Meditation. Prayer
.7 Devotional literature. Prayers

Mysticism
.8 General works
.85 Contemplation. Samadhi

Special modifications, schools, sects, etc.
1379 General works
1380 Individual, A-Z
.A55 Aṇuvrata

.S8 Śvetāmbara
.T4 Terehpanth

Buddhism, see BQ

Religion
History and principles of religions
Asian. Oriental
By religion - Continued
Zoroastrianism (Mazdeism). Parseeism
For Mithraism, see BL1585
For Parseeism, see BL1530
1500 Periodicals. Societies. Serials
1505 Collections (Nonserial)

1510 Sacred books. Sources
Avesta (or Zend-Avesta)
1515 Original text. By date
.2 Translations. By language, A-Z, and date

.4 Commentaries. By author
For philological commentaries, see PK
.5 Parts. By name or part, A-Z
Under each:
.xA2 Original text. By date
.xA4-49 Translations. By language and date
.xA5-Z Commentaries. By author

.H8 Husparam nask
.K5 Khordah Avesta
.V4 Vendidad

.Y28 Yashts
.Y3 Yasna

1520 Other, A-Z
Subarranged like BL1515.5
.D5 Dinkard

1525 History. Iran (Persia)
By region or country
1530 India
Iran (Persia), see BL1525
1535 Other regions or countries, A-Z

Biography
1550 Collective
Individual
1555 Zoroaster
1560 Other, A-Z

Religion
History and principles of religions
Asian. Oriental
By religion
Zoroastrianism (Mazdeism) - Continued
Relation to other religions
1565 General works
1566 Special religions, A-Z
Buddhism, see BQ4610.Z6
.J8 Judaism

General works
1570 Early through 1950
1971 1951-

1575 Addresses, essays, lectures
Special topics
1580 Mazda or Ormazd
1585 Mithras (God). Mithraism

1590 Other, A-Z
.F73 Fravashis
Government, see .S73
.H36 Haoma
.M9 Mysticism
Politics, see .S73

.P7 Prayers
.R5 Rider-gods

.S73 State. Politics and government
.S95 Symbolism

1595 Yezidis
Semitic religions
For Judaism, see BM
For Islam, see BP
1600 General works

1605 Special topics, A-Z
.A5 'Anat
.A7 Asherah
.I8 Ishtar
Including Astarte, Ashtoreth, etc.
.L55 Lilith
.M6 Moloch
.N3 Names (Semitic)
.N35 Navel

Religion
History and principles of religions
Asian. Oriental
By religion
Semitic religions
1605 Special topics, A- Z - Continued
Ocean, see .W3
.P7 Prophets
.R5 Ritual

.S65 Spring
.W3 Water. Ocean

1610 Aramean
Sumerian
1615 General works
1616 Special topics, A-Z
.I5 Inanna (Sumerian deity)
Assyro-Babylonian
1620 General works
1625 Special topics, A-Z
.A5 Anu (Deity)
.A8 Assur (Assyrian deity)
.C6 Cosmogony

Deities, see .G6
.D4 Deluge
.F8 Future life

.G6 Gods
Ishtar, see BL1605.I8
.M6 Monotheism

.N32 Nabu
.N37 Nergal
.N4 New Year

.O2 Oaths
.P3 Panbabylonism
.P7 Prophets

.S38 Shirkûtu
.S49 Sin (Deity)

.S5 Sin (Doctrine)
.T3 Tammuz
.T42 Temples
1630 Chaldean
1635 Harranian. Pseudo-Sabian
1640 Syrian. Palestinian. Samaritan
Class here ancient religions only
Cf. BL2340, Syria and Palestine

Religion
History and principles of religions
Asian. Oriental
By religion
Semitic religions - Continued
1650 Hebrew
Judaism, see BM
Phenician, Carthaginian, etc.
1660 General works

1665 Special topics, A-Z
Astarte, see BL1605.I8
.T3 Tanith

Canaanite
1670 General works
Special topics
1671 Baal
1672 Other, A-Z
Ashtoreth, see BL1605.I8
.R47 Rešep

1675 Moabite. Philistine
Arabian (except Islam)
1680 General works
1685 Pre-Islamic
Islam, see BP

1695 Druses
Cf. DS94.8.D8, Ethnography (Syria)
1710 Ethiopian
Other, see BL1750+

By region or country
1750 Afghanistan
Arabia, see BL1680+

1760 Armenia
Assyria and Babylonia, see BL1620

China
General works
1800 Early through 1800
1801 1801-1950
1802 1951-
1810 Addresses, essays, lectures
1812 Special topics, A-Z
.F87 Future life
.G63 Gods
.H44 Hell
.M68 Mountains
.M94 Mysticism
.Y55 Yin-yang cults

Religion
History and principles of religions
Asian. Oriental
By region or country
China - Continued
Special religions
Buddhism, see BQ
1825 Primitive religion of China

Confucianism
Cf. B127.C65, Confucian philosophy
B128.C8, Confucius
1830 Sources
1840 History. China

By region or country
China, see BL1840
1842 Korea
1843 Japan
1844 Other, A-Z

General works
1850 Early through 1800
1851 1801-1950
1852 1951-

1855 Addresses, essays, lectures
Biography
Confucius, see B128.C8
1870 Mencius
1875 Other, A-Z

Shrines
1880 General works
1882 By region or country, A-Z
Under each country:
.x General works
.x2 Local, A-Z

Taoism
1899 Periodicals. Societies. Serials
Sacred books. Sources
For philosophical commentaries, see PL

1900.A1A-Z Collected works (nonserial). Selections

Religion
History and principles of religions
Asian. Oriental
By region or country
<u>China</u>
Special religions
<u>Taoism</u>
<u>Sacred books. Sources</u> - Continued

1900.A3-Z Individual works. By author when known

Under each work, unless otherwise indicated:

.x	Original text. By date
.x2	Translations. By language, A-Z, and date
.x3	Selections. By date
.x4	Translations. By language, A-Z, and date
.x5	Criticism
.x6	Special topics (not A-Z)
.x7	Dictionaries, terminology, indexes, concordances

e. g.

.C45-576	Chuang-tzŭ. Nan-hua ching
.C45	Original text. By date
.C46	Translations. By language, A-Z, and date
.C48	Selections. By date
.C5	Translations. By language, A-Z, and date
.C576	Criticism
.L25-37	Lao-tzŭ. Tao te ching
.L25	Original text. By date
.L26	Translations. By language, A-Z, and date
.L28	Selections. By date
.L3	Translations. By language, A-Z, and date
.L35	Criticism
.L36	Special topics (not A-Z)
.L37	Dictionaries, terminology, indexes, concordances

Religion
History and principles of religions
Asian. Oriental
By region or country
China
Special religions
Taoism - Continued
1910 History. China
By region or country
China, see BL1910

1912 Korea
1913 Japan
1914 Other, A-Z

1920 General works
1923 General special
1925 Addresses, essays, lectures
Biography
1929 Collective
1930 Lao-tzŭ (Lao-tse, Lao-tsu, Laou-tsze)
1940 Other, A-Z

Temples. Shrines, etc.
1941 General works
1942 By region or country, A-Z

1943 Other religions in China, A-Z
Bon (Tibetan religion), see BQ7960+
.C5 Chên K'ung Chaio

.C55 Ch'üan Chen Chiao
1945 By country division, A-Z
e. g. .M6 Mongolia
Cf. BQ7530+, Lamaism
BL2370.M7, Mongols
.T5 Tibet
Cf. BQ7530+, Lamaism
BQ7960+, Bonpo (Sect)

1950 Chinese religions in countries other than China, A-Z
e. g. .S5 Singapore
.T5 Tibet
.U6 United States
Cf. BL1842+, Confucianism in countries other than China
1975 Taiwan

Religion
History and principles of religions
Asian. Oriental
By region or country - Continued
India
General works
2000 Early through 1800
2001 1801-1950
.2 1951-

2003 General special
2010 Addresses, essays, lectures

2015 Special topics, A-Z
.A6 Ancestor worship
.A65 Animals
.A8 Asceticism

.F2 Fakirs
.F3 Fasts and feasts
.F55 Fire. Heat

.G63 Gods
.G85 Gurus
.I4 Idolatry

.I6 Immortality
.K3 Karma
.K5 Kings and rulers

.M27 Mahāvrata
.M3 Mandala
.M4 Meditation

.M68 Mother goddesses
.M9 Mysticism
.N3 Nativistic movements

.N64 Nonviolence
.P3 Pantheism
.P57 Politics and religion

.P6 Poverty (Virtue)
.R4 Reincarnation
.R48 Rites and ceremonies
.R5 Rivers
Rulers, see .K5
.S3 Saints
.S4 Serpent worship

Religion
History and principles of religions
Asian. Oriental
By region or country
India
2015 Special topics, A-Z - Continued
Shrines, see .T4
.S6 Society and religion
.S9 Sun. Sun worship

.T4 Temples and shrines
.T7 Trees. Tree worship
.V5 Visions

.W6 Women
.Y6 Yogis
2016 Local, A-Z
Individual religions
Brahmanism, see BL1100+
Buddhism, see BQ

Jainism, see BL1300+
Islam, see BP1+

Parseeism, see BL1500+
Sikhism. Sikh religion
2017 Periodicals. Societies. Collections
.4 Ādi-Granth
.A2 Original texts. By date
.A32 Selections. By date
Translations
.A4A-Z English. By translator
.A7-Z Other languages
Assign second Cutter for translator

.42 Special parts
Texts and criticism
.421 Introductory parts
.422 Nānak's Jap Ji

.424 Nānak's Sidha gosati
The Rāgs
.427 General works
.428 Special authors of Rāgs, A-Z
.43 Special Rāgs, A-Z
.44 Arjun's Sukhamunī
.45 General works. Criticism

Religion
History and principles of religions
Asian. Oriental
By region or country
India
Individual religions
Sikhism. Sikh religion - Continued

2017.46-48 Sikh literature. Sikh authors 1/
Including devotional or theologico-philosophical works of Sikh authors not limited specifically by subject
For works on specific subjects, regardless of authorship, see the appropriate subjects
For works by founders of special sects or movements, see BL2018.7
Cf. BJ1290.5, Sikh ethics
For Ādi-Granth, see BL2017.4+
Biography, see BL2017.8+

.6 History

Biography

.8 Collective

.9 Individual, A-Z

2018 General works. Treatises
Cf. BL2017.46+, Devotional or theologico-philosophical works of Sikh authors not limited specifically by subject

.15 Relation to other religions, etc.
Special
Christianity, see BR128.S6
Islam, see BP173.S5

Theology

.2 General works

.22 God

Cultus. Ritual. Worship

.3 General works

.32 Hymns

.36 Temples and shrines
Subarranged like BL1227

Sikh religious life (Descriptive works)

.37 General works

.38 Devotional literature

.39 For special classes, A-Z

1/ Subarranged like BL1415-1417

Religion
History and principles of religions
Asian. Oriental
By region or country
India
Individual religions
Sikhism. Sikh religion
Cultus. Ritual. Worship - Cont.
Devotion. Meditation. Prayer

2018.4 General works
.42 Devotions. Meditations. Prayers
.43 Mysticism

.5 Special topics, A-Z
- .A47 Amrit
- .B4 Bangle
- .C4 Charities
- .D4 Death
- .D5 Dietary laws
- .G85 Gurus
  - For biography, see BL2017.8+
- .H3 Hair. Haircutting
- .N65 Nonviolence
- .P75 Psychology
- .R44 Religious tolerance
- .S3 Salvation
- .S35 Science

.7 Special sects, modifications, etc., A-Z
- .A1 General works
- .N34 Namdharis
- Sant Mat, see BP605.R335

2020 Other, A-Z (Table VI) 1/

- .A4 Ajivikas
- .D47 Ḍerā Saccā Saudā
- .D7 Dravidian religion
- .K3 Kabirpanthis
  - Founded by Kabir, 15th cent.
- .M3 Mahima Dharma
- .P7 Prānnāthīs
  - Founded by Prānanātha
- .V7 Vratyas

1/ For table, see p. 288

Religion
History and principles of religions
Asian. Oriental
By region or country
India - Continued
2030 By country division, A-Z
Including former divisions
e. g. .B8 Burma
.C5 Sri Lanka

.C6 Coorg
.M3 Malabar

2032 By ethnic group, etc., A-Z
.A2 Abors
.A35 Ahoms
.G6 Gonds

.K3 Kandhs
.K45 Khasis
.M4 Meitheis

.M5 Minas
.R34 Rajputs
.S45 Sherpas

.S55 Sinhalese
.T3 Tamils

2035 Pakistan
Southeast Asia
2050 General works
2055 Vietnam
Cf. BL2065, Cochin China
BL2070, Tongking

2060 Cambodia
2065 Cochin China

2067 Laos
2070 Tongking (Tonkin)

2075 Thailand
Malaysia
2080 General works
2082 By state, region, etc., A-Z
2085 Singapore

Religion
History and principles of religions
Asian. Oriental
By region or country
Southeast Asia - Continued
Indonesia
2110 General works
2112 General special

2120 By island, etc., A-Z
e. g. .B2 Bali (Island)
.B6 Borneo

.C4 Celebes
.F5 Flores

.J3 Java
.M4 Mentawai Islands
.S8 Sumatra

2122 Special sects, cults, etc., A-Z
.P3 Paguyban Sumarah

2123 By ethnic group, A-Z
.B38 Batak
2130 Philippine Islands
2150 By ethnic group, A-Z
Japan
General works
2200 Early through 1800
2201 1801-1950
2202 1951-

2203 General special
By period
2204 Early through 592
2205 593-1185
2206 1185-1600
2207 1600-1868
.3 19th century
.5 1868-
2208 1868-1912
.5 20th century
2209 1945-

2210 Addresses, essays, lectures
.5 Study and teaching

Religion
History and principles of religions
Asian. Oriental
By region or country
Japan - Continued

2211 Special topics, A-Z
.A5 Ancestor worship
.C67 Cosmogony
.D35 Death and life
.D4 Demons and demonology
.D68 Dōsojin
.F47 Fetishism
.F86 Funeral rites and ceremonies
.G6 Gods
Cf. BL2226+, Shinto deities
.H4 Hermits
.I5 Inari cult
.I53 Incantations
Life, see .D35
.K35 Kamagami
.K6 Kōshin cult
.M59 Mountain gods
.M6 Mountains
.P48 Phallicism
.P5 Pilgrims and pilgrimages
.P7 Prison
.R34 Rainmaking rite
.R44 Reward
.R47 Rice gods
.R5 Rites and ceremonies
.S36 Seven gods of fortune
.S38 Shamanism
.S4 Shrines
Cf. BL2225+, Shinto shrines
.T3 Takamagahara
.T8 Tutelaries
.V6 Votive offerings
.W48 Wetlands
.Y56 Yin-yang cults

Religion
History and principles of religions
Asian. Oriental
By region or country
Japan - Continued
2215 Local, A-Z
e. g. .O4 Okinawa Island
Individual religions
For special Christian denominations and sects, see BX
Christianity, see BR1300+
Buddhism, see BQ670+
Shinto
2216 Periodicals. Serials. Societies
.1 Dictionaries. Encyclopedias
Collections. Collected works
For Shinto authors, see BL2217.6+
.2 Several authors
.3 Individual authors, A-Z
2217 Sources. Sacred books
.2 Kojiki. Nihon shoki
Including studies of these works from the point of view of religion and mythology, and texts accompanied by such studies
For original texts, translations, and general and historical studies of these works, see DS855
For literary and linguistic studies of these works, see PL784

.3 Kojiki
.4 Nihon shoki
.5 Other, A-Z
Under each work, unless otherwise indicated:
.x Original text. By date
.x2 Translations. By language, A-Z, and date
.x3 Selections. By date
.x4 Translations. By language, A-Z, and date
.x5 Criticism

.K6 Kogo shui (by Imbe, Hironari, fl. 808)
.K8 Kujiki
.U3 Uetsufumi

Religion
History and principles of religions
Asian. Oriental
By region or country
Japan
Individual religions
Shinto - Continued

2217.6-8 Shinto literature. Shinto authors 1/
Including devotional or theologico-philosophical works of Shinto authors, not limited specifically by subject
For works on specific subjects, regardless of authorship, see the appropriate subject
For works by founders of special sects, see BL2222

Sacred books, see BL2217.2+
Biography, see BL2219.7+

.9 Study and teaching. Research
History. Japan (General)
2218 General works
.2 General special
By period
.3 Origins through 1868
.4 1868-1945
.5 1945-

By country
Japan
General, see BL2218+
2219 Local, A-Z
Other countries
.6 General
.65 Special countries, A-Z

Biography
.7 Collective
.8 Individual, A-Z

2220 General works
.3 General special
.5 Addresses, essays, lectures

1/ Subarranged like BL1316-1317

Religion
History and principles of religions
Asian. Oriental
By region or country
Japan
Individual religions
Shinto - Continued

2220.6 Controversial works against Shinto
.7 Philosophical theology. The essence, genius, and nature of Shinto

Doctrines. Theology
2221 General works
.7 Creeds and catechisms. Questions and answers
.9 Special schools, A-Z
.I8 Ise Shintō
.S5 Shirakawa Shinto

.S9 Suika Shinto
.Y6 Yashikawa Shintō

.Y67 Yoshida Shintō

2222 Individual sects, A-Z (Table VI) 1/

.F8 Fuso
.H5 Hinomoto
.H6 Honmiti

.I9 Izumo Taisha
.J5 Jikko
.K6 Konko

.K8 Kurozumi
.M3 Maruyama
.M5 Misogi

.M6 Mitake
.O4 Oomoto
.S37 Sekai Shinto

.S4 Shinri
.S5 Shinshu
.S6 Shinto-Honkyoku

.S63 Shintō Taiseikyō
.S65 Shizensha
.S7 Shusei

.T2 Taisei
Taisha, see .I9
.T26 Taiwa Kyōdan

1/ For table, see p. 288

Religion
History and principles of religions
Asian. Oriental
By region or country
Japan
Individual religions
Shinto
2222 Individual sects, A-Z - Continued
.T39 Tenno
.T4 Tenri

.Y3 Yamakage

Relation to other religions, etc.
.2 General works
Special
.23 Buddhism
Christianity, see BR128.S5
Judaism, see BM536.S5

2223 Relation to other subjects, A-Z
.S8 State
.5 Apologetics
Forms of worship. Shinto practice
2224 General works
Ceremonies and rituals
.2 General works

.25 Special, A-Z
.D4 Dedication services
.D46 Dengaku

.F8 Funeral rites
.H3 Harai

.K3 Kagura
.M57 Misogi
.O5 Onie no Matsuri (Daijo-sai)
.3 Devotional literature. Meditations. Prayers (Norito)
.35 Altars, liturgical objects, etc.

Ministry. Organization. Government
.4 General works
Priests. Priestesses
.5 General works
.55 Pastoral theology. Counseling
Shrine management
.6 General works
.63 Miyaza
.7 Religious life

Religion
History and principles of religions
Asian. Oriental
By region or country
Japan
Shinto
Forms of worship. Shinto practice - Cont.
Shrines
Cf. BL2224.6, Shrine management

2225 Japan

.3 Other countries, A-Z
Under each country:
.A1-29 General works
.A3-Z By city (or by name if non-urban)

Special deities. Shinto mythology

2226 General works
.2 Individual deities, A-Z
.A5 Amaterasu Omikami
.H3 Hachiman

.O48 Okuninushi no kami

2227.8 Topics not otherwise provided for, A-Z
.A45 Amulets, talismans, charms, etc.
.A5 Antiquities
.P7 Psychical research

2228 Other, A-Z (Table VI) 1/

.E5 Ennōkyō

.F8 Fuji (Sect)

.K9 Kyūseikyō

.P2 PL Kyōdan

.S4 Seichō-no-Ie
Including biographies of its founder Masaharu Taniguchi
.S43 Sekai Kyūseikyō

.S5 Shinri Jikkokai

.S54 Shūyōdan

.S94 Sukyo Mahikari
.T45 Tenshō Kōtaijingū Kyō

1/ For table, see p. 288

Religion
History and principles of religions
Asian. Oriental
By region or country - Continued
Korea
2230 General works
2231 General special
By period
2232 Early to 1864
2233 1864-1945
.5 1945-

2234 Addresses, essays, lectures
2236 Special topics, A-Z
.C6 Cults
.G62 Goddesses
.R58 Rites and ceremonies
.S5 Shamanism
.T35 Tan'gun

2238 Local, A-Z
2240 Individual religions, A-Z (Table VI) 1/

Buddhism, see BQ
.C5 Ch'undogyo
.C6 Ch'onji Taean'gyo
.C63 Ch'ŏnjin'gyo
Confucianism, see BL1842
.H36 Hanŏlgyo
.T33 Taejonggyo

.T34 Taesun chillihoe
.Y64 Yonghwagyo

2250 Media. Magi
Iran
2270 General works
Individual religions
Zoroastrianism, see BL1500+
2280 Other, A-Z

2290 Phrygia
2300 Soviet Union in Asia. Siberia
2320 Turkey in Asia. Asia Minor
For Islam, see BP1+
For Semitic religions, see BL1600+
2325 Cyprus
2330 Armenia

1/ For Table, see p. 288

Religion
History and principles of religions
Asian. Oriental
By region or country - Continued
Syria and Palestine
Cf. BL1640, Ancient religions
2340 General works
2345 By province, region, city, etc., A-Z
e. g. .H3 Hauran
2350 Other, A-Z
e. g. .I7 Iraq
.M7 Mosul
2370 Other special, A-Z
.A5 Ainu
.C5 Circassians
.H5 Hittites

.K8 Kurds
.M7 Mongols
.S25 Saka

.S3 Samoyeds
.S5 Shamanism
.T19 Tajiks
.T23 Tamang (Nepalese people)
.T25 Tamils

.T3 Tartars
.T8 Tunguses
.T84 Turks (General)
.Y34 Yakuts

African
2400 General works
2410 Hamitic
Egyptian
General works
2420 Early through 1800
2421 1801-1950
2422 1951-

Ancient Egypt
Cf. DT68+, Religious antiquities of ancient Egypt
2428 Dictionaries. Encyclopedias
2430 Sacred books. Sources
For philological commentaries, see PJ

General works
2440 Early through 1800
2441 1801-1950
.2 1951-
2443 General special

Religion
History and principles of religions
African
Egyptian
Ancient Egypt - Continued
2445 Addresses, essays, lectures
2450 Special deities and topics, A-Z
.A6 Animism
.A62 Anubis
.A64 Apedemak

.A89 Atum
.B2 Ba
Birth, see .C65

.C3 Camephis
.C65 Conception. Birth
.E8 Eschatology

Eternity, see .T55
.F3 Fate and fatalism
.F5 Fish

.F8 Funeral rites
.F83 Future life
.F84 Future punishment

.G6 Gods
.H3 Hathor
.H35 Heaven

.H5 Hippopotamus
.H6 Horus
.I44 Imiut

.I5 Immortality
.I7 Isis
.L5 Lions

.M4 Mert-seger
.M9 Mysteries
.N3 Navel
.N45 Neith
.O7 Osiris
.P3 Palms
.P7 Ptah

.R2 Ra
.R25 Renenet
.R3 Reshpu

Religion
History and principles of religions
African
Egyptian
Ancient Egypt
2450 Special deities and topics, A-Z - Cont.
.R4 Resurrection
.S23 Sacrifice
.S34 Sekhmet

.S37 Serapis
.S4 Set (Seth)
.S55 Shadows

.S56 Shai
.S6 Shu
.S65 Sky

.T37 Tatenen
.T43 Temples
.T5 Thoth
.T55 Time. Eternity
2455 Greco-Roman period
Including from Alexander's conquest to the Islamic conquest
For special topics that are survivals from the ancient period, see BL2450
2460 Modern Egypt

By region
2462 North Africa
2463 Southern Africa
2464 East Africa
2465 West Africa
2466 Central Africa

2470 By region or country, A-Z
e. g. Benin, see .D3
.D3 Dahomey. Benin
Egypt, see BL2420+
.G6 Gold Coast. Ghana

.G8 Guinea
.M3 Madagascar

.M6 Morocco
.N5 Nigeria

Religion
History and principles of religions
African - Continued

2480 By ethnic group, etc., A-Z

.A3 Abidji
.A4 Akans
.A5 Anlo

.A8 Ashantis
.B22 Bachama
.B23 Bakoko
.B244 Bakossi
.B24 Bakongo
.B25 Baluba
.B26 Bambara

.B27 Bamileke
.B3 Bantus
.B33 Baoulé

.B34 Basakata
.B35 Basuto
.B37 Batetela

.B4 Bembas
.B47 Beti
.B49 Betsimisaraka
.B5 Birifor

.B64 Bobo
.B8 Bushmen

.C5 Chokwe
.D3 Dagari

.D5 Dinka
.D6 Dogons
.F3 Fang

.G3 Gā
.H28 Hadjerai
.H3 Hausas

.H4 Hereros
Hottentots, see .K45
Ibos, see .I2
.I2 Igbo
.I37 Ijo
.K45 Khoikhoi
.K54 Kikuyu
.K6 Kono

Religion
History and principles of religions
African
2480 By ethnic group, etc., A- Z - Continued
.L8 Luo
.M25 Manala
.M28 Mandari
.M3 Mashona
.M33 Mbala
.M4 Mende
.M43 Meru
.M63 Moba
.N3 Ndembu
.N45 Ngbaba-Ma'bo
.N7 Nuer

.N8 Nupe
.N9 Nzima
.O77 Ovambo
.O8 Owegbe Society
.S25 Sara
.S8 Suku
.T27 Taita

.T3 Tallensi
.T5 Tivi
.T76 Tswana
.Y34 Yanzi
.Y6 Yorubas
.Z4 Zezuru
.Z56 Zinza
.Z8 Zulus
2490 Survival of African religions in America
Including voodooism in general
For works limited to individual cults, see BL2530+

American
For religion of American Indians, see E-F
2500 General works
2510 Pre-Columbian
North America
Including Canada, Mexico, United States, West Indies
2520 General works
2530 By country, etc., A-Z
e. g. .C9 Cuba
.H3 Haiti
.M4 Mexico

Religion
History and principles of religions
American
North America - Continued
2532 Special cults, etc., A-Z
.E86 Espiritualistas Trinitarios Marianos
.G33 Gagá
.O23 Obeah
.R37 Rastafarians

.S3 Santeria. Lucumí
.S5 Shango

2540 Latin America
Central America
2550 General works
2560 By country, etc., A-Z
e. g. .G8 Guatemala
.M3 Mayas

South America
2580 General works
2590 By country, etc., A-Z
e. g. .B7 Brazil
.P4 Peru. Incas

2592 Special cults, etc., A-Z
.B3 Batuque
.B45 Benito

.C34 Campanha do Quilo
.C38 Catimbó

.F73 Fraternidade Eclética Espiritualista Universal
.L4 Legião da Boa Vontade

.M3 Malê
Umbanda
.U4 Museums. Exhibitions
.U5 General works. History
.U512 Dictionaries
.U513 Doctrine. Rituals
.U514 Special topics, A-Z
.U515G6 Gods
.U514P55 Plants. Trees. Flowers
.W56 Winti

Religion
History and principles of religions - Continued
Oceanian
2600 General works
By country or island group
2610 Australia
2615 New Zealand
Including Maoris
2620 Other, A-Z
e. g. .A4 Admiralty Islands
.H3 Hawaiian Islands

.M4 Melanesia
.N45 New Guinea

.P6 Polynesia
.T8 Tuamotu Islands

2630 By ethnic group, etc., A-Z

.A72 Arapesh

.H82 Hua

.K85 Kwaio

.P3 Papuans

.T64 Tolai
2670 Arctic regions
Eskimos, see E99.E7
Local, see BL875.F5, Finland; BL980.L3, Lapland; BL2530, North America; etc.

Religions of preliterate peoples (General), see GN470+
Gypsies, see DX151

RATIONALISM

Including agnosticism, deism, free thought, atheism, secularims, etc.

Cf. B808, Agnosticism in philosophy
B833, Rationalism in philosophy
B837, Skepticism in philosophy
BR128.A5, Christianity and atheism
BR160.3, Early ancient writers against Christianity
BT1095+, Apologetics

2700 Periodicals. Societies. Serials
2703 Congresses
2705 Dictionaries. Encyclopedias

Collected works
2710 Several authors
Individual authors
Cf. BL2773+, Individual works except those of Ingersoll and Paine
2715 A - Ingersoll
e. g. .D4 Denton, William
.I3 I͡Aroslavskiĭ, Emelʹi͡an
Ingersoll, Robert Green
Cf. AC8, Collected works (General)

Works on religious subjects
Collected works
English
2720.A2 General
.A4 Other
.A5-Z Other languages
2725 Individual works, A-Z
e. g. .A3 About the Holy Bible
.L5 Liberty of man, woman, and child
.S6 Some mistakes of Moses
.W4 What must we do to be saved?

2727 Controversial works against Ingersoll
2728 Controversial works in favor of Ingersoll

2730 Ingersoll - Paine
e. g. .M5 Mills, Benjamin Fay

Rationalism
Collected works
Individual authors - Continued
Paine, Thomas
Cf. JC177+, Works on political theory
Works on religious subjects
2735 Collected works
Individual works

Age of reason
English
2740.A1 Editions. By date
.A2 Special parts. By number and date
.A3 French
.A4 German
.A5 Other languages, A-Z
.A7 Collections of criticisms
.A8-Z History and criticism
2741 Other works, A-Z

2742 Controversial works against Paine
2745 Paine - Z
2747 General works

Special theories
.2 Agnosticism
.3 Atheism
.4 Deism
.5 Free thought
.6 Humanism
.7 Rationalism
.8 Secularism

History
General works
2749 Early through 1800
2750 1801-1950
2751 1951-
2755 Other

By period
2756 Early and medieval
Modern
2757 General works
2758 16th-18th centuries
2759 19th-20th centuries

By region or country
2760 United States
2765 Other regions or countries, A-Z

Rationalism - Continued
Works by agnostics, atheists, freethinkers, etc.
For collected works, see BL2715+
General works
2773 Early through 1800

2775 1801-1950
.2 1951-

2776 General special
2777 Special topics, A-Z
.B8 Burial services for freethinkers
.P7 Prayers

.R4 Religious training of children
.R5 Ritual, hymns, etc., for freethinker meetings

2778 Joint debates and discussions
2780 Addresses, essays, lectures
Works against deists, see BT1180
Works against agnostics, atheists, etc., see BT1209+

Biography
2785 Collective
2790 Individual, A-Z
e. g. .C5 Chubb, Thomas
.I6 Ingersoll, Robert Green
Cf. BL2727+, Controversial works for and against Ingersoll
Paine, Thomas, see JC178.V2

For works on Jewish history, see DS101+
For biblical texts and exegesis, see BS

1 Periodicals. Societies. Serials
11 Yearbooks
21 Societies
30 Congresses. Conferences

Collected works
40 Several authors
42 Addresses, essays, lectures
43 Extracts from several authors
44 Pamphlet collections
45 Individual authors
50 Dictionaries. Encyclopedias
51 Questions and answers
52 Pictorial works
Directories
55 General
By region or country
60 United States
65 Other regions or countries, A-Z

Study and teaching
70 General works
Cf. BM570, Manuals of religious instruction
71 General special

By region or country
United States
75 General works
77 By state, A-W
80 By city, A-Z
85 Other regions or countries, A-Z
For Talmudic academies in Babylonia and Palestine (through 11th century), see BM502
Biography
88 Collective
Individual, see BM755+
By school
90 American (United States), A-Z
95 Other, A-Z
Religious education of the young. Sabbath schools
100 Periodicals. Societies. Serials
101 Congresses. Conferences

102 Biography, A-Z
103 General works

Study and teaching
Religious education of the young. Sabbath schools - Continued
105 Textbooks
107 Stories, etc.
108 Teacher training

109 Special types of schools, A-Z
For general education, see LC720+
e. g. .C6 Congregational Hebrew School
.H4 Heder
.T3 Talmud Torah

110 Individual schools, A-Z
Entertainments, exercises, etc.
125 General works
127 Special days, A-Z
Social life, recreation, etc., in the synagogue
135 Camps

History
General works
150 Early through 1800
155 1801-1950
.2 1951-

156 Handbooks, manuals, etc.
157 General special
160 Addresses, essays, lectures
By period
Ancient
165 General works

170 General special
173 Addresses, essays, lectures
175 Individual sects, parties, etc., A-Z
Including the tenets of each
.A1 General works
.A2 Unidentified sects
.E8 Essenes

.P4 Pharisees
.Q6 Qumran community
.S2 Sadducees

Samaritans, see BM900+
.T5 Therapeutae
.Z3 Zadokites

History
By period
Ancient - Continued
Religion of the Old Testament, see BM165; BM605

176 Last centuries before Christian Era
Including period between Old and New Testaments, Hellenistic movements, etc.

177 Judaism in the early centuries of Christian Era
Including the influence of Philo, etc.
Cf. BM504.3, Theology of the Talmud

178 Other
e. g. Ancestor worship

Medieval

180 General works

182 Ashkenazim. Sephardim 1/

185 Individual sects, parties, etc., A-Z
e. g. .K3 Karaites

Modern

190 General works

By period

193 16th-18th centuries

194 Haskalah

195 19th-20th centuries

Special movements
Including the tenets of each

196 General works

197 Reform movements
For individual congregations, see BM225+

.5 Conservative Judaism

.7 Reconstructionist Judaism

198 Hasidism
Including Assideans, Chasidim, Chasidism, Hasidim
Cf. BM532, Hasidic tales and legends

199 Other, A-Z
e. g. .S3 Sabbathaians

201-449 By region or country
Including history of individual synagogues

201 America

1/ The Ashkenazim are treated as standard Judaism. Class here works dealing with the Sephardim alone or in relation to the Ashkenazim

History
By region or country - Continued
203 North America
205 United States
By region
208 New England
211 South
214 Central
218 West
221 Pacific coast
223 By state, A-W
225 By city, A-Z
Under each:
.x General works
.x2 Individual synagogues or congregations, A-Z

Canada
227 General works
228 By province, A-Z
229 By city, A-Z 1/
Mexico
230 General works
231 By state, A-Z
232 By city, A-Z 1/

233 Central America
Under each country:
(1) General works
(2) Local, A-Z 1/
234-235 British Honduras
236-237 Costa Rica
238-239 Guatemala
240-241 Honduras
242-243 Nicaragua
244-245 Panama
246-247 Salvador

248 West Indies
Under each island or group of islands:
(1) General works
(2) Local, A-Z 1/
250-251 Bahamas
252-253 Cuba
254-255 Haiti
256-257 Jamaica
258-259 Puerto Rico
260 Other islands, A-Z

1/ Divided like BM225

History
By region or country - Continued
261 South America
Under each country:
(1) General works
(2) Local, A-Z 1/
262-263 Argentina
264-265 Bolivia
266-267 Brazil
268-269 Chile
270-271 Colombia
272-273 Ecuador
Guianas
274 General works
276-277 Guyana
278-279 Surinam
280-281 French Guiana
282-283 Paraguay
284-285 Peru
286-287 Uruguay
288-289 Venezuela

290 Europe
Under each country:
(1) General works
(2) By political division, A-Z
(3) By city, A-Z 1/

292 Great Britain. England
294 By English county, A-Z
By English city, A-Z
London
.8 General works
295 Individual synagogues or congregations, A-Z
296 Other, A-Z 1/
297-299 Scotland
300-302 Ireland
303-305 Wales

307-309 Austria
Hungary, see BM376.H8+
310-312 Belgium
313-315 France
316-318 Germany
319-321 Greece
322-324 Italy
325-327 Netherlands
328-330 Portugal

1/ Divided like BM225

History
By region or country - Continued
Europe

331-333	Soviet Union
334-336	Finland
337-339	Poland
	Scandinavia
340	General works
342-344	Denmark
345-347	Iceland
348-350	Norway
351-353	Sweden
354-356	Spain
357-359	Switzerland
360-362	Turkey
363	Other Balkan States
364-366	Bulgaria
370-372	Romania
373-375	Yugoslavia
376	Other European countries, A-Z Under each: .x General works .x2 Individual synagogues or congregations. By place, A-Z e. g. .H8-82 Hungary

Asia
Under each three-number country:
(1) General works
(2) By political division, A-Z
(3) By city, A-Z 1/

377	General works
379	Southwestern Asia
381	Turkey in Asia
382	By Turkish vilayet, region, etc., A-Z
383	By city, A-Z 1/
384-386	Armenia
386.4-6	Mesopotamia. Iraq

1/ Divided like BM225

History
By region or country
Asia
Southwestern Asia - Continued

387-389	Syria. Palestine Cf. BM165+, Ancient history of Judaism
390-392	Israel (The modern state)
393-395	Arabia
396-398	Iran
	Central Asia
399	General works
400	Afghanistan
402	Bokhara (Bukhara)
403	Khiva. Khorezm
404	Other, A-Z
	Southern Asia
405	General works
406	India
407	Burma
408	Sri Lanka
409	By political division, A-Z
410	By city, A-Z 1/
411-413	Indochina. Malay Peninsula Including Cambodia, Cochin China, Malaya, Thailand, Vietnam, etc.
	Indonesia. Malay Archipelago
414	General works
415-417	Indonesia
418-420	Philippine Islands
422	Eastern Asia
423-425	China
426-428	Japan
429-431	Northern Asia. Siberia
	Africa
432	General works
434-436	Egypt
437	South Africa
440	Other political divisions, A-Z
	Australia and New Zealand
443	General works
444	By political division, A-Z
445	By city, A-Z 1/
	Pacific islands
447	General works
449	By individual island or group of islands, A-Z 1/

1/ Divided like BM225

Pre-Talmudic Jewish literature (non-Biblical)
480 Collections
485 History and criticism
Special texts or groups of texts
For Apocrypha and Apocryphal books, see BS1691+
For Aristeas' epistle, see BS744.A7

Dead Sea scrolls
Texts
487.A05 Facsimiles. By date
.A1 Original language. By date
Translations
.A2 Hebrew. By date
.A3 English. By date
.A4 French. By date
.A5 German. By date
.A6A-Z Other languages. By language, A-Z, and date
.A62A-Z Periodicals
.A7-Z History and criticism
Language, see PJ4901+
488 Individual scrolls, A-Z
Subarranged like BM487
Biblical texts, see BS
.C6 Copper Scroll
Genesis Apocryphon, see BS1830+
Habakkuk commentary, see BS1635.H26+

.M3 Manual of discipline
.T44 Temple scroll
.T5 Thanksgiving scroll
.W3 War of the Sons of Light against the Sons of Darkness

Elephantine papyri, see PJ5208.E4+
Sources of Jewish religion. Rabbinical literature
Including Bible, Mishnah, Palestinian Talmud, Babylonian Talmud, Baraita, Tosefta, Midrash
Collections. Selections. Extracts, quotations, etc.
495 Several authors
.5 Individual authors

Works about the sources
496.A1 Periodicals. Societies. Serials
Treatises
.A4-Z Early through 1900
.5 1901-

Sources of Jewish religion. Rabbinical literature - Continued

496.8 Publication and distribution

.9 Special topics in Rabbinical literature, A-Z

.E9 Elijah, the prophet

.H4 Hell. Gehenna

.K5 Kings and rulers

.M87 Mysticism

.R66 Rome

.S48 Sex

.S93 Suffering of God

Bible, see BS701+

Talmudic literature 1/

Mishnah

Original language (Hebrew and Aramaic)

497 Complete texts. By date

.2 Selections. Miscellaneous tractates
By editor or date

.5 Translations. By language, A-Z
Under each language:
(1) Complete texts. By date
(2) Selections. Miscellaneous tracts.
By editor or date

Works about the Mishnah

.7 Early through 1900

.8 1901-

(.9) Gemara

498 Palestinian Talmud
Divided like BM497-497.8

Babylonian Talmud

Original language (Hebrew and Aramaic)

499 Complete texts. By date

.2 Selections. Miscellaneous tractates
By editor or date

1/ The bulk of Talmudic literature is devoted to the Babylonian Talmud. The classification for the Babylonian Talmud (BM499+) is therefore carried out in detail and is to be used for all Talmudic material unless any work is limited to the Mishnah or the Palestinian Talmud.

Sources of Jewish religion. Rabbinical literature
Talmudic literature 1/
Babylonian Talmud - Continued

499.5 Translations. By language, A-Z
Under each language:
.x Complete texts. By date
.x2 Selections. Miscellaneous tractates. By editor or date

Works about the Babylonian Talmud
Including the Palestinian Talmud, if necessary

500 Periodicals. Serials. Societies
.2 Collections. Collected works
Including addresses, essays, etc.

.5 Concordances. Subject dictionaries
Indexes, etc.
Language, see PJ4901+, PJ5201+, PJ5251+, PJ5301+
Language dictionaries, see PJ4935+

501 General works
Development of the Talmud
.15 Collective biography of Talmudists (General)
Under each group of Talmudists include collective biography
The evaluation of individual Talmudists is classed in BM502.3; their biography is classed in BM755
.17 Soferim
.2 Tannaim
.25 Beth Hillel and Beth Shammai
.3 Amoraim
For Baraita, see BM507+
For Tosefta, see BM508+
.4 Saboraim
.5 Geonim

1/ The bulk of Talmudic literature is devoted to the Babylonian Talmud. The classification for the Babylonian Talmud (BM499+) is therefore carried out in detail and is to be used for all Talmudic material unless any work is limited to the Mishnah or the Palestinian Talmud.

Sources of Jewish religion. Rabbinical literature
Talmudic literature 1/
Babylonian Talmud
Works about the Babylonian Talmud
Development of the Talmud - Continued

501.6 "Rishonim" (Early authorities)
.7 North African and Spanish scholars
Cf. BM545, Maimonides
.8 French and German scholars
e. g. Rashi, 1040-1105, and his school; Tosafists

.9 "Aharonim" (Later authorities, 16th century to date)
502 Talmudic academies in Babylonia and Palestine (through 11th century)
.3 Criticism and evaluation of individual Talmudists, A-Z
For Biography, see BM755

Study and teaching
.5 General works
.7 Hadranim
Individual institutions, see BM90+
503 Authority. Tradition. Oral tradition
Cf. BM529, Jewish tradition

.3 Apologetics
Cf. BM648, Judaism
For "Anti-Talmud", see BM585+
.5 Introductions

Methodology
.6 General works
.7 Hermeneutics
.8 Philpul

.9 Textual criticism
Commentaries
504 General works
.2 Novellae (Hidushim)
.3 Theology

1/ The bulk of Talmudic literature is devoted to the Babylonian Talmud. The classification for the Babylonian Talmud (BM499+) is therefore carried out in detail and is to be used for all Talmudic material unless any work is limited to the Mishnah or the Palestinian Talmud.

Sources of Jewish religion. Rabbinical literature
Talmudic literature 1/
Babylonian Talmud
Works about the Babylonian Talmud - Continued
504.5 Addresses, essays, lectures
.7 Juvenile works
Cf. BM530+, Jewish myths, legends, and traditions
Aggada, see BM516

506 Special orders and tractates of the Mishnah and the Palestinian and Babylonian Talmuds, A-Z
For list of Orders and Tractates, see Table I following BM990
Minor tractates (Not part of the Mishnah)
.2 Collections
.3 Works on the minor Tractates
.4 Special tractates, A-Z
Subarranged as in Table I following BM990

.A15-17	Abadim
	Aboth de-Rabbi Nathan, see .A94+
.A94-943	Avot de-Rabbi Nathan (Aboth de-Rabbi Nathan)
.D4-6	Derek ereg
.G4-43	Gerim
.K3-33	Kallah
.K35-353	Kallah rabbati
.K8-83	Kutim
.M48-483	Mezuzah
.S4-43	Semahot
.S6-63	Soferim
.Z5-53	Zizit

Baraita
507 Collections
.2 Works on the Baraita
.5 Special Baraitot, A-Z
For list of Baraitot, see Table II following BM990

1/ The bulk of Talmudic literature is devoted to the Babylonian Talmud. The classification for the Babylonian Talmud (BM499+) is therefore carried out in detail and is to be used for all Talmudic material unless any work is limited to the Mishnah or the Palestinian Talmud.

Sources of Jewish religion. Rabbinical literature

Talmudic literature 1/ - Continued

Tosefta

508 Editions. By editor, A-Z

.12 Selections. Miscellaneous tractates. By editor or date

.13 Translations. By language, A-Z
Divided like BM497.5

.15 Concordances. Subject dictionaries, indexes, etc.

.2 Works on the Tosefta

.5 Special Orders and Tractates, A-Z
Divided like BM506 except for .A2+, Aboth; .K7+, Kinnim; .M5+, Middot; .T3+, Tamid
For list of Orders and Tractates, see Table I following BM990

509 Special topics in Talmudic literature (not otherwise provided for), A-Z

.A5 Animals
.A7 Astrology
.A72 Astronomy

.B6 Botany
.C3 Caesarean section
.C4 Ceramics

.C5 Christians
.D5 Dialectic
.E27 Economics

.E3 Education
.E8 Eschatology
.G4 Geography
.G63 Gods

.H4 Hermaphroditism
.H54 Hides and skins
.I6 Iran
.J48 Jews

1/ The bulk of Talmudic literature is devoted to the Babylonian Talmud. The classification for the Babylonian Talmud (BM499+) is therefore carried out in detail and is to used for all Talmudic material unless any work is limited to the Mishnah or the Palestinian Talmud.

Sources of Jewish religion. Rabbinical literature

Talmudic literature 1/

509 Special topics in Talmudic literature (not otherwise provided for), A-Z - Continued

.L2 Labor and laboring classes

.M3 Mathematics

.M4 Messiah

.M6 Mnemonic devices

.N3 Names

.N4 Natural history

.P3 Palestine

.P8 Psychology

Skins, see .H54

.T5 Titus, emperor of Rome

.W4 Weights and measures

.W7 Women

Midrash

510 Original language (Hebrew or Aramaic)

Translations

511 English

512 Selections

513 Other languages, A-Z

514 Works about the Midrash

515 Halacha in the Midrash

Aggada

Including Talmudic Aggada

516 Texts. By author or title, A-Z

Under each:

.x Original. By date

.x2 Translations. By language, A-Z, and date

.x3 Criticism, commentaries, etc. By author, A-Z

.5 Works about the Aggada

1/ The bulk of Talmudic literature is devoted to the Babylonian Talmud. The classification for the Babylonian Talmud (BM499+) is therefore carried out in detail and is to be used for all Talmudic material unless any work is limited to the Mishnah or the Palestinian Talmud.

Sources of Jewish religion. Rabbinical literature

Midrash - Continued

517 Special Midrashim, A-Z

For list of Midrashim, see Table III following BM990

518 Special topics in the Midrash, A-Z

.A2 Abraham

.A4 Adam

.A45 Allegory

.B87 Burning bush

.C5 Circumcision

.I8 Isaac

.J4 Jerusalem

.K5 Kings and rulers

.M6 Moses

.P25 Palestine

.P3 Parables

.S24 Sabbath

.T5 Titus, emperor of Rome

Halacha

520 Periodicals. Societies. Serials

Collected works

.2 Several authors

.3 Individual authors

.4 Dictionaries

.5 History

.6 Philosophy

.65 Sources. Halakic portions of the Bible, Talmudic literature, and Midrash

Cf. BM515, Holacha in the Midrash

Commandments

.7 General works

.73 Noahide Laws

.75 Ten commandments

.8 Six hundred and thirteen commandments

Codes (Poskim)

.82 Alfasi, Isaac ben Joseph, 1013-1103. Halakhot

.A2 Original texts. By date

.A21-219 Translations. By language

Subarranged by translator

.A3-Z Criticism, commentaries, etc.

Sources of Jewish religion. Rabbinical literature
Halacha
Codes (Poskim) - Continued

520.84 Maimonides, Moses, 1135-1204 (Moses ben Maimon). Mishneh Torah
Subarranged like BM520.82

.86 Jacob ben Asher, ca. 1269-ca. 1340. Arba'ah turim
Subarranged like BM520.82+

.88 Caro, Joseph, 1488-1575. Shulhan 'arukh
.A2 Original texts. By date
.A3-39 Original selections. By date
.A4-49 Translations. By language
Subarranged by translator

Special parts
Each subarranged like BM520.88.A52+

.A52-53 Oraḥ ḥayim
.A52 Texts
.A53 Criticism, commentaries, etc.
.A54-55 Yoreh de'ah
.A56-57 Even ha'ezer
.A58-59 Ḥoshen mishpat
.A6-Z Criticism, commentaries, etc.

.9 Other codes
521 General works
Responsa
522.A1 Several authors
.A2-Z Individual authors
See Table IV following BM990 for special arrangement in use at the Library of Congress

Works on Responsa. History. Criticism
523 General works
Orah hayim law
.2 General works
.3 Special topics, A-Z
.B4 Benedictions
Festivals, see BM690+

.F7 Fringes
.I5 International date line
.P5 Phylacteries

.P7 Prohibited work
Sabbath, see BM685

Sources of Jewish religion. Rabbinical literature
Halacha
Responsa
Works on Responsa. History. Criticism
Orah hayim law
523.3 Special topics, A-Z - Continued
Synagogue, see BM653
.T9 Twilight
Work, see .P7

Yoreh de'ah law
.4 General works
.5 Special topics, A-Z
.B4 Benevolence (Gemilut ḥasadim)
Circumcision, see BM705

Dietary laws, see BM710
.H3 Hallah
.I3 Idolatry

.I5 Interest
Mourning, see BM712
Purity, see BM703

Redemption of the firstborn, see BM720.R4
.R4 Respect to parents and teachers

.S5 Shaatnez
.S53 Shaving
Slaughter of animals, see BM720.S6

Visiting the sick, see BM729.V5
.W5 Wine and wine making

Even ha-'ezer law
.6 General works
.7 Special topics, A-Z
Agunah, see K
Common law marriage, see K
Divorce, see K

Marriage
Civil aspects, see K
Religious aspects, see BM713
.P3 Parent and child

Sources of Jewish religion. Rabbinical literature
Halacha - Continued
Hoshen mishpat law, see K
Cabala
Cf. BF1585+, Cabala and magic
Sources
525.A2A-Z Collections
Individual texts
Under each:
(1) Original language (Aramaic or Hebrew). By date
(2) English
Subarranged by translator
(3) French
Subarranged by translator
(4) German
Subarranged by translator
(5) Hebrew (if translation)
Subarranged by translator
(6) Other languages, A-Z
Subarranged by date
(9) Criticism, alphabetically by critic

.A3-319 Bahir
.A36-3619 Book of Raziel
.A37-3719 Sefer ha-Razim
.A4-419 Sefer Yezirah
.A43-4319 Sword of Moses
.A5-59 Zohar
Zohar supplements
.A6A-2 Collections
.A6A3-Z Individual
Subarranged like .A6T5-579
.A6H4 Hekhalot
.A6122-2279 Idra de-mashkena
.A613 Idra raba
.A615 Idra zuta
.A6M5 Midrash ha-ne 'elam
.A6R2 Ra'ya mehemna
.A6S5 Sifra di-tseni'uta
.A6T5-579 Tikune ha-Zohar
.A6T5 Aramaic original. By date
.A6T52-529 English, alphabetically by translator
.A6T53-539 French, alphabetically by translator
.A6T54-549 German, alphabetically by translator
.A6T55-559 Hebrew, alphabetically by translator
.A6T56-569 Other languages, alphabetically by language
.A6T57-579 Criticism, alphabetically by critic
.A6Z6 Zohar ḥadash

Sources of Jewish religion. Rabbinical literature
Cabala - Continued
525.A7-Z Modern Cabalistic works. By author, A-Z
e. g. Issac ben Solomon Luria
.L83 Works
.L835 History and criticism
Including biography of Luria as a cabalist

526 History and criticism
529 Jewish tradition
530 Myths and legends
531 Golem
532 Hasidic tales and legends

Relation of Judaism to special subject fields
Ethics, see BJ1280+
Religions
534 General works
535 Christianity. Jews and Christianity
Cf. BM590, Jewish works against Christianity
BM620, Jewish attitude toward Christ
BT93, Judaism (Christian theology)
BT590.J34, Attitude of Jesus Christ to Jewish law
BT590.J8, Relation of Jesus Christ to Judaism
BV2619+, Christian missions among Jews

Judaism and Mormonism, see BX8643.J84
Judaism and Islam, see BP134.J4, Jews in the Koran; BP173.J8, Relations of Judaism and Islam

536 Other religions, A-Z

.A8 Assyro-Babylonian
Buddhism, see BQ4610.J8

.E3 Egyptian
.G54 Gnosticism

.G7 Greek
.H5 Hinduism

.P5 Phenician
.S5 Shinto

Relation of Judaism to special subject fields - Continued

537 Civilization
Including influence of Judaism

538 Other, A-Z
.A4 Agriculture
.A7 Art
Cf. N7415+, Jewish art

.A75 Astronautics
.A8 Atomic warfare

Communism, see HX550.J4
.E8 Evolution
.H85 Human ecology
.P2 Parapsychology
.P3 Peace

Philosophy, see B154+
.P68 Psychoanalysis. Psychology
.S3 Science (General)

Socialism, see HX550.J4
.S7 State and society
Cf. HN40.J5, Social history and the Jews
.S8 Superstition

.V43 Vegetarianism

540 Relation of Judaism to special classes, groups, etc., A-Z

.Y6 Youth

General works on the principles of Judaism
Cf. B154+, B755+, Jewish philosophy
Early to 1800

545 Maimonides. Moses ben Maimon
Cf. B759.M3, Maimonides as philosopher
BM755.M6, Biography
For Mishneh Torah, see BM520.84

550 Other early writers
For Caro, Joseph, see BM520.88
e. g. .J79 Judah, ha-Levi
.S25 Saadiah ben Joseph, gaon

General works on the principles of Judaism - Cont.
Modern works
560 1801-1950
561 1951-

565 General special
570 Manuals of religious instruction
573 Juvenile works
Cf. BM105, Textbooks
580 Addresses, essays, lectures
582 Other

Controversial works against the Jews
Cf. BT1120, Christian apologetics
585 General works
.2 Blood accusation cases

590 Jewish works against Christianity
.A1 Collections
591 Jewish works against Islam
.A1 Collections

Dogmatic Judaism
For early works, see BM545+
General works
Cf. BM150+, History of Judaism
600 Early through 1950
601 1951-

603 History of theology
Cf. BS1192.5, Theology of the Old Testament
607 Thirteen articles of faith
610 Conception of God

612 Revelation on Sinai
.5 Covenants. Covenant theology
.7 Holy Spirit

Mission of Israel. Election. Chosen people
613 General works
.5 The diaspora in relation to Israel's election

Messiah
Cf. BS680.M4, Biblical conception of Messiah
615 General works
620 Attitude toward Jesus Christ
621 Attitude toward Virgin Mary

Dogmatic Judaism - Continued
Messianic era
625 General works
.5 The State of Israel in relation to the Messianic era
627 Man
630 Sin
Eschatology. Future life
635 General works
.4 Death
.7 Transmigration
645 Other topics, A-Z
.A6 Angels
.A8 Atonement
.C6 Conversion

.E9 Exodus, The
.F4 Fear
.F7 Freedom

.H6 Holocaust
.I5 Immortality
.J67 Joy
.J8 Justice

.M34 Martyrdom
.M4 Merit
.P7 Providence and government of God

.R3 Race
.R4 Redemption
.R45 Repentance

.R47 Resurrection
.R5 Revelation
.R55 Reward

.S6 Soul
.S9 Suffering

646 Heresy, heresies, heretics, etc.
Cf. BM720.H5, Treatment of heretics, etc.
648 Apologetics
Including the history of apologetics
Practical Judaism
650 General works
Priests, rabbis, etc.
651 History
Cf. BS1199.P7, Priests in the Old Testament
652 Office of the rabbi
Including ordination, etc,; also his work, if included

Practical Judaism
Priests, rabbis, etc. - Continued
Work of the rabbi
652.3 General works
.4 Professional development, study, etc.
.5 Psychology and psychiatry for the rabbi. Counseling

.6 Conduct of services, meetings, etc.
Cf. BM676, Rabbinical manuals
.7 Participation in community affairs, interfaith movements, etc.

Congregations. Synagogues
653 Organization and administration
.2 Synagogue seating. Mixed pews. Mehitsah. Separation of sexes

.3 Management of financial affairs
.5 Management of subsidiary organizations
Including sisterhoods, men's clubs, etc.
.7 Management of educational activities and youth work

654 The tabernacle
Including history, structure, etc.

The temple
Including function, purpose, etc.
Cf. BS649.J4, Jerusalem Temple (Prophecy)
BS680.T4, Temple of God (Symbolism)
DS109.3, History of the temple
NA243, Architecture of the temple

655 General works
.4 The Sanhedrin
Cf. BM506.S2+, Tractate Sanhedrin
.45 The Nasi

.5 The French Sanhedrin under Napoleon
.6 Proposals for restoration

Forms of worship
656 General works
657 Special objects and instruments, A-Z
.A1 Collective
.A5 Altars

.A8 Ark of the covenant
.A85 Ark of the law

Practical Judaism
Forms of worship
657 Special objects and instruments, A-Z - Continued
.B7 Breastplate of the High Priest (Hoshen)
.C3 Candles and lights

.C5 Citron
.E7 Ephod

.F7 Fringes
.H3 Hanukkah lamp

Lights, see .C3
.L8 Lulab

.M35 Menorah
.M4 Mezuzah

.P5 Phylacteries
.S5 Shofar (Shophar)
.S64 Spice boxes
.T6 Torah scrolls
.U7 Urim and Thummim

Symbols and symbolism
Cf. N7415+, Jewish art
.2 General works
.5 Special symbols, A-Z
.M3 Magen David
Music in Jewish worship
Cf. ML3195, Jewish sacred vocal music
658 General works
.2 Cantors

659 Other religious functionaries, A-Z
.G3 Gabai
.M3 Magid (Preacher)
Mohel, see BM705
.S3 Scribe (Sofer)
.S5 Shamesh (Sexton)
Shochet, see BM720.S6

Liturgy and ritual
660 General works
663 Reading of the Bible
General and miscellaneous prayer and service books
General collections
665.A2 By title where editor, compiler, or translator is unknown

Practical Judaism
Liturgy and ritual
General and miscellaneous prayer and service books
General collections - Continued

665.A3 Local. By synagogue, A-Z
Cf. BM673, Liturgy and ritual of special places

.A4-Z By editor, etc.

Works for special classes

666 Children

667 Other classes, A-Z

Armed forces, see .S6
.G5 Girls

.S4 School prayers
.S55 Sick
.S6 Soldiers. Armed forces
.W6 Women

669 General works on prayer

670 Special elements of the liturgy, A-Z
Including individual prayers
Cf. BM675, Special liturgical books

Under each: 1/
.xA3 By date (if author or editor is unknown)
.xA5-Z By author or editor

.A42 Akdamut millin
.A8 Azharot
.H28 Had gadya
.H3 Haftaroth
.H35 Hallel
.H67 Hosha'not

.K3 Kaddish
.K39 Kavanot
.K6 Kol nidre
.M33 Mah tovu
.P5 Piyyutim (Piyutim)
For biography of authors, see BM678.4+
.S4 Seder hakafot
.S45 Shema
.S5 Shemoneh 'esreh
.S55 Shir ha-yiḥud
.U25 U-netanneh tokef

1/ .x=Cutter number. Substitute the Cutter number of the special element for .x in the table.

Practical Judaism
Liturgy and ritual - Continued

672 Special rites, A-Z

For special liturgical books with cross reference here, see BM675

e. g. .A8 Ashkenazic. Mitnaggedic
.A82 Hasidic
.F3 Falasha
Karaite, see BM185+
.S4 Sephardic
.Y4 Yemenite

673 Special places, A-Z

For special liturgical books with cross reference here, see BM675

Cf. BM665.A3, General collections by synagogue

e. g. .T9 Tunis

675 Special liturgical books, A-Z

Under each:

Texts 1/
Ashenazi or unspecified rite
Hebrew only
.xA3 By date (if editor is unknown)
.xA5-Z5 By editor
.xZ52-529 Manuscripts in facsimile. By name
Translations
.xZ55-559 English. By editor or translator
.xZ56-569 French. By editor or translator
.xZ57-579 German. By editor or translator
.xZ58-589 Other languages
.xZ62-629 Other traditional rites. By rite as given in uniform title
Non-traditional rites
.xZ64-649 Conservative. By editor or institution given in uniform title
.xZ65-659 Reconstructionist. By editor or institution given in uniform title
.xZ66-669 Reform. By editor or institution given in uniform title
Including European liberal
.xZ68-689 Adaptations for children. By editor or institution given in uniform title
.xZ7-9 Criticism

1/ .x=Cutter number. Substitute the Cutter number of the liturgical book for .x in the table.

Practical Judaism
Liturgy and ritual

675 Special liturgical books, A-Z - Continued

Atonement. Kol nidre, see .Y58
Ayelet ha-shahar, see .R412
.B4 Benedictions
Birkat ha-ḥamah, see .B53
.B53 Blessing of the sun
.D3 Daily prayers
Day of Atonement prayers, see .Y58
.F3 Fast-day prayers

.F45 Festival prayers
.G7 Grace at meals
Hagadah, see .P4

.H33 Hanukkah prayers
.H35 Hatarat nedarim
.H5 High Holy Day prayers

.H6 Hosha'nah Rabbah prayers
.I87 Israel Independence Day prayers
.K5 Kinot

Likute tsevi, see .R42
Ma'amadot, see .R44
.M4 Memorial services

.M7 Mourners' prayers
Including Book of life, etc.
.N45 New moon prayers

New Year prayers, see .R67
.O25 Occasional prayers
.P3 Passover
Cf. BV199.P25, Christian observance

.P4 Seder service (The Haggadah (Hagadah) of Passover)
.P45 Miscellaneous adaptations

.P5 Pentecost
.P59 Pilgrimage Festival prayers
.P6 Pirke shirah

.P8 Purim prayers
.R4 Readings
.R412 Ayelet ha-shahar
.R42 Likute Tsevi

.R44 Ma'amadot
.R46 Sha'are Tsiyon
.R48 Tikun (except Pentecost)

Practical Judaism
Liturgy and ritual
675 Special liturgical books, A- Z - Continued
.R67 Rosh ha-Shanah (New Year) prayers
.S3 Sabbath prayers
.S4 Selihot

Sha'are Tsiyon, see .R46
Siddur, see .D3
.S5 Simḥat Torah prayers
.S9 Synagogue dedication services

.T2 Tabernacle service
.T38 Tefilat ha-derekh
.T4 Teḥinot

Tikun (General), see .R48
Tikun lel Shavu'ot (Pentecost), see .P5
.T5 Tiḳun hatsot
.T52 Tikun shovavim
.Y55 Yom ha-zikaron prayers
.Y58 Yom Kippur (Day of Atonement, Kol nidre) prayers

.Y6 Yom Kippur Katan prayers
.Z4 Zemirot

676 Selections for the use of rabbis, etc.
Rabbinical manuals
Hymns
Cf. BM670.P5, Piyyutim (Piyutim)
History and criticism
678.A1 Periodicals. Societies. Serials
.A3-Z General works

Biography
Including authors of Piyyutim (Piyutim)
.4 Collective
.5 Individual, A-Z
679 By language, A-Z
685 The Sabbath
Festivals and fasts
Cf. BM125+, Sbbath school exercises
690 General works
693 Special groups, A-Z

.H5 High Holy Days
.H64 Hol ha-Moed
.P5 Pilgrimage Festivals
Three Festivals, see .P5
.T6 Tishri

Practical Judaism
Festivals and fasts - Continued
695 Individual festivals and fasts, A-Z

.A8 Atonement, Day of (Yom Kippur)
.H3 Hanukkah (Feast of Lights)
.L3 Lag b'Omer

.N4 New moon
.N5 New Year (Rosh ha-Shanah)
Cf. BS1199.R6, Old Testament

Passover
Cf. BS680.P33, Passover in the Bible
BV199.P25, Christian liturgy and ritual
.P3 General works
.P35 Ritual ceremonies
Pentecost, see .S5

.P8 Purim (Feast of Esther)
.S4 Sefirah period

.S5 Shabu'ot (Shavu'oth; Pentecost)
.S6 Simḥat Torah
.S8 Sukkot (Sukkoth)

.T4 Three Weeks
.T9 Tu bi-Shevat
Yom Kippur, see .A8

Rites and customs
For halacha, see BM523.2+
700 General works
Ritual purity. Purification
702 General works
703 Ritual baths. Mikveh. Baptism

705 Berit milah (Circumcision)
Bar Mitzvah. Confirmation
707 General works
.2 Instruction and study. Manuals

.3 Sermons. Addresses, essays, etc.
.4 Services, etc.

710 Dietary laws
Cf. BM720.S6, Slaughter of animals
TX724, Jewish cookery
712 Funeral rites. Mourning customs
Cf. BM675.M7, Mourners' prayers

Practical Judaism
Rites and customs - Continued

713 Marriage
715 Sacrifices
720 Other, A-Z
.C6 Clothing and dress
.C65 Cohanim
.D2 Dancing, Religious

.E9 Excommunication. Herem
.F3 Fasting
.F4 Fellowship

.H3 Halitsah
Herem, see .E9
.H5 Heretics, apostates, etc. (Treatment)
Cf. BM720.M3, Treatment of Maranos
BM646, Heresy, heresies, heretics (Dogmatic Judaism)

.H6 Hospitality
.I6 Incense
.K3 Karaites (Treatment)

.K5 Kissing
.M3 Maranos (Treatment)
.N3 Nazarite

.N6 Non-Jews (Goyim, Gentiles, Heathen), Position of
.O3 Oaths
.R3 Rain. Prayers for rain

.R4 Redemption of the firstborn
.S2 Sabbatical year. Shemitah

.S23 Special observances
e. g. Reading of Deuteronomy
.S4 Sex
Shehitah, see .S6
.S6 Slaughter of animals
.S6A1-4 Societies. Organizations, boards, etc.
.S6A5-Z Ritual. Procedure

.S62 History. Politics
.S63 Humanitarian aspects

.T4 Tithes. Terumah
.T7 Travel

Practical Judaism - Continued

Jewish way of life. Spiritual life. Personal religion

723 General works

.5 Admonition

.7 Confession

724 Devotional works. Meditations

Religious duties

725 General, and men

.5 Duties of fathers and children

726 Women. Motherhood

727 Children and youth. Students

.5 Soldiers

728 Moral theology

Halacha, see BM523.4-5

Cf. BJ1280+, Jewish ethics

729 Other special topics, A-Z

.A4 Amulets. Talismans

.A5 Animals (Protection and treatment)

Cf. BM509.A5, Animals in Talmudic literature

.C4 Censorship

.C6 Consolation

.D92 Dybbuk

.E45 Electric apparatus and appliances

.F3 Faith

.H35 Handicraft

.J4 Jewish science (Applied psychology: health, happiness, etc.)

.N3 Name (Jew, Israel, Hebrew)

Cf. CS3010, Jewish personal names

Nonviolence, see .P4

.P3 Palestine. Jerusalem, etc.

.P35 Parchment

.P4 Peace. Pacifism. Conscientious objectors. Nonviolence

.P65 Printing

.P7 Proselytes and proselyting

.S85 Summer

.S6 Social ideals

.S7 Social service

Talismans, see .A4

.V5 Visiting the sick

.W6 Women

Practical Judaism - Continued
Preaching. Homiletics

730.A1 Periodicals. Societies. Serials
.A2 Collections. Collected works
.A3 History
.A4 By country, A-Z
.A5-Z General works

731 Addresses, essays, lectures
732 Outlines, texts, etc.
733 Illustrations for sermons

Sermons. Addresses, etc.
735 Collective
Individual authors
740 Works through 1950
.2 1951-
742 To the young
743 To children

Occasional sermons. Special sermons
744 General works
.3 Funeral sermons. Memorial sermons
.5 Wedding sermons

Bar mitzvah sermons, see BM707.3
.6 Dedication sermons
.7 Installation and ordination sermons of rabbis
.8 Installation sermons of synagogue officials

Festival day sermons
For Sabbath and festival sermons combined in one volume, see BM735+
745 General works
746 High Holy Day sermons
.5 Three Festival sermons
747 Individual festivals, A-Z

.H3 Hanukhah
.P3 Passover sermons

.P8 Purim
.R6 Ros ha-Shanah sermons

Reform movements, see BM197
Biography
Cf. BM88, Religious educators
BM102, Sabbath school teachers
DS151, Zionist biography

750 Collective
752 Pseudo-Messiahs
753 Women

755 Individual, A-Z

.A2 Abba Arika, called Rab
.A25 Abravanel, Isaac

.A28 Abulafia, Abraham
.A87 Aviḥatsira, Jacob, 1808-1880
Bar Cocheba, see DS122.9
Bar Kokba, see DS122.9
.C28 Caro, Joseph

.E6 Elijah ben Solomon, gaon of Vilna
.G4 Geiger, Abraham

.I8 Israel ben Eliezer, Ba'al-Shem-Tob, called BeSHT
.J8 Judah Low ben Bezaleel

.K25 Kahan, Israel Meir
.L45 Levinsohn, Isaac Baer
.L54 Lipkin, Israel
.L8 Luzzatto, Samuele Davide

Maimonides, Moses, see .M6
.M6 Moses ben Maimon
Naḥman, of Bratslav, see .N25
.N25 Naḥman ben Simḥah, of Bratzlav
Ouziel, Ben-Zion Meir Hai, see .U72
Rashi, see .S6
.R6 Rosenzweig, Franz
.S2 Saadiah ben Joseph, gaon

Salanter, Israel, see .L54
.S33 Schreiber, Moses

.S45 Shabbethai Zebi
Sofer, Moses, see .S33
.S6 Solomon ben Isaac, called RaSHI

.U72 Usiel, Ban-Zion Meir Hai
.W5 Wise, Isaac Mayer

.Z8 Zunz, Leopold

	<u>Samaritans</u>
900	Periodicals. Serials
903	Societies
	Collections
905	Collective authors
907	Individual authors
	History
910	General works
913	Special sects, etc., A-Z
915	Relation to Judaism
	Sources of Samaritan religion
917	General works
	Samaritan Pentateuch
920	Original texts. By date of printing
922	Manuscripts. History and criticism of manuscripts
923	Facsimiles
924	Samaritan and Hebrew versions paralleled. By editor
.5	Samaritan and Latin versions paralleled. By editor
925	Translations. By language, A-Z
927	History and criticism
	Including comparison with Masoretic Pentateuch
930	Samaritan Targum
933	Samaritan-Arabic version of Targum
935	General works
940	General special
945	Dogmas
	Practical religion
950	Priesthood
	Liturgy and ritual
960	General works
.3	Special liturgical books. By title, A-Z
	Under each:
	.x Texts. By date
	.x3A-Z Criticism. By author
	.D33 ha-Daftar
	.S52 Shabat hol mo'ed Sukot
	.S53 Shemini 'atseret
970	Festivals and fasts
980	Rites and ceremonies
	Biography
990.A1	Collective
.A3-Z	Individual

TABLE I 1/

Special Orders and Tractates of the Mishnah and the Palestinian and Babylonian Talmuds (BM506)

Each Order and Tractate subarranged like .A15-17, .A2-23 or .D3-5

.A15-17 'Abodah zarah
  .A15 Original texts (Hebrew and Aramaic). By date
  .A15A-Z Translations. By language
    e. g. .A15E5 English
    .A15E65 English paraphrases
  .A16 Selected works. By date
  .A17 Criticism. Commentaries, etc. 2/
.A2-23 Aboth (Abot or Pirke Abot)
  .A2 Original texts (Hebrew or Aramaic). By date
  .A2A-Z Translations. By language
    e. g. .A2G4 German
    .A2Y5 Yiddish
  .A22 Selected works. By date
  .A23 Criticism. Commentaries, etc. 2/
Ahilot, see .03+
.A7-73 'Arakin
Avodah zarah, see .A15+
.B15-17 Bavot (Baboth)
.B2-23 Bava kamma (Baba ḳamma)
.B3-33 Bava meẓia (Baba meẓi'a)
.B4-43 Bava batra (Baba batra)
.B5-53 Bekorot
.B6-63 Berakhot (Berakot)
.B7-73 Bezah
.B8-83 Bikkurim
Chagigah, see .H3+
.D3-5 Demai
  .D3 Original texts (Hebrew and Aramaic). By date
  .D3A-Z Translations. By language
    e. g. .D3L3 Latin
  .D4 Selected works. By date
  .D5 Criticism. Commentaries, etc.

1/ The forms of the names of the orders and tractates follow the usage of the Encyclopaedia Judaica, 1971 edition

2/ Commentaries without text are arranged by commentator. Commentaries with text are arranged by commentary by title, or by whatever form is used for the catalog entry of the work.

TABLE I - Continued

.E3-5	'Eduyot
.E7-9	Eruvin ('Erubin)
.G5-53	Giṭṭin
.H3-33	Hagigah (Chagigah)
.H4-43	Ḥallah
.H5-7	Horayot
.H8-83	Ḥullin
.K2-23	Ḳelim
.K3-33	Keritot
.K4-43	Ketubbot (Ketubot)
.K5-53	Ḳiddushin
.K6-63	Kil'ayim
.K7-73	Ḳinnim
.K8-83	Ḳodashim (Order)
.M13-15	Ma'aser sheni
.M17-19	Ma'aserot
.M2-23	Makhshirin
.M3-33	Makkot
	Mashkin, see .M8+
.M4-43	Megillah
.M44-46	Me'ilah
.M47-49	Menaḥot
.M5-53	Middot
.M6-63	Miḳwa'ot (Micva'ot, Mikwot)
	Minor tractates, see BM506.4
.M7-73	Mo'ed (Order)
.M8-83	Mo'ed kaṭan. Mashkin
.N2-23	Nashim (Order)
.N3-33	Nazir
.N4-43	Nedarim
.N5-53	Nega'im
.N6-63	Neziḳin (Order)
.N7-73	Niddah
.O3-5	Ohalot (Ahilot)
.O6-8	'Orlah
.P2-4	Parah
.P5-7	Pe'ah
.P8-83	Pesaḥim

TABLE I - Continued

	Pirḳe Abot, <u>see</u> .A2+
.R5-7	Rosh ha-Shanah
.S2-23	Sanhedrin
.S25-27	Shabbat
.S3-33	Shebi'it
.S4-43	Shebu'ot
.S5-53	Sheḳalim
.S7-73	Soṭah
.S9-93	Sukkah
.T2-23	Ta'anit
.T3-33	Tamid
.T4-43	Ṭebul yom
.T5-53	Temurah
.T6-63	Terumot
.T7-73	Ṭohorot (Order)
.T8-83	Tohorot
.U5-7	'Uḳẓin
.Y2-4	Yadayim
.Y5-7	Yevamot (Yebamot)
.Y8-83	Yoma
.Z2-4	Zabim
.Z5-7	(Zebaḥim) Zevaḥim
.Z8-83	Zera'im (Order)

TABLE II

SPECIAL BARAITOT (BM507.5)

(Subarranged as in Table I)

.A2-4	Baraita on the Aboth (Abot)
.A5-7	Baraita of Rabbi Ada
	Baraita of Rabbi Eli'ezer, see Midrash. Pirke de Rabbi Eli'ezer
.E6-8	Baraita on the Erection of the tabernacle
.F5-7	Baraita of the Forty-nine rules
.I7-9	Baraita of Rabbi Ishmael
.M7-9	Baraita of the Mystery of the calculation of the calendar
.N4-6	Baraita de-Niddah
.P4-6	Baraita of Rabbi Phinehas ben Jair Including sayings on Messianic times and on Soṭah IX.15
	Baraita of Rabbi Phinehas ben Jair (Genesis), see Midrash. Tadshe
.S2-4	Baraita on Salvation
.S6-7	Baraita of Samuel
.T4-6	Baraita of the Thirty-two rules

TABLE III

SPECIAL MIDRASHIM (BM517)

(Subarranged as in Table I)

.A1-13	Abba Gorion
.A2-23	Abkir
.A3-33	Midrash Aggadat Bereshit
.A34-36	Agadat Ester
.A4-6	Al yithallel
.A7-9	Midrash Aseret ha-Dibrot
	Bamidbar rabbah, <u>see</u> .M68
	Baraita of Rabbi Eli'ezer, <u>see</u> BM517.P7+
	Baraita of Rabbi Phinehas ben Jair (Genesis), <u>see</u> BM517.T3+
.B7-73	Bereshit rabati
	Bereshit rabbah, <u>see</u> .M65
.B8-83	Bereshit zuta
	Debarim rabbah, <u>see</u> .M69
.D4-43	Midrash Debarim zuta
.D5-7	Dibre ha-yamin shel Mosheh
	Ekah rabbati, <u>see</u> .M74
.E5-53	Midrash Elek ezkerah
.E6-63	'Eser galiyyot
.E7-73	Esfah
	Esther rabbah, <u>see</u> .M76
	Midrash ha-gadol, <u>see</u> .M5-53
.I7-9	Midrash Iyyob
.K5-7	Kohelet
.K8-83	Midrash Konen
.M2-23	Ma'aseh Torah
.M4-43	Mekhilta of Rabbi Ishmael (Mekilta)
.M45-47	Mekilta de-Rabbi Shim'on

TABLE III - Continued

.M5-53	Midrash ha-gadol
.M54-59	Special parts
	Divided like .M64-69
.M6-63	Midrash rabbah
.M64-76	Special parts
	Each part subarranged like Genesis
.M64	Pentateuch
	Genesis
.M65	Texts. By date
	Translations
.M65A3	English. By date
.M65A32-49	Other languages, alphabetically. By date
.M65A5-Z	Criticism. Commentaries, etc.
.M66	Exodus
.M67	Leviticus
.M68	Numbers
.M69	Deuteronomy
.M7	Five Scrolls
.M72	Song of Solomon
.M73	Ruth
.M74	Lamentations
.M75	Ecclesiastes
.M76	Esther
.M77-79	Midrash Mishle
.08-83	Otiyyot de-Rabbi Aḳiba (Otiyot de-rabi Akiva)
.P1-13	Panim aḥerim
.P2-23	Midrash Peliah
.P3-33	Pesiḳta
.P34-36	Pesiḳta de-Rab Kahana
.P4-43	Pesiḳta rabbati
.P5-53	Peṭirat Aharon
.P6-63	Peṭirat Mosheh
.P7-73	Pirḳe de-Rabbi Eliezer
	Midrash rabbah, <u>see</u> .M6+
	Ruth rabbah, <u>see</u> .M73
	Shemot rabbah, <u>see</u> .M66
.S4-43	Shemu'el (Shemuel)
.S45-47	Midrash Shir ha-shirim

TABLE III - Continued

	Shir ha-shirim rabbah, see .M72
	Midrash Shoḥer tov, see .M77+, .S4+, .T5+
.S6-63	Sifra (Torat kohanim)
.S7-73	Sifre. Sifrei
	Special parts
	Each part subarranged like .M64
.S74	Numbers
.S75	Deuteronomy
.S85-87	Sifre zuta
.T2-23	Ta'ame ḥaserot ve-Yeterot (we-Yeterot)
.T3-33	Tadshe
.T35-37	Midrash Tanḥuma (Midrash Yelammedenu)
.T4-43	Tanna debe Eliyahu
	In two parts:
	(1) Seder Eliyahu Rabbah
	(2) Seder Eliyahu zuṭa
.T5-53	Midrash Tehillim (Midrash Shoḥer tov)
.T6-8	Temurah (Temuroth)
	Torat kohanim, see .S6+
.V2-23	Va-yekullu (Wayekullu)
	Vayikra (Wayikra) rabbah, see .M67
.V4-43	Vayissa'u (Wayissa'u)
.V5-53	Vayosha' (Wayosha')
.V6-8	Ve-hizhir (We-hizhir)
.Y2-23	Yalḳut ha-Makir
.Y3-33	Yalḳut Shim'oni
	Midrash Yelammedenu, see .T35+
.Y4-6	Yeshayah
.Y7-9	Midrash Yonah
.Z8-83	Midrash zuṭa

TABLE IV

AUTHORS OF RESPONSA

This table is necessitated by the large number of authors of Responsa who are entered under the same forename. Special numbers are therefore assigned to all forenames. However, if a forename has become a family name, Cutter numbers are assigned as usual for family names.

Directions for establishing Cutter number:

Forenames

(1) Cutter number for author is based on name following the forename, disregarding "ben," i. e., son of ...

Family names

(2) Cutter number for author is based on fourth letter in the name
(3) Cutter number for author is based on third letter in the name
(4) Cutter number for author is based on second letter in the name

.17	Aa-Aaron (3)
.18	Aaron (1) (Forename)
.19	Aaron, A (Family name)-Abraham (4)
.2	Abraham (1) (Forename)
.21	Abraham, A-Aryeh Loeb (4)
.22	Aryeh Loeb (1)
.23	Aryeh Loeb, A-Az (4)
.24	Ba-Baruch (3)
.25	Baruch (1)
.26	Baruch, A-Bz (4)
.27	C (4)
.28	Da-David (3)
.29	David (1)
.3	David, A-Dz (4)
.31	Ea-Eliezer (4)
.32	Eliezer (1)
.33	Eliezer, A-Elijah (2)
.34	Elijah (1)
.35	Elijah, A-Ez (4)
.36	F (4)
.37	Ga-Gabriel (3)
.38	Gabriel (1)
.39	Gabriel, A-Gz (4)
.4	Ha-Ḥayyim (3)
.41	Ḥayyim (1)
.42	Ḥayyim, A-Hz (4)
.43	Ia-Isaac (4)
.44	Isaac (1)

TABLE IV

AUTHORS OF RESPONSA - Continued

.45	Isaac, A-Israel (3)
.46	Israel (1)
.47	Israel, A-Iz (4)
.48	Ja-Jacob (3)
.49	Jacob (1)
.5	Jacob, A-Jehiel (4)
.51	Jehiel (1)
.52	Jehiel, A-Joseph (4)
.53	Joseph (1)
.54	Joseph-Joshua (2)
.55	Joshua (1)
.56	Joshua, A-Juaah (4)
.57	Judah (1)
.58	Judah, A-Jz (4)
.59	K (4)
.6	L (4)
.61	Ma-Meir (4)
.62	Meir (1)
.63	Meir, A-Menahem (3)
.64	Menahem (1)
.65	Menahem, A-Meshullam (3)
.66	Meshullam (1)
.67	Meshullam, A-Mordecai (4)
.68	Mordecai (1)
.69	Mordecai, A-Moses (3)
.7	Moses (1)
.71	Moses, A-Mz (4)
.72	Na-Nathan (3)
.73	Nathan (1)
.74	Nathan, A-Nz (4)
.75	O (4)
.76	P (4)
.77	Q (4)
.78	Ra-Raphael (3)
.79	Raphael (1)
.8	Raphael, A-Rz (4)
.81	Sa-Samson (3)
.82	Samson (1)
.83	Samson, A-Samuel (2)
.84	Samuel (1)
.85	Samuel, A-Solomon (4)
.86	Solomon (1)
.87	Solomon, A-Sz (4)
.88	T (4)
.89	U (4)

TABLE IV

AUTHORS OF RESPONSA - Continued

.9	V (4)
.91	W (4)
.92	X (4)
.93	Y (4)
.94	Za-Ze'ev (4)
.95	Ze'ev (1)
.96	Ze'ev, A-Zevi (3)
.97	Zevi (1)
.98	Zevi-Zz (4)

ISLAM
Cf. DS35.3+, The Islamic world

1 Periodicals
9 Yearbooks
10 Societies. Conferences. Clubs
15 Congresses
Collected works
20 Several authors
25 Individual authors
40 Dictionaries. Encyclopedias

Study and teaching. Research
Including general and advanced
Cf. BP130.8+, Koran
42 General works
43 Individual countries, A-Z
Under each (using two successive Cutter numbers):

.x General works
.x2 Individual schools, A-Z

Religious education of the young
44 General. Organization, method, etc.
45 Textbooks. Stories, catechisms, etc.
48 Individual schools, A-Z
Historiography
49 General works
.5 Biography of students and historians
.A1 Collective
.A2-Z Individual, A-Z
History
50 General works
52 General special
.5 Muslims in non-Muslim countries
53 Addresses, essays, etc.
By period
55 Origins. Early through 1800
60 1801-

62 By race, ethnic group, tribe, etc., A-Z
Prefer country, region, etc.

.B56 Blacks. Afro-Americans
Cf. BP221+, Black Muslims
Negroes, see .B56

Islam
History - Continued
By continent and country
Under each continent:
.A1 General works
.A3 By ethnic group, etc., A-Z
Prefer country, region, etc.
.A4 By region, A-Z
.A5-Z By country
Under each (using two successive Cutter numbers):
.x General works
.x2 Local, A-Z

63 Asia
e. g. .C5 China
.I5 Indonesia (Republic). Dutch East Indies

64 Africa
e. g. .A4W3 West Africa
.A5 Algeria

65 Europe
e. g. .S6 Spain
.Y8 Yugoslavia

66 Australia and Pacific islands
67 America. North America
68 South America

Biography
70 Collective
Cf. BP136.46, Companions of Muḥammad (Sahaba)
BP136.47, Followers (Al-Tabi'in)
BP136.48, Guarantors, reporters, transmitters of Hadith
Saints, see BP189.4
Local, see BP63+
72 Martyrs
73 Women

Individual
Muḥammad, d. 632
Cf. BP135.8, Hadith literature
BP166.5, Muḥammad in Islamic theology
By language
75 English
.13 French
.16 German
.2 Arabic
.22 Bengali

Islam
Biography
Individual
Muḥammad, d. 632
By language - Continued
75.24 Indonesian
.26 Persian
.27 Turkish
.28 Urdu
.29 Other, A-Z

.3 Historiography
Including history and criticism of biographies
Biographies of Muḥammad
.4 Collective
Individual, see BP80

Companions (Sahaba)
.5 Collective
Cf. BP136.46, Hadith literature
Individual, see BP80

Special topics
.8 Miracles
Cf. BP166.65, Islamic theology
.9 Relics
Mission, see BP166.55
76.2 Panegyrics

Teachings, see BP132
Special doctrines, see BP166.2+
.3 Attitude toward paganism
.4 Relations with Jews
.45 Relations with Hinduism. Hindu interpretations of Muḥammad

.7 Domestic life
.8 Family. Wives and daughters
.9 Friends and associates

Special events
77.2 Birth and childhood
Period at Mecca
.4 General works
.43 Call and early revelations
.47 Public appearance. Persecution and emigration of his followers to Abyssinia
.5 Hijrah. Flight to Medina

Islam
  Biography
    Individual
      Muḥammad, d. 632
        Special events - Continued
          Period at Medina
77.6 General works
.63 Attempted assassination
.65 Escape to Mt. Thaur
.67 Return to Medina as ruler of the city
.68 Farewell pilgrimage. Ḥajjat al-wadā'
.69 Political career
.7 Military campaigns. Truce with the Meccans
.75 Death
80 Other, A-Z
  e. g. .G3 al-Ghazzāli
    Cf. B753.G3, al-Ghazzāli as philosopher
  .I6 Iqbal, Sir Muhammad
    Cf. B5129.I5+, Iqbal as a philosopher

87-89 Islamic literature. Islamic authors
  Including devotional or theologico-philosophical works of Islamic authors not limited specifically by subject.
  Cf. B740+, Islamic philosophy
  For works on specific subjects, regardless of authorship, see the appropriate subject
  Sacred books, see BP100+
  Biography, see BP70+

Sacred books
  Koran
    Texts. By language
      Under each language where applicable:

2 no.	Cutter no.	
(1)	.x	Complete text. By date
(2)	.x2	Selections. By date Including two or more selected suras (surahs)

History and criticism, see BP130+

Arabic
100 Texts
.3 Works on manuscripts
.5 Facsimiles of manuscripts
101 Selections

Islam
Sacred books
Koran
Texts. By language
Arabic - Continued

History and criticism, see BP130+
Philological works, see PJ6696

Other Oriental languages
102-103 Turkish
104-104.2 Hebrew

104.3-32 Chinese

.4-42 Indonesian
.5-52 Pahlavi

.6-62 Persian

.7-72 Sundanese
.8-82 Urdu

.9-92 Bengali

105 Other languages. By language, A-Z, and date

.5 Oceanic, African, American, and artificial languages. By language, A-Z, and date

Western languages
106-107 Dutch
109-110 English

112-113 French

115-116 German
118-119 Italian

121-122 Scandinavian

124-125 Spanish and Portuguese
127 Other languages. By language, A-Z, and date

Islam
Sacred books
Koran - Continued
Special parts and chapters
Under each:

.A2	Original texts. By date.
	Translations
.A3	English. By translator, A-Z
.A4A-Z	Other languages, A-Z
.A5-Z	Criticism, etc.

128.15	Juz' al-ḥamd (Pt. I)
.16	Sūrat al-fātiḥoh (Chap. 1)
.17	Sūrat al-baqarah (Chap. 2)
.18	Juz' sayaqūlu (Pt. II)
.19	Juz' tilka al-rusul (Pt. III)
.2	Sūrat āl 'Imrān (Chap. 3)
.22	Juz' Kull al-ṭa 'ām (Pt. IV)
.23	Sūrat al-nisā' (Chap. 4)
.24	Juz' wa-al-muḥṣanāt (Pt. V)
.25	Juz' lā yuḥibbu (Pt. VI)
.26	Sūrat al-mā'idah (Chap. 5)
.27	Juz' latajidanna (Pt. VII)
.28	Sūrat al-an 'ām (Chap. 6)
.29	Juz' wa-law annanā (Pt. VIII)
.3	Sūrat al-a 'rāf (Chap. 7)
.32	Juz' qāla al-mala' (Pt. IX)
.33	Sūrat al-anfāl (Chap. 8)
.34	Juz' wa-i 'lamū (Pt. X)
.35	Sūrat al-tawbah (Chap. 9)
.36	Juz' innamā al-sabīl (Pt. XI)
.37	Sūrat Yūnus (Chap. 10)
.38	Sūrat Hūd (Chap. 11)
.39	Juz' wa-māmin dābbah (Pt. XII)
.4	Sūrat Yūsuf (Chap. 12)
.42	Juz' wa-mā ubarri' (Pt. XIII)
.43	Sūrat al-ra'd (Chap. 13)
.44	Sūrat Ibrāhīm (Chap. 14)
.45	Sūrat al-ḥijr (Chap. 15)
.46	Juz' alif lāmrā (Pt. XIV)
.47	Sūrat al-naḥl (Chap. 16)
.48	Juz' subḥān (Pt. XV)
.49	Sūrat al-isrā' (Chap. 17)
.5	Sūrat al-kahf (Chap. 18)

Islam
Sacred books
Koran
Special parts and chapters - Continued

128.52 Juz' qāla alam aqul (Pt. XVI)
.53 Sūrat Maryam (Chap. 19)
.54 Sūrat ṭā'hā' (Chap. 20)
.55 Juz' iqtaraba (Pt. XVII)
.56 Sūrat al-anbiyā' (Chap. 21)
.57 Sūrat al-ḥajj (Chap. 22)
.58 Juz' qad aflaḥa (Pt. XVIII)
.59 Sūrat al-mu'minūn (Chap. 23)
.6 Sūrat al-nūr (Chap. 24)
.62 Sūrat al-furqān (Chap. 25)
.63 Juz' wa-qāla alladhīna (Pt. XIX)
.64 Sūrat al-shu 'arā' (Chap. 26)
.65 Sūrat al-naml (Chap. 27)
.66 Juz' fa-mā kāna (Pt. XX)
.67 Sūrat al-qaṣaṣ (Chap. 28)
.68 Sūrat al-'ankabūt (Chap. 29)
.69 Juz' wa-lā tujādilū (Pt. XXI)
.7 Sūrat al-Rūm (Chap. 30)
.72 Sūrat Luqmān (Chap. 31)
.73 Sūrat al-sajdah (Chap. 32)
.74 Sūrat al-aḥzāb (Chap. 33)
.75 Juz' wa-man yaqnat (Pt. XXII)
.76 Sūrat Saba' (Chap. 34)
.77 Sūrat fātir (Chap. 35)
.78 Sūrat ya' sin (Chap. 36)
.79 Juz' wa-mā anzalnā (Pt. XXIII)
.8 Sūrat al-sāffāt (Chap. 37)
.82 Sūrat ṣād (Chap. 38)
.83 Sūrat al-zumar (Chap. 39)
.84 Juz' fa-man aẓlam (Pt. XXIV)
.85 Sūrat ghāfir (Chap. 40)
.86 Sūrat fuṣṣilat (Chap. 41)
.87 Juz' ilayhi (Pt. XXV)
.88 Sūrat al-shūra (Chap. 42)
.89 Sūrat al-zukhruf (Chap. 43)
.9 Sūrat al-dukhān (Chap. 44)
.92 Sūrat al-jāthiyah (Chap. 45)
.93 Juz' ḥā' mīm (Pt. XXVI)
.94 Sūrat al-aḥqaf (Chap. 46)
.95 Sūrat Muḥammad (Chap. 47)
.96 Sūrat al-fatḥ (Chap. 48)
.97 Sūrat al-hujurāt (Chap. 49)
.98 Sūrat qāf (Chap. 50)
.99 Sūrat al-dhāriyāt (Chap. 51)

Islam
Sacred books
Koran
Special parts and chapters - Continued

129 Juz'qāla fa-mā khaṭbukum (Pt. XXVII)
.12 Sūrat al-ṭūr (Chap. 52)
.13 Sūrat al-najm (Chap. 53)
.14 Sūrat al-qamar (Chap. 54)
.15 Sūrat al-Raḥmān (Chap. 55)
.16 Sūrat al-wāqi 'ah (Chap. 56)
.17 Sūrat al-ḥadīd (Chap. 57)
.18 Juz' qad sami'a (Pt. XXVIII)
.19 Sūrat al-mujādalah (Chap. 58)
.2 Sūrat al-hashr (Chap. 59)
.22 Sūrat al-muntaḥinah (Chap. 60)
.23 Sūrat al-ṣaff (Chap. 61)
.24 Sūrat al-jumu 'ah (Chap. 62)
.25 Sūrat al-munāfiqūn (Chap. 63)
.26 Sūrat al-taghābun (Chap. 64)
.27 Sūrat al-ṭalāq (Chap. 65)
.28 Sūrat al-taḥrīm (Chap. 66)
.29 Juz' tabāraka (Pt. XXIX)
.3 Sūrat al mulk (Chap. 67)
.32 Sūrat al-qalam (Chap. 68)
.33 Sūrat al-ḥāqqah (Chap. 69)
.34 Sūrat al-ma 'ārij (Chap. 70)
.35 Sūrat Nūh (Chap. 71)
.36 Sūrat al-jinn (Chap. 72)
.37 Sūrat al-muzzammil (Chap. 73)
.38 Sūrat al-muddaththir (Chap. 74)
.39 Sūrat al-qiyāmah (Chap. 75)
.4 Sūrat al-insān (Chap. 76)
.41 Sūrat al-mursalāt (Chap. 77)
.42 Juz' 'amma (Pt. XXX)
.43 Sūrat al-naba' (Chap. 78)
.44 Sūrat al-nāzi 'at (Chap. 79)
.45 Sūrat 'abasa (Chap. 80)
.46 Sūrat al-takwīr (Chap. 81)
.47 Sūrat al-infiṭar (Chap. 82)
.48 Sūrat al-muṭa ffifīn (Chap. 83)
.49 Sūrat al-inshiqāq (Chap. 84)
.5 Sūrat al-burūj (Chap. 85)
.52 Sūrat al-ṭariq (Chap. 86)
.53 Sūrat al-a'lā (Chap. 87)
.54 Sūrat al-ghāshlyah (Chap. 88)
.55 Sūrat al-fajr (Chap. 89)

Islam
Sacred books
Koran
Special parts and chapters
Juz' 'amma - Continued

129.56 Sūrat al-balad (Chap. 90)
.57 Sūrat al-shams (Chap. 91)
.58 Sūrat al-layl (Chap. 92)
.59 Sūrat wā-al-ḍuḥa (Chap. 93)
.6 Sūrat al-sharḥ (Chap. 94)
.62 Sūrat al-tīn (Chap. 95)
.63 Sūrat al- 'alaq (Chap. 96)
.64 Sūrat al-qadr (Chap. 97)
.65 Sūrat al-bayyinah (Chap. 98)
.66 Sūrat al-zalzalah (Chap. 99)
.67 Sūrat al-'adiyāt (Chap. 100)
.68 Sūrat al-qāri'ah (Chap. 101)
.69 Sūrat al-takāthur (Chap. 102)
.7 Sūrat al-'aṣr (Chap. 103)
.72 Sūrat al-humazah (Chap. 104)
.73 Sūrat al-fīl (Chap. 105)
.74 Sūrat Quraysh (Chap. 106)
.75 Sūrat al-mā'un (Chap. 107)
.76 Sūrat al-Kawthar (Chap. 108)
.77 Sūrat al-Kafirūn (Chap. 109)
.78 Sūrat al-naṣr (Chap. 110)
.79 Sūrat almasad (Chap. 111)
.8 Sūrat al-ikhlāṣ (Chap. 112)
.82 Sūrat al-falaq (Chap. 113)
.83 Sūrat al-nās (Chap. 114)

Works about the Koran
For languages of the Koran, including glossaries, vocabularies, etc., see PJ6696+

130 General works
.1 Criticism
Principles of criticism. Hermeneutics
.2 General works
.3 Abrogator and abrogated verses
.4 Commentaries. Exegesis. Interpretation
.45 History of criticism and exgesis
.5 History of events in the Koran
.58 Koran stories
.6 Addresses, essays, lectures
Appreciation. Excellence. Inspiration. Authority. Credibility
.7 General works
.73 I'jāz. Inimitability

Islam
Sacred books
Koran
Works about the Koran - Continued

130.8 Study and teaching
.82 Textbooks
.84 Advanced
.86 Juvenile. Catechisms

131 History of the Koran
.13 Translating the Koran. Theory, methods, problems, etc.
.14 History of translations of the Koran
.15 Special languages, A-Z
.18 Publication and distribution

.A1A-Z General works
.A2-Z By region or country, A-Z

.2 Geography
Language, see PJ6696+

.3 Metaphors
.4 Peculiar dialectal words

.5 Readings (Qirā'āt)
.6 Melodic reading
.8 Koran as literature

Theology. Teachings of the Koran
132 General works
.5 Symbols. Symbolism
133 Concordances. Dictionaries. Indexes, etc.
Men, women, and children of the Koran
Biography
Collective
.5 General works
.6 Special groups, A-Z

.E5 Enemies of Muḥammad

.W6 Women

.7 Individual, A-Z

.J65 John the Baptist. Yaḥyá
.M35 Mary, Blessed Virgin, Saint. Maryam

Maryam, see .M35
Yaḥyá, see .J65

Islam
Sacred books
Koran
Works about the Koran - Continued

134 Special topics, A-Z
.A38 Aesthetics
.A5 Angels
.A8 Astronomy

.B4 Bible and the Koran
.B5 Bible characters in the Koran
.C6 Cosmogony. Cosmology. Creation

.D35 Death
.D4 Demonology
.D43 Devil. Shayṭān. Iblīs
.E5 Egypt
.E7 Eschatology
.E8 Ethics

Evil, see .G65
.F25 Family. Family relations
.F3 Fasting

.F58 Food
.F6 Forgiveness of sin
.F8 Future life

.G6 God
.G65 Good and evil
.H5 Historiography

.H57 History
.I72 Iran. Iranians
.J37 Jesus Christ
.J4 Jews. Judaism
.J52 Jinn
.K6 Knowledge. Theory of knowledge
.M3 Man
.N3 Nature. Natural history

.P5 Philosophy. Koran and philosophy
.P6 Political science
.P7 Prayer

.P74 Prophecies
.P745 Prophets. Pre-Islamic prophets
.P747 Psychology

.P8 Punishment
.R35 Religious life
.R4 Resurrection

Islam
Sacred books
Koran
Works about the Koran

134 Special topics, A-Z - Continued

.S3 Science
.S6 Social teachings
.S67 Soul

.S7 Spirit
.W6 Women (Attitude toward)

Hadith literature. Traditions. Sunna
Cf. BP193.25+, Shiite hadith literature
Canonical collections

135.A1 General
Special. By compiler
Under each, subarranged like BP135.A12-128
.A12 al-Bukhārī, Muḥammad ibn Ismā'īl
.A122 Selections
.A124 Translations. By language, A-Z
Including selections under each
.A126 Concordances. Dictionaries. Indexes, etc.
.A128 Commentaries. Criticism

.A13 Abū Dā'ūd Sulaymān ibn al-Ash'ath al-Sijistānī
.A14 Muslim ibn al-Ḥajjāj al-Qushayrī
.A15 al-Tirmidhī, Muḥammad ibn 'Isā
.A16 al-Nasā'ī, Aḥmad ibn Shu'ayb
.A17 Ibn Mājah, Muḥammad ibn Yazīd

.A2 Other compilations
Subarranged by author
.A3 Selections. Extracts, etc.
Subarranged by author
.A4-Z General works
.2 Concordances. Dictionaries. Indexes, etc.
Language, including glossaries, vocabularies, etc., see PJ6697

.8 Special topics, A-Z

.A7 Arabs
.E3 Education. Knowledge
.I7 Iran

.J54 Jihad
Knowledge, see .E3
.M85 Muḥammad, the prophet

Islam
Sacred books
Hadith literature. Traditions. Sunna
135.8 Special topics, A-Z - Continued

.P66 Prayer
.P7 Predestination
.R3 Ramadan

.R4 Religious life
.S24 Salvation

.W6 Women
.Y46 Yemen
History
136 General works
.2 Origin
Organization of Hadith
.3 General works
.33 Ascription and chain of transmission (Isnad)
.36 Subject matter (Matn)

Authority of Hadith
.4 General works
.42 Conditions to be met to establish authority
.44 Ascription to Muḥammad or a companion
.46 Companions of Muḥammad (Sahaba)
Individual companions, see BP80

.47 Followers (al-Tabi'in)
.48 Guarantors. Reporters. Transmitters

.5 Quality of the transmission of the tradition into "sound, fair, or weak" transmission
.6 Methods of testing the transmission of a tradition by "wounding, impugning, interpolating"

Special critical problems
.7 General works
.72 Interpolation
.74 Forgery

.76 Misconstruction
.78 Abrogating and abrogated Hadith

.8 Commentaries on the Hadith
.9 Hadith stories. Retellings of the Hadith
Teaching, theology, see BP160+

Islam
Sacred books - Continued
Koranic and other Islamic legends
Including Biblical legends
137 General works
.5 Individual legends, A-Z

.D3 David, King of Israel
.K5 al-Khaḍir

Islamic law (Fiqh) 1/
(140) Periodicals. Societies, etc.
(141) Collections
(.A1) Several authors
(.A2-Z) Individual authors

(142) Dictionaries
Study and teaching
(143.A1) General works
(.A2-Z) Individual institutions for the teaching of law, A-Z

(144) General works
(145) Sources, roots, foundations (Usul)
Koran, see BP100+
Hadith, see BP135+

(146) Idjma. Consensus
(147) Kiyas. Analogy
(148) Other

Law schools
(150) General works
By school
(151) Sunnite
(152) Hanafite
(153) Shafiite

(154) Malikite
(155) Hanbalite
(156) Shiite
(157) Kharijite

1/ At the Library of Congress all works except those dealing with ceremonial and religious law are classed in K.

Islam
Islamic law (Fiqh) 1/- Continued
By subject matter
Ceremonial and religious law, see special topics in BP
Civil, criminal, and other law, see K

General works on Islam. Treatises
Cf. B740+, Islamic philosophy
BP87+, Devotional or theologico-philosophical works of Islamic authors not limited specifically by subject

160 Early through 1800
161 1801-1950
.2 1951-

163 General special
165 Addresses, essays, lectures
.5 Dogma ('Aqā'id)
.7 Authority

Theology (Kalam)
Including Sunnite theology
166 General works
.1 History of theology
.14 Special schools, A-Z
Cf. BP194, Shiite theology

.D4 Deoband school
.H2 Hanafite

.H3 Hanbalite
.M3 Malikite
.S4 Shafiite

Special doctrines
.2 God. Unity of God
.22 Polytheism. Shirk
.23 Creation. Cosmology. Cosmogony
.3 Fatalism. Determinism. Predestination
.33 Merit
.4 Prophets prior to Muhammad

1/ At the Library of Congress all works except those dealing with ceremonial and religious law are classed in K.

Islam
Theology (Kalam)
Special doctrines - Continued
Muḥammad, d. 632
166.5 General works
.55 Mission
.57 Mi'rāj. Ascension. Isrā'. Night journey to Jerusalem

Revelation
.6 General works
.65 Miracles
Cf. BP75.8, Muḥammad, the prophet
Man
.7 General works
.72 Health and sickness. Islam and medicine
.73 Soul
.75 Sin
.76 Mediation between God and man. Shafā'ah
Salvation
.77 General works
.78 Faith. Faith and works
Eschatology. Future life
.8 General works
.815 Death
.82 Intermediate state
.825 Intercession
.83 Resurrection
.85 Judgment
.87 Paradise
.88 Hell

.89 Spirit world: Angels, demons, jinn, devil
Cf. BP134.A5, Angels (Koran)
Other
.9 Caliphate
.93 Mahdism
.94 Imamate

Ethics, see BJ1291
167 Addresses, essays, lectures. Pamphlets, etc.
.3 Blasphemy
.5 Heresy, heresies, heretics
Including the charge of heresy

168 Apostasy from Islam
169 Works against Islam and the Koran
Cf. BM591, Jewish works against Islam
BT1170, Christian works against Islam
170 Works in defense of Islam. Islamic apologetics
.2 Benevolent work. Social work. Welfare work, etc.

Islam - Continued
170.3 Missionary work of Islam
Cf. BV2625+, Christian missions to Moslems
.5 Converts to Islam
Cf. BV2626.3+, Converts to Christianity from Islam

.A1 Collective
.A3-Z Individual

.8 Universality of Islam
.82 Unity of Islam
.85 Da'wah. Mission of Islam. Summons, invitation, etc.
Cf. BP166.55, Mission of Muḥammad

Relation of Islam to other religions
Cf. BP170.3+, Missionary work of Islam
171 General works
.5 Toleration
Relation to Christianity
Cf. BT1170, Apologetics
172 General works
.5 Special denominations, sects, A-Z

e. g. .C6 Coptic Church

173 Other, A-Z
.B9 Buddhism
.H5 Hinduism
Cf. BP76.45, Muḥammad's relations with Hinduism
Special sects, etc.
.H58 Vaishnavism
.J8 Judaism
Cf. BP76.4, Muḥammad's relations with Jews
BP134.J4, Judaism in the Koran
.S5 Sikhism

.2 Sources of Islam
Islamic sociology
For islam and social problems, see HN40.M6
For islam and socialism and communism, see HX550.I8
.25 General works
.3 Children in Islam

.4 Women in Islam
.43 Social justice in Islam. Theology of justice
.45 Equality in Islam
Cf. BP190.5.R3, Race

Islam - Continued
173.5 Islam and world politics
.6 Islam and the state
Cf. JC49, Political science
.65 Islam and religious liberty
.7 Islam and politics
Cf. BP134.P6, Political science in the Koran

.75 Islam and economics
Islam and labor, <u>see</u> HD6338.4
.77 Islam and work

<u>The practice of Islam</u>
174 General works
175 Psychology of Islam
Including the psychology of religious experience

The five duties of a Moslem. Pillars of Islam
176 General works
177 Profession of faith
Cf. BP166.2, God
BP166.5, Muhammad, d. 632

178 Prayer
Cf. BP183.3, Prayers
BP184.3, Prayer, the call to prayer

179 Fasting
Cf. BP184.5, Mode of fasting
BP186, Fast days
180 Alms (Zakat)
181 Pilgrimage to Mecca
Cf. BP184.7, Pilgrimages in general
BP187.3+, Descriptive works of the pilgrimage to Mecca
DS248.M4, Mecca

182 Jihad (Holy War)
The Jihad is on a par with the five duties among the Kharijites
Symbols and symbolism
Cf. N6260+, Islamic art
.5 General works
.6 Special symbols, A-Z
<u>The formularies of worship, texts, etc.</u>
183 General works
.3 Prayers, invocations, quatrains, praises, religious preludes
.4 Calls to prayer
.5 Hymns, songs
.6 Sermons

Islam
The practice of Islam
The formularies of worship, texts, etc. - Cont.
183.63-.66 Sermons for special days, seasons, etc.
Subdivided like BP186.3-6
.7 Other, A-Z

.B3 Basmalah
Tasmiyah, see .B3

Religious ceremonies, rites, actions, customs, etc.
184 General works
.2 Public worship
Including mode and manner
.25 Preaching. Homiletics
.3 Prayer
Including the call to prayer, the hours of prayer, the manner of prayer

.4 Purifications and ablutions
.5 Fasting
For special days, see BP186
.6 Sacrifices
For special days, see BP186
.7 Pilgrimages
For special places, see BP187
.8 Circumcision

.9 Other, A-Z

.B5 Blood as food or medicine
.D5 Dietary laws

.F8 Funeral rites and ceremonies

Religious functionaries. Polity. Government
185 General works
.3 Muezzin
.4 Imam
.5 Other, A-Z

.S53 Shaykh al-Islam

Special days and seasons, fasts, feasts, festivals, etc.
Cf. BP194.5, Shiite festivals, etc.
186 General works
.15 Fridays. al-Jum'ah
.2 New Year's Day (The first of Muḥarram)

Islam
The practice of Islam
Special days and seasons, fasts, feasts, festivals, etc. - Continued

186.3 'Ashūrā (The tenth of Muḥarram)
For Shiite Tenth of Muḥarram, see BP194.5.T4
.34 Mawlid al-Nabī
.36 Laylat al-Mi'rāj
.38 Laylat al Barā'ah (Beret gecesi)
Night of mid-Sha'ban
.4 Ramadan
.43 Laylat al-Qadr
.45 'Īd al-Fitr
Fast-breaking at the end of Ramadan
.6 'Id al-Aḍḥā (Day of sacrifice)
.9 Other, A-Z
.97 Relics. Veneration, etc.
Cf. BP75.9, Relics of Muḥammad, the prophet

Shrines, sacred places, etc.
187 General works
Mecca and its pilgrimages
.3 General works
.4 The Kaaba
.45 Qiblah. Direction of prayer
.5 Non-Meccan shrines, sanctuaries, etc.
Subdivided like BL1227
Cf. BP194.6, Shiite shrines, etc.
.6 Mosques, monasteries
Subdivided like BL1227
Cf. BJ2019.5.I8, Islamic etiquette, Mosque etiquette
For mosques on Temple Mount Jerusalem, see DS109.32
.9 Other, A-Z

188 Islamic religious life (Descriptive works)
Sins. Vices
.13 General works
.14 Individual sins, A-Z
.E58 Envy
.F3 Falsehood
.S55 Slander

Islam
The practice of Islam
Islamic religious life (Descriptive works) - Cont.
Virtues
188.15 General works
.16 Individual virtues, A-Z
.G7 Gratitude
.L68 Love

.M3 Magnanimity
.M59 Moderation. Tawazun
.M6 Modesty. Nazar
Devotional literature
.2 General works
.3 For special classes, A-Z
.C5 Children
.F3 Families

.M3 Married people
.S5 Sick
.S6 Soldiers
.W6 Women
.Y6 Youth

.4 History and criticism of devotional literature
Sufism. Mysticism. Dervishes
.45 Periodicals. Societies. Congresses
.48 Dictionaries and encyclopedias
History
.5 General works
.55 Addresses, essays, lectures
By period
.6 Through 1900
.7 1901-
.8 By region or country, A-Z
Under each country:
.x General works
.x2 Local, A-Z
General works
.9 Early works through 1900
189 1901-
.2 General special
.23 Addresses, essays, lectures
Doctrine
.26 Early works through 1900
.3 1901-
Special topics
.33 Sainthood
Other special topics, see BP166+
.36 Controversial works about the sect. Polemics

Islam
The practice of Islam
Islamic religious life (Descriptive works)
Sufism. Mysticism. Dervishes - Continued
Biography
189.4 Collective (Saints, etc.)
For biography of individual orders, see BP189.7. Collective biography of individual region, country, city, see BP188.8
Individual, see BP80
Shrines, sacred places, etc., see BP187.5
Sufi practice
.5 General works
Special topics
.52 Asceticism
.55 Formularies of worship, texts, etc.
.58 Ceremonies, rites, actions, etc.
e. g. Recital of the Names of God, etc.
Religious life
.6 General works
.62 Devotional literature
.65 Other special topics, A-Z
.A47 Alphabet. Symbolism and numeric value of letters
.F35 Faith-cure. Spiritual healing
Letters, Symbolism and numeric value of, see .A47
.L68 Love
.P78 Psychology
Spiritual healing, see .F35
Monasticism. Sufi orders. Brotherhoods
.68 General works
.7 Individual orders, A-Z 1/
Under each:
(1) General works
(2)A2 Collective biography
(2)A3 Works by the founder or central figure
(2)A5-Z Criticism and biography of the founder or central figure
Including devotional literature, cultus, etc.
Other individual biography, see BP80
.B3-32 Badawiyah. Ahmadiyah (Sufism)
.B4-42 Bektashi

1/The orders are listed under the heading Tarikah in the Handwörterbuch des Islam, Enzyklopädie des Islams, etc.

Islam
The practice of Islam
Islamic religious life (Descriptive works)
Sufism. Mysticism. Dervishes
Monasticism. Sufi orders. Brotherhoods

189.7 Individual orders, A- Z 1/ - Continued

.C47-472 Cerrahiye
.H3-32 Haddāwā
.H34-342 Ḥamadsha

.I7-72 al-Isāwīyah
.K46-462 Khānaqāh-i Ni'mat Allāhī. Ni'mat Allāhī Order
.K5-52 al-Khatmiyah

.M3-32 al-Malāmatīyah
.M4-42 Mevlevi

.M5-52 al-Mīrghanīyah
.N35-352 al-Naqshabandīyah
Ni'mat Allāhī Order, see .K46+
.Q3-32 al-Qadirīyah
.R5-52 al-Rifā'īyah

.S4-42 Senussites (al-Sanūsīyah)
.S5-52 al-Shādhilīyah

.T5-52 al-Tijanīyah

190 Communal religious activities

For asylums, see RC443+; benevolent and welfare societies, see HS1556+; hospitals, see RA960+; orphanages, see HV959+; red crescent, see HV859, RT120, UH543+; religious corporations, see K; religious endowments, property, wakfs, see K

.5 Topics not otherwise provided, A-Z

.A5 Amulets. Talismans
.A6 Animism

1/ The orders are listed under the heading Tarikah in the Handwörterbuch des Islam, Enzyklopädie des Islams, etc.

Islam

190.5 Topics not otherwise provided, A-Z - Continued

.A67 Arabs in Islam
Including Arab contributions to Islam, Islam as an Arab religion, and Arab status in Islam
.A7 Art. Images. Photography

.A75 Asceticism
For Sufi asceticism, see BP189.52
.A8 Astronautics

.B3 Barakah
Beard, see .H3

.C6 Costume. Clothing and dress
.E86 Evolution
.F7 Freedom

.H3 Hair. Haircutting. Beard
.H5 History

.H7 Homosexuality
.H8 Humor in Islam
Images, see .A7

Jerusalem, see .P3
.M3 Martyrdom

.M8 Music
.P3 Palestine. Jerusalem, etc.

.P4 Performing arts
Photography, see .A7

.P6 Poverty
.R3 Race. Race problems

.R4 Reason
.S3 Science

.S4 Sex
.S5 al-Shuʻūbīyah

Talismans, see .A5
.V3 Values

.W35 War

Islam - Continued
Branches, sects, and modifications
Cf. BP63+, By country
191 General works
Sunnites, see BP166
Shiites
History
192 General works
.2 General special
.3 Addresses, esssays, lectures
By period
.4 661-1502
.5 1502-1900
.6 1901-

.7 By region, country, city, etc., A-Z
Biography
.8 Collective
Imams
193 Collective
Individual
Under each:

.A1	Collected works. By editor, A-Z
.A2	Works by the Imam of a Shiite nature, apocryphal works, collections of his hadith, etc. For orthodox Muslim works, see BP166
.A3A-Z	Biography, criticism
.A5-Z	Devotional literature, cultus, tomb, etc.

.1 1st, 'Alī ibn Abī Ṭālib
.12 2nd, al-Ḥasan ibn 'Alī, d. ca. 669
.13 3rd, al-Ḥusayn ibn 'Alī, d. 680
.14 4th, Zayn al-'Ābidīn 'Alī ibn al-Husayn
.15 5th, Muḥammad al-Bāqir ibn 'Alī Zayn al-'Ābidīn
.16 6th, Ja'far al-Ṣādiq
Ismā'īl ibn Ja'far, see BP195.I8+
.17 7th, Mūsā al-Kāẓim ibn Ja'far
.18 8th, 'Alī al-Riḍā ibn Mūsā
.19 9th, Muḥammad al-Jawād ibn 'Alī al-Riḍā
.2 10th, 'Alī al-Hādī ibn Muḥammad
.21 11th, al-Ḥasan al-'Askarī ibn 'Alī al-Hādī
.22 12th, al-Mahdī, Muḥammad ibn al-Ḥasan

Other individual, see BP80

Islam
Branches, sects, and modifications
Shiites - Continued
Hadith literature. Traditions
Class here the collective sayings, etc., of the Imams and Muḥammad, the prophet. For the Hadith of Muḥammad, the prophet, see BP135+; for the Hadith of individual Imams, see 193.1+

193.25 Collections. By compiler, A-Z
.26 Selections. Extracts, etc.
.27 General works
For works on the science of Hadith, see BP136.3+
.28 Authorities. Transmitters
Class here only Shiite authorities

General works
.3 Early works through 1800
.5 1801-
.7 Addresses, essays, etc.

Theology. Doctrine
194 General works
Special topics, see BP166+

.1 Controversial literature, apologetics, etc.
Shiite practice
.2 General works
.3 Formularies of worship, texts, etc.
.4 Ceremonies, rites, actions, etc.
.5 Special days and seasons, fasts, feasts, festivals, etc., A-Z

.G45 al-Ghadīr. 'Id al-Ghadīr
.T4 Tenth of Muḥarram

.6 Shrines, sacred places, etc.
.A2 Collective
.A3-Z Individual. By place, A-Z
For shrines, tombs, etc. related to an individual Imam, see BP193.1+

.7 Shiite religious life
Including devotional literature

Islam
Branches, sects, and modifications
Shiites
Shiite practice - Continued
194.9 Other special topics, A-Z

.E3 Education. Religious education
.P7 Prayer. Prayers

Branches, sects, and modification of the Shiites, see BP195
195 Other (to 1900), A-Z
Subarranged like BP189.7

.A3-32 Ahl-i Hadīth
.A4-42 Ahl-i Haqq
.A5-6 Ahmadiyya. Qadiyani
Founded by Ahmad, Ghulam, Hazrat Mirza, 1839?-1908

.A8-82 Assassins
.A84-85 Azraqites (Azāriqah)
Babism, Bahaism, see BP300+
.B3-32 Batinites

.D5-52 Dīn-i Ilāhī
Founded by Akbar, Emperor of Hindustan, 1542-1605
Druses, see BL1695
.H3-32 Ḥashwīya

.H8-82 Hurufis
.I3-32 Ibadites
.I8-82 Ismailites

.J3-32 al-Jahmiyah
.K3-32 Karmathians
.K35-36 Karramites. Karrāmīyah

.K38-382 Kaysānīyah
.K4-42 Kharijites
.K45-46 Khojahs

.M6-62 Motazilites
.M66-67 Murīdīyah. Murids
.M7-72 Murjites

.N7-72 Nosairians
.S2-22 Sālimīyah
.S5-52 Shabak

Islam
Branches, sects, and modifications
195 Other (to 1900), A-Z - Continued

.S55-56 Shaykhī
.S6-62 Sifatites
.W2-22 Wahhabis

Yezidis, see BL1595
.Z2-22 Zaidites

Other, 1900-
221-223 Black Muslims. (Table II) 1/
231-233 Moorish Science Temple of America (Table II) 1/
251-253 Nurculuk (II) 1/

1/ For table II, see p. 287

BAHAISM

300 Periodicals
310 Societies

Collections. Collected works
320 Several authors
325 Individual authors

327 Dictionaries. Encyclopedias
History
330 General works
340 Babism

By region or country
350 United States
352 By state, A-W
355 Other regions or countries, A-Z

e. g. Iran, see BP330

360 Works by 'Alī Muḥammad, Shīrāzī, called ul-Bāb; Bahā Ullāh, 1817-1892; Abdul Baha, 1844-1921
365 General works
370 General special

375 Addresses, essays, etc.
377 Miscellaneous
380 Devotions. Directions, etc.

Biography
390 Collective
Individual
391 'Alī Muḥammad, Shīrāzī, called ul-Bāb
392 Bahā Ullāh
393 'Abd ul-Bahā ibn Bahā Ullāh
395 Other, A-Z

THEOSOPHY

500 Periodicals
509 Yearbooks
510 Societies. Institutions

e. g. .T52 Theosophical Society, Covina, California

Collections
520 Several authors
525 Individual authors

527 Dictionaries. Encyclopedias
528 Study and teaching. Schools
History
530 General works
By region or country
540 United States
545 Great Britain
550 Other regions or countries, A-Z
e. g. India, see BP530

General works
Works by Helene Petrovna (Hahn-Hahn) Blavatsky
561.A1 Collected works
.A5-Z Individual works
Subarranged by title, A-Z
563 Works by Annie (Wood) Besant
Subarranged by title

565 Works by other writers. By author and title, A-Z
567 General special

570 Addresses, essays, etc.
573 Special topics, A-Z

.A5 Angels. Angelic communion
.A7 Astral body
.A8 Aura
.B5 Blood
.B7 Breath
.C2 Causal body

.C5 Chakras
.C7 Concentration
.D4 Death

.D5 Discipleship
.E7 Etheric double
.E8 Evolution

Theosophy

573 Special topics, A-Z - Continued

.E9 Extrasensory perception
.F8 Future life
.G4 Gems

.G6 God
.H4 Health. Mental healing
.H5 Hierarchies

.H8 Human body
.I5 Immortality
.K3 Karma

.M3 Man
.M4 Memory
.N5 Nirvana

.P3 Peace
.P4 Periodicity
.P7 Political science

.R5 Reincarnation
.S4 Self-preparation
.S6 Sociology

.S95 Sun
.T5 Thought

575 Works against the theosophists
Cf. BT1240, Apologetics

Biography

580 Collective

585 Individual, A-Z

e. g. .B3 Besant, Annie (Wood)
.B6 Blavatsky, Helene Petrovna (Hahn-Hahn)

.K7 Krishnamurti Jiddu
.T5 Tingley, Katherine Augusta (Westcott)

ANTHROPOSOPHY

595.A1 Periodicals. Societies. Yearbooks. Collections
.A2 Dictionaries. Encyclopedias
History
.A25 General works
.A26 By region or country, A-Z
.A3-Z General works
Works by and about Rudolf Steiner

.S894 Works. By title
Cf. B3333, Philosophical works
.S895 Biography and criticism

596 Special topics, A-Z

.C4 Christmas. Christmas trees
.E25 Economics
Eurythmy, see .R5

.F85 Future life
.G7 Grail
.H57 History and Anthroposophy

.J4 Jesus Christ
Medicine, see RZ409.7
.073 Organic farming
.P47 Physiology

.R5 Rhythm. Eurythmy
.S4 Second advent
.S63 Soul
.S65 Spirits

.V5 Virtues
.Z6 Zodiac
.Z66 Zoology

Biography
597.A1 Collective
.A3-Z Individual

e. g. .B3 Bauer, Michael
Steiner, Rudolf, see BP595.S895

OTHER BELIEFS AND MOVEMENTS

Cf. BF1995+, Other beliefs and movements occult in nature

BX9998, Other beliefs and movements akin to Christianity

600 Periodicals
601 Dictionaries
602 Directories. Yearbooks
603 General works
605 Works. By movement, A-Z
.A2 Abrahamites (Bohemia)
.A4 Ametsuchi no Kai
Ananda Cooperative Village, see .S38A52
.A67 Arete Truth Center
.A7 Arica Institute
.A8 Astara

Grail movement
.B4-49 Works by Bernhardt
.B5 Works by other adherents
.B52 General works. History
Biography
.B53 Collective
.B54 Individual, A-Z

e. g. .B54B4, Bernhardt, Oscar Ernst
Bhagwan Shree Rajneesh, see .R34
.B63 Black Hebrew Israelite Nation
.C42 Christ Foundation
.C43 Christ Ministry Foundation
Founded by Eleanor Mary Thedick, 1883-1973
.C45 Christengemeinschaft (Friedrich Rittelmeyer)
.C5 Christward ministry (Newhouse)
.C53 Church of Creative Bio-dynamics
.C55 Church of the Creator
.C57 Círculo Esóterico da Comunhão do Pensamento
Dawn Horse Communion, see BP610.B8+

.D48 Deutschgläubige Gemeinschaft
Dianetics, see .S2

.D58 Divine Light Mission
Divine-Love, International Society of, see .I55

.E27 Echerian Church
.E3 Eckankar
.E4 Emissaries of Divine Light
.E84 Ethical culture movement
.F44 Fellowship of Isis
.F5 Findhorn Community
.G68 Great White Brotherhood

Other beliefs and movements

605 Works. By movement, A-Z - Continued

.H5 Ḥikmati-i nuvīn

.H6 Holy Order of Mans

.I45 International Community of Christ

.I5 International Friends

.I55 International Society of Divine-Love

.I8 Ittōen

Founded by Nishida, Tenkō, 1872-

.K6 Koreshanity

Founded by Teed, Cyrus Reed, 1839-1908

.L56 Lindisfarne Association

.M37 Mazdaznan

.M68 Movement of Spiritual Awareness

.N3 Naropa Institute

New Universal Union, see .H5

.O73 Ordo Novi Templi

.P46 Peoples Temple

Founded by Jim Jones, 1931-1978

.P68 The Power (Society)

.P8 Pure Life Society

.R33 Radhasoami Satsang

Including Radhasoami Satsang (Agra); Radhasoami Satsang (Beas); Radhasoami Satsang (Dayalhagh); Radhasoami Satsang (Soamibagh)

.R335 Sant Mat

.R34 Rajneesh Foundation (International). Bhagwan Shree Rajneesh

.R35 Ramala Centre

.R85 Ruhani Satsang

.S12 Sant Nirankari Mandal

.S18 Le Scarabée (Association)

.S2 Scientology. Dianetics

Founded by Hubbard, La Fayette Ronald, 1911

Self-Realization movement

.S35 Periodicals

Societies

.S36 Self-Realization Fellowship. Yogoda. Sat-sanga Society

.S37 Local organization, A-Z

.S38 Other, A-Z

.S38D63 Doctrine of Truth Foundation

.S38A52 Ananda Cooperative Village

.S39 History

.S4 General works

Cf. B132.Y6, Yoga

Biography

.S42 Collective

.S43 Individual

e. g. .S43L9 Lynn, James Jesse

.S43Y6 Yogananda Paramhansa

Other beliefs and Movements
605 Works. By movement, A-Z - Continued

.S53 Shikōkai
.S55 Shinri no Kai
Shree Rajneesh Ashram, Pune, India, see .R34
.S6 Sōgōgaku Gakuin
.S65 Solar Quest (Organization)
.S66 Spiritual Frontiers Fellowship
Spiritual Inner Awareness Movement, see .M68
.S7 Subud
.S74 Sunburst Communities
Swami Order of America
.S8 Periodicals
.S82-829 Works by Swami Premananda
.S83 Works by other adherents
.S84 General works. History
.S85 Local organizations, A-Z
.S85W3 Washington, D. C. Self-Revelation Church of Absolute Monism
Biography
.S86 Collective
.S87 Individual
.U53 United Church of Religious Science
Urantia Brotherhood
.U7 Periodicals
.U71 Official documents, governing boards, conferences
.U72 Study and teaching
.U73 History

The Urantia Book
.U74 Text
.U75 Commentary, criticism, theology
.U76 Topics, A-Z
.U76S3 Science
.U77 General works
.U78 Local organizations, A-Z
Biography
.U79A1-19 Collective
.U79A2-Z Individual
.W48 White Brotherhood
610 Works. By author (where name of movement cannot be determined)
Under each:
.x-x19 Works by author
.x2 Works about author, A-Z
.A32-322 Abubabaji
.A35-352 Aïvanhov, Omraam Mikhaël
.B8-82 Bubba Free John
John, Bubba Free. John, Da Free, see .B8+

Other beliefs and movements

610 Works. By author (where name of movement cannot be determined) - Continued

.K8-82 Kushi, Michio

.S5-52 Sherman Ingrid, 1919-

.V6-62 Voorthuyzen, Louwrens, (the man and his following)

Periodicals (General)

For works limited to a sect, see BQ7001+; for works limited to a particular country, see the country in BQ251+

1 Polyglot
2 English
3 Chinese
4 French
5 German
6 Japanese
8 Other languages, A-Z

10 Yearbooks (General)

Societies, councils, associations, clubs, etc.

For works limited to a sect, see BQ7530+

International (General)
12 General works. History
Young Buddhist associations
14 General works. History

Young men's associations
16 General works. History
Women's associations
18 General works. History
20 Individual associations, councils, etc., A-Z

Under each:
.x Periodicals. Yearbooks
.x2 Congresses. Conferences. Documents. By date

.x3 Directories
.x4 General works. History

.x5 Biography (Collective)
.x6 National branches. By country, A-Z

.E8 European Congress
.W5 World Buddhist Sangha Council
Headquarters in Colombo, Ceylon

.W6 World Buddhist Union
Headquarters in Seoul, Korea
.W7 World Fellowship of Buddhists
Headquarters in Bangkok, Thailand

Societies, councils, associations, clubs, etc. - Cont.

By region or country

Under each country:

(3)	(1)	(Cutter number)	
1	.A1A-Z	.x	General works. History
2	.A2A-Z	.x2	Local, A-Z
3	.A3-Z	.x3	Individual societies, A-Z

Asia

21-23 India

24-26 Ceylon

27-29 Burma

31-33 Thailand

34-36 Vietnam

37-39 Malaysia

41-43 Indonesia

44-46 China

47-49 Korea

50-52 Japan

53 Other Asian countries, A-Z

Europe

54-56 Great Britain

e. g. Sangha Sabhā (Council) of the United Kingdom

57-59 Belgium

61-63 France

64-66 Germany

67-69 Netherlands

71-73 Sweden

74-76 Soviet Union

77 Other European countries, A-Z

78 Africa

America

81-83 United States

Including Hawaii and Alaska

84-86 Canada

87-89 Brazil

90 Other American countries, A-Z

91 Australia

92 New Zealand

93 Pacific islands

For works dealing with Hawaii, see BQ82.H3

Financial institutions. Trusts

96 General works. History

98 General special

99 By country, A-Z

Under each country:
.x General works. History
.x2 Local, A-Z
.x3 Individual, A-Z

Bibliography, see Z7860+

100 Congresses. Conferences (General)
Cf. BQ290+; BQ304, Early Councils
BQ315; BQ317, Modern councils
For works limited to a sect, see BQ7001+

102 Organization, methods, etc.

Directories (General)
For individual associations, see BQ12+
For directories limited to a sect, see BQ7001+

104 International

105 By region or country, A-Z

Under each country:
.x General
.x2 Local, A-Z

Museums. Exhibitions

107 General works

109 By region or country, A-Z

Under each country:
.x General works
By city
.x2 General
.x3 Individual museums, A-Z

General collections. Collected works
For collections limited to a particular country, see BQ320+

Several authors

Comprehensive volumes

115 Early works through 1800

118 1801-

120 Minor collections. Collected essays. Festschriften

122 Selections. Excerpts

General collections. Collected works - Cont.
Individual authors
For works by founders (original and local) and other important leaders of sects, see BQ7001+
For individual works of Pāli and Sanskrit writers in the Tripiṭaka, see BQ1170+
For individual works other than Pāli and Sanskrit originals, see the subject

Under each:
.x Collected works. By date
.xA-Z Translations. By language, A-Z
.x2 Addresses, essays, etc. By title, A-Z

124 Authors through 1800
126 1801-

128 Encyclopedias (General)
For encyclopedias limited to a sect, see BQ7001+
130 Dictionaries (General)
For dictionaries limited to a sect, see BQ7001+

133 Terminology
135 Questions and answers. Maxims (General)
For works limited to a sect, see BQ7001+

Religious education (General)
Cf. BQ5251+, Education for the ministry (General)
BQ7001+, Works limited to a sect
LC921+, General education managed by Buddhist institutions

141-148 Periodicals. Yearbooks. Societies
Divided like BQ1+
150 Conventions, conferences, etc.
152 Collections

154 Encyclopedias. Dictionaries
156 Theory, philosophy, etc.
158 Methods of study and teaching
.5 Aids and devices
160 History (General)
162 By region or country, A-Z

Under each country:
.x General works. History
.x2 Local, A-Z

Religious education (General) - Continued

164 Biography (Collective)

General works

166 Early works through 1945

167 1946-

168 General special

169 Addresses, essays, lectures, etc.

Religious education of the young. Sunday schools, etc.

For works limited to a sect, see BQ7001+

171-178 Periodicals. Societies. Serials

Divided like BQ1-8

180 Congresses

182 History

184 General works

186 General special

188 Methods of teaching, organization, etc.

190 Aids and devices

192 Textbooks for children

194 Teachers' manuals

196 Stories, catechisms, etc.

198 Teacher training

199 By region or country, A-Z

Under each country:

.x General works. History

.x2 Local, A-Z

.x3 Individual schools, A-Z

Including monasteries and temples

Religious education in the home

200 General works

202 General special

204 History

209 By region or country, A-Z

Under each country:

.x General works. History

.x2 Local, A-Z

Research

Class here works limited to methodology and programs

210 General works. International

219 By region or country, A-Z

Under each country:

.x General works

.x2 Local, A-Z

Antiquities. Archaeology
Class here works limited to religious points of view only
For descriptive works, see DS

221-228 Periodicals. Societies. Collections
Divided like BQ1-8
230 Dictionaries
232 General works. Methodology

236 General special
239 By region or country, A-Z

Under each country:
.x General works
.x2 By province, A-Z
.x3 By city, A-Z

Literary discoveries
240 General works. History and criticism
242 General special
244 Individual, A-Z

Under each:
.x Collections
.x2 Original texts. By date
Including facsimiles
Translations and adaptations (with or without original text)
Subarranged by translator or adaptor
.x3 Polyglot
.x35 Individual languages, A-Z
.x4 General works. Criticism, etc.

.G5 Gilgit manuscripts

.T8 Tun-huang manuscripts

Inscriptions, etc.
Class here works limited to religious points of view only
For philological works, see PK and PL, e. g. PK1480+, Aśoka inscriptions

246 General works. History and criticism
248 General special

Antiquities. Archaeology
Inscriptions, etc. - Continued
249 By region or country, A-Z
Under each country:
.x General works
.x2 Local, A-Z
.x3 Individual inscriptions, A-Z

History
251-258 Periodicals. Societies. Serials
Divided like BQ1-8
260 Collections. Collected works. Sources
For works limited to a sect, see BQ7001+

General works
262 Early works through 1800
e. g. History written by Bu-ston
264 1801-1945
266 1946-

270 General special
272 Textbooks, compends, etc.
274 Outlines, syllabi, chronological tables, etc.

276 Popular works
277 Juvenile works
278 Addresses, essays, lectures, etc.

280 Historiography
282 Philosophy
284 Biography of historians (Collective)

By period
286 Early and medieval (Early to ca. 1200 A.D.)
Including Buddhist history of India to ca. 1200 A.D.
287 Early to rise of Mahāyāna Buddhism (ca. 100 A.D.)
288 Origin of Buddhism
For the biography of Gautama Buddha, see BQ860+

289 Ca. 486 B.C.-ca. 100 A.D. (Early Buddhism and Hīnayāna Ābhidharma to the rise of Mahāyāna Buddhism)
Early councils
290 General works
291 First Council (Rājagrha) ca. 486 B.C.
292 Second Council (Vaiśālī) ca. 380 B.C.
293 Third Council (Pātaliputra) ca. 246 B.C.
Fourth Council (Kaśmīra), see BQ304

History
By period
Early and medieval (Early to ca. 1200 A.D.)
Early to rise of Mahāyāna Buddhism (ca. 100 A.D.)
Ca. 486 B.C.-ca. 100 A.D. -(Early Buddhism and Hīnayāna Abhidharma to the rise of Mahāyāna Buddhism) - Continued
295 Aśoka, Mauryan king, ca. 264-227 B.C., and Buddhism
For biography of Aśoka, see DS451.5
296 First missionaries to foreign lands (General)
By country, see BQ365, etc.
Inscriptions, see BQ249.I4

298 Menander, Indo-Greek king, fl. 150 B.C. and Buddhism
Cf. BQ2610+, Milindapañhā

300 Ca. 100-ca. 550 A.D. (Development of Mahāyāna Buddhism and the introduction of Buddhism to other parts of Asia)
Kaniṣka, Kushan emperor, ca. 144-170, and Buddhism
302 General works
304 Fourth Council (Kaśmīra) ca. 150

306 Ca. 550-ca. 1200 (Rise of Tantric Buddhism and the decline of Buddhism in India)
308 Harṣavardhana, King of Thānesar and Kanauj, fl. 606-647, and Buddhism
Modern (ca.1200-)
310 General works
312 ca. 1200-1850
1851-1945
314 General works
315 Fifth Council (Mandalay) 1868-1871
1945-
316 General works
317 Sixth Council (Rangoon) 1954-1956
By region or country
Asia
General, see BQ251+
South Asia
320 Periodicals. Collections, etc. Sources
General works
Early works through 1800, see BQ262
322 1801-
325 General special
327 Addresses, essays, lectures, etc.
328 Biography (Collective)

History
By region or country
Asia
South Asia - Continued
Special regions or countries
India
330 Periodicals. Collections, etc. Sources
General works
332 Early works through 1800
334 1801-1946
336 1947-

339 General special
340 Addresses, essays, lectures
342 Biography (Collective)
By period
Early to 1203 A.D., see BQ286+
344 1204-1761 (Muslim era)
345 1761-1947 (British era)
346 1947-
349 Local, A-Z

Sri Lanka
350 Periodicals. Collections, etc. Sources
General works
352 Early works through 1800
Cf. BQ2570+, Dāthāvaṃsa
BQ2580+, Dīpavaṃsa
BQ2600+, Mahāvaṃsa

354 1801-1947
356 1948-

359 General special
360 Addresses, essays, lectures
362 Biography (Collective)

By period
364 Early to 1152, the end of Cholas rule
365 First missionaries to Sri Lanka, 3rd century B.C.
366 Buddhaghosa and his activities
367 Cholas invasion, 1073
Including Cholas rule

369 1153-1504 (Restoration of Buddhism)
372 1505-1850 (European era)
374 1851-1947 (Buddhist revival)
376 1948-
379 Local, A-Z

History
By region or country
Asia
South Asia
Special regions or countries - Continued
Nepal
380 Periodicals. Societies. Serials
382 General works
384 General special

386 Addresses, essays, lectures
388 Biography (Collective)

By period
390 Early through 1845
392 1846-1951 (Rana period)
394 1951-
396 Local, A-Z
400 Other regions or countries, A-Z

Under each country:
.x Periodicals. Collections, etc. Sources
.x2 General works. History
.x3 General special
.x4 Biography (Collective)
.x5 Local, A-Z

.A5 Afghanistan
.B3 Bangladesh

.B5 Bhutan
.H54 Himalaya region
.K37 Kashmir

.L33 Ladakh
.P3 Pakistan
For history to 1946, see BQ330+
.S5 Sikkim

Southeast Asia
402 Periodicals. Collections, etc. Sources
General works
406 Early works through 1800
408 1801-

410 General special
412 Addresses, essays, lectures
414 Biography (Collective)

History
By region or country
Asia
Southeast Asia - Continued
Special regions or countries
Burma
416 Periodicals. Collections, etc. Sources
418 General works

420 General special
422 Addresses, essays, lectures
424 Biography (Collective)

By period
426 Early through 1043
428 1044-1287 (Pegan dynasty to Mongol invasion)
430 1287-1486 (Shan period)
432 1486-1752 (Toungoo dynasty)
434 1752-1885 (Alaungpaya dynasty)
436 1886-1947 (British era)
438 1948-
439 Local, A-Z

Indochina
440 Periodicals. Collections, etc. Sources
442 General works
444 General special
446 Addresses, essays, lectures, etc.
448 Biography (Collective)

Special regions or countries
Cambodia
450 Periodicals. Collections, etc. Sources
452 General works
454 General special

456 Addresses, essays, lectures
458 Biography (Collective)

By period
460 Early to 1432
Including Khmer era
462 1432-1864 (Thai era)
464 1864-1949 (French era)
466 1949-
469 Local, A-Z

History
By region or country
Asia
Southeast Asia
Special regions or countries
Indochina
Special regions or countries - Continued
Laos

470 Periodicals. Collections, etc. Sources
472 General works
474 General special
476 Addresses, essays, lectures
478 Biography (Collective)
By period
480 Early through 1884
482 1885-1946 (French era)
484 1947-
489 Local, A-Z

Vietnam. South Vietnam
For material concerned with North Vietnam, see BQ509.N6

490 Periodicals. Collections, etc. Sources
492 General works
494 General special
496 Addresses, essays, lectures
498 Biography (Collective)

By period
500 Early to 939 (Chinese era)
502 939-1787
504 1788-1945 (French era)
506 1946-
509 Local, A-Z
e. g. .N6 North Vietnam

Indonesia
510 Periodicals. Collections, etc. Sources
512 General works
514 General special
516 Addresses, essays, lectures
518 Biography (Collective)
By region
Bali
520 Periodicals. Collections, etc. Sources
522 General works
524 General special
526 Biography (Collective)

History
By region or country
Asia
Southeast Asia
Special regions or countries
Indonesia
By region - Continued
Java
530 Periodicals. Collections, etc. Sources
532 General works
534 General special
536 Biography (Collective)
538 Local, A-Z
539 Other local, A-Z

Malaysia. Malaya
540 Periodicals. Collections, etc. Sources
542 General works
544 General special

546 Addresses, essays, lectures
548 Biography (Collective)
549 Local, A-Z
For material concerned with Singapore, see BQ569.S5

Thailand (Siam)
550 Periodicals. Collections, etc. Sources
552 General works
554 General special

555 Addresses, essays, lectures
556 Biography (Collective)
By period

558 Early through 1237
560 1238-1350 (Sukhōthai period)
562 1350-1782 (ʻAyutthayā period)
Including Thonburī period, 1767-1782
564 1782-1932 (Rattanakōsin (Bangkok) period)
566 1932-
568 Local, A-Z

569 Other regions or countries, A-Z
Divided like BQ400

.P5 Philippine Islands

.S5 Singapore

History
By region or country
Asia - Continued
Central Asia
570 Periodicals. Collections, etc. Sources
572 General works
574 General special

576 Addresses, essays, lectures
579 Biography (Collective)

Special regions or countries
Mongolia. Mongolian People's Republic.
Outer Mongolia
580 Periodicals. Collections, etc. Sources
582 General works
584 General special
586 Addresses, essays, lectures
588 Biography (Collective)

By period
590 Early through 1260
591 1261-1576
593 1577-1750
595 1751-1923
597 1924-

599 Local, A-Z
For material concerned with Inner Mongolia, see BQ649.I7
Tibet, see BQ7530+

609 Other regions or countries, A-Z
Including ancient kingdoms of Central Asia
Divided like BQ400

.K5 Khotan
.K8 Kucha

.L6 Lou-lan
Siberia, see BQ709.S655S53
.S6 Soviet Central Asia

Far East
610 Periodicals. Collections, etc. Sources
General works
612 Early works through 1800
614 1801-
616 General special
618 Addresses, essays, lectures
619 Biography (Collective)

History
By region or country
Asia
Far East - Continued
Special countries
China

620 Periodicals. Collections, etc. Sources
General works
622 Early works through 1800
624 1801-1948
626 1949-

628 General special
630 Special topics, A-Z

.K8 Ku-i Buddhism

632 Addresses, essays, lectures
634 Biography (Collective)

By period
636 Early to 581 A.D.
638 581-960 (Sui, Tang and Five dynasties)
640 960-1368 (Sung and Yüan dynasties)
641 1368-1644 (Ming dynasty)
643 1644-1912 (Manchu (Ch'ing) dynasty)
645 1912-1949
647 1949-

649 Local, A-Z

Formosa, see .T32
.H6 Hongkong
.I7 Inner Mongolia

.M3 Manchuria
.T32 Taiwan. Formosa
.T86 Tun-huang, Kansu

Korea. South Korea
650 Periodicals. Collections, etc. Sources
General works
652 Early works through 1800
654 1801-1945
656 1946-

658 General special
659 Addresses, essays, lectures
660 Biography (Collective)

History
By region or country
Asia
Far East
Special countries
Korea. South Korea - Continued
By period
661 Early to 935 A.D.
Including Silla Kingdom
662 935-1392 (Koryŏ (Koryu) period)
664 1392-1910 (I (Yi) dynasty)
665 1910-1945 (Chōsen. Japanese era)
667 1945-
669 Local, A-Z
e. g. .N6 North Korea

Japan
670 Periodicals. Collections, etc. Sources
General works
672 Early works through 1800
674 1801-1945
676 1946-

678 General special
680 Special topics, A-Z

.H6 Honji Suijaku
Cf. BL2222.23, Relations to Shinto

682 Addresses, essays, lectures
683 Biography (Collective)

By period
684 Early to 794 A.D.
685 794-1185 (Heian period)
687 1185-1600 (Kamakura through Momoyama period)
689 1600-1868 (Tokugawa period)
691 1868-
693 1868-1912
695 20th century
697 1945-
699 Local, A-Z
Europe
700 Periodicals. Colllections, etc. Sources
702 General works
704 General special
706 Addresses, essays, lectures
708 Biography (Collective)
709 By region or country, A-Z
Divide like BQ400
e. g. .S655S53 Siberia

History

By region or country - Continued

Africa

710 Periodicals. Collections, etc. Sources

712 General works. History

714 General special

716 Addresses, essays, lectures

718 Biography (Collective)

719 By region or country, A-Z

Divided like BQ400

America

Including both North and South America

720 Periodicals. Collections, etc. Sources

722 General works

724 General special

726 Addresses, essays, lectures, etc.

728 Biography (Collective)

Special countries

United States

730 Periodicals. Collections, etc. Sources

732 General works

734 General special

736 Addresses, essays, lectures

738 Biography (Collective)

739 By region or state, A-Z

Divided like BQ400

e. g. .C2 California

.H2 Hawaii

Canada

740 Periodicals. Collections, etc. Sources

742 General works

744 General special

746 Addresses, essays, lectures

748 Biography (Collective)

749 By region or province, A-Z

Divided like BQ400

Brazil

750 Periodicals. Collections, etc. Sources

752 General works

754 General special

756 Addresses, essays, lectures

758 Biography (Collective)

759 By region or state, A-Z

Divided like BQ400

760 Other American regions or countries, A-Z

Divided like BQ400

History
By region or country - Continued
Australia
770 Periodicals. Collections, etc. Sources
772 General works
774 General special
776 Addresses, essays, lectures
778 Biography (Collective)
779 By state or territory, A-Z
Divided like BQ400

New Zealand
780 Periodicals. Collections, etc. Sources
782 General works
784 General special
786 Addresses, essays, lectures
788 Biography (Collective)
789 By island or district, A-Z
Divided like BQ400

Pacific islands
790 Periodicals. Collections, etc. Sources
792 General works
794 General special
796 Addresses, essays, lectures
798 Biography (Collective)
799 By island groups, A-Z
Divided like BQ400

Persecutions
For classification with individual modifications, schools, etc., see BQ7001+
800 Collections
810 General works

815 General special
820 History
829 By region or country, A-Z

Under each country:
.x General works. History
.x2 Local, A-Z

Biography
840 Collective (General)
Cf. BQ164, Educators
BQ284, Historians
BQ900, Gautama Buddha's disciplines
BQ7920+, Lamaists
etc.
843 Monks. Priests. Novices. Bhikṣu. Bhikkhu
Cf. Tables IV and V, 48, Special modifications, sects, etc.

Biography
Collective (General) - Continued
Laymen, see BQ840
846 Upāsaka (Men believers)
Women
850 General works
855 Nuns. Bhikṣunī. Bhikkhunī
Cf. Tables IV and V, 48, Special modifications, sects, etc.
858 Upāsikā (Women believers)

Individual
Gautama Buddha
General works
For Buddhakāya, see BQ4180; for Śākyamuni Buddha, see BQ4690.S3
860 Early works through 1200
For Avadānas, see BQ1530+; for Jātakas, see BQ1460+
Gautama Buddha in the Tripiṭaka
865 History and criticism
Individual texts, see BQ1300+

868 1201-1800
871-878 1801-1945
Divided like BQ1-8
881-888 1946-
Divided like BQ1-8

890 Pictorial works
892 Juvenile works
893 Popular works
894 General special
895 Addresses, essays, lectures
897 Historiography
899 Chronology
Disciples. Friends and associates, etc.
900 Collective

905 Individual, A-Z
.N2 Nanda
e. g. .N2A7 Saundarananda (by Aśvaghoṣa)

910 His attitude toward contemporary religions or philosophies
912 Sermons about the life of Gautama Buddha
915 Selections of his sayings and teachings. Parables
Class here descriptive works only
For doctrinal works on his teachings, see BQ4061

Biography
Individual
Gautama Buddha - Continued
918 Special topics, A-Z

.G6 God

Cultus
920 General works
Special topics
922 Footprints
923 Iconography. Physical attributes
Class here works limited to religious points of view only
Cf. N8193.2, Gautama Buddha in art

924 Relics
925 Stūpas
Including descriptive works on Stūpa worship
Cf. BQ6460+, Sacred shrines in India, etc.
For works concerned with the meaning of the Stūpa, see BQ5125.S8

927 Symbolism
929 Other, A-Z

.P7 Prophecies

Special events
930 Former lives (mythological)
932 Birth. Youth. Married life

933 Family
934 Renunciation and ascetic life
935 Enlightenment

937 First sermon and deliverance of teachings
Including life with followers
For works limited to doctrines, see BQ4230, etc.

938 Last years. Last illness. Death (Pari-nirvana). Cremation
For works limited to doctrinal points of view, see BQ4263
939 Other, A-Z

Biography - Continued

Other individuals (VIII)

For works limited to founders and important persons of individual sects, see the sect

For works limited to the disciples of Gautama Buddha, see BQ900+

The author number is determined by the letter following the letter or letters for which each class number stands

940	A
942	B
944	Ca - Cg
946	Ch
948	Ci - Cz
950	D
952	E
954	Fa - Ft
956	Fu
958	Fv - Fz
960	G
962	H
964	I
966	J
968	K
970	L
972	M
974	N
976	O
978	P
980	Q
982	R
984	Sa - Sg
986	Sh
988	Si - Sz
990	T
992	U
994	V
995	Wa
996	Wb - Wz
997	X
998	Y
999	Z

Buddhist literature

For devotional literature, see BQ5535+

For works limited to a particular sect, see BQ7001+

1001-1008 Periodicals. Societies. Serials

Divided like BQ1-8

1010 Dictionaries

1011-1018 Collections. Collected works

Divided like BQ1-8

Individual works, see BQ4000+, etc.

1020 History and criticism

1029 By region or country, A-Z

Under each country:

.x Collections

.x2 History and criticism

Juvenile works

1031-1038 Collections

Divided like BQ1-8

Individual works, see BQ4032, etc.

1040 History and criticism

1045 By region or country, A-Z

Under each country:

.x Collections

.x2 History and criticism

Tripiṭaka (Canonical literature)

Class here texts originally transmitted (though not necessarily extant) in Pāli, Sanskrit, or Prākrit (including translations and commentaries) as well as anonymous sutras originally written in Tibetan, Chinese, etc.

This classification schedule does not reflect the internal organization of any one version or edition, but it is rather a practical working synthesis

1100 Collections. Collected works

1105 General works

1107 General special

1110 Introductions. Popular works

1112 Addresses, essays, lectures, etc.

1113 Origins and development. History

1115 Philological studies

.5 Hermeneutics. Exegetics. Principles of interpretation

History of publication

1117 General works

1118 General special

1119 By region or country, A-Z

Tripiṭaka (Canonical literature) - Continued
History of translation
1120 General works
Bibliography, see Z7862
1122 By region or country, A-Z
1124 By language, A-Z

Preservation of manuscripts, books, etc.
Kyōzō
1126 General works
1128 General special

e. g. Mainōkyō, kyōzuka, kyōzutsu

1129 By region or country, A-Z
Under each country:
.x General works
.x2 Local, A-Z

1130 Dictionaries, indexes, etc.
Biography in the Tripiṭaka (Collective)
1132.A1A-Z Dictionaries
.A2-Z General works. Sermons on characters
1133 Special classes, groups, etc., A-Z

.W6 Women

1136 Special topics, A-Z

.C6 Copying
.N38 Natural history

.P35 Parables
.P56 Plants

1138 General collections or selections from the Tripiṭaka not related to a special piṭaka or version
By piṭaka
Class here general editions, commentaries, etc., covering more than one version
Each division is subdivided by Table I (10 numbers), Table II (1 number), and Table III (Cutter numbers)

1140-1149 Sūtrapiṭaka
1150-1159 Vinayapiṭaka
1160-1169 Abhidharmapiṭaka

Tripiṭaka (Canonical literature) - Continued
By version
Each division is subdivided by Table I (10 numbers), Table II (1 number), and Table III (Cutter numbers)

1170-1179 Pāli version (Tipiṭaka)
1180-1189 Vinayapiṭaka
1190-1199 Suttapiṭaka
1200-1209 Abhidhammapiṭaka

1210-1219 Chinese version (Ta tsang ching)
Including those works composed in Korea and Japan
1220-1229 Ching tsang (Sūtrapiṭaka)
1230-1239 Lü tsang (Vinayapiṭaka)
1240-1249 Lun tsang (Abhidharmapiṭaka)

1250-1259 Tibetan version
1260-1269 Kanjur. Bkaḥ-ḥgyur
1270-1279 Tanjur. Bstan-ḥgyur

Divisions not limited to a particular linguistic version
Sutrapitaka
1280-1289 Early Buddhist suttas 1/
Class here the five Nikāyas or four Āgamas which include the nine or twelve Aṅgas
1290-1299 Dīghanikāya
1295 Early commentaries

e. g. Sumaṅgalavilāsinī (by Buddhaghosa)

.5 Major divisions

Mahāvagga, see BQ2370+
.P35-359 Pāṭikavagga
.S56-569 Sīlakkhanda

1/ The originals are mainly in Pāli. As this classification is based on the Pāli version, individual texts in the Chinese version should be converted according to the catalog by Akanuma, Chizen: Kan-Pa shibu shiagon goshōroku. The comparative catalogue of Chinese Āgamas and Pāli Nikāyas.

Tripiṭaka (Canonical literature)
By version
Divisions not limited to a particular linguistic version
Sūtrapiṭaka
Early Buddhist suttas 1/
Dīghanikāya - Continued

1300 Individual suttas, A-Z

.A35-359 Aggañña suttanta
.A45-459 Ambaṭṭha sutta

.B73-739 Brahmajālasutta
.C35-359 Cataṣapariṣatsūtra

.M34-349 Mahāpadānasuttanta
.M35-359 Mahāparinibbānasuttanta

.M36-369 Mahāsatipaṭṭhānasutta
.S56-569 Siṅgalovadāsuttanta

1310-1319 Majjhimanikāya
1320 Individual suttas, A-Z

.A53-539 Aṅgulimāla Sutta
.C85-859 Cūlamālunkyasuttanta

.I53-539 Indriyabhāvanāsutta
.S25-259 Satipatthana sutta

.U63-639 Upālisutta

1330-1339 Saṁyttanikaya
1339.5 Individual suttas, A-Z

.D45 Dhammacakkapavattana sutta
.V45-459 Verahaccānisutta

1340-1349 Anguttaranikāya
1349.5 Individual suttas, A-Z

.G57-579 Girimānanda Sutta
.K35 Kālakārāma Sutta

1/ The originals are mainly in Pāli. As this classification is based on the Pāli version, individual texts in the Chinese version should be converted according to the catalog by Akanuma, Chizen: Kan-Pa shibu shiagon goshōroku. The comparative catalogue of Chinese Āgamas and Pāli Nikāyas.

Tripiṭaka (Canonical literature)
By version
Divisions not limited to a particular linguistic version
Sūtrapiṭaka
Early Buddhist suttas 1/ - Continued

1350-1359	Khuddakanikāya
1360-1369	Khuddakapāṭha
1369.5	Individual suttas, A-Z
	.M35-359 Maṅgala Sutta
1370-1379	Dhammapada
1375	Early commentaries
	e. g. Dhammapadaṭṭhakathā
1380-1389	Udānavarga (by Dharmatrāta)
1390-1399	Udāna
1400-1409	Itivuttaka
1410-1419	Suttanipāta
1419.5	Individual suttas, A-Z
	.P36-369 Pārāyanasutta
	.U72-729 Uragasutta
1420-1429	Vimānavatthu
1430-1439	Petavatthu
1440-1449	Theragāthā
1450-1459	Therīgāthā
1460-1469	Jātakas
	Including Jātakamāla (by Āryaśūra)
1470	Individual Jātakas. By title, A-Z
	.C34-349 Candakumāra
	.G53-539 Ghāsī Vimaladattajātaka
	.M35-359 Mahā Ummagga Jataka
	.M3594-35949 Mahājanakajātaka
	.M38-389 Maṇicūḍajātaka
	.N53-539 Nidanakatha
	.S27-279 Sasajātaka
	.S93-939 Sudhābhojanajātaka
	.V48-489 Vessantarājātaka
1480-1489	Niddesa
1490-1499	Paṭisambhidāmagga
1495	Early commentaries
	e. g. Saddhammapakāsinī

1/ The originals are mainly in Pāli. As this classification is based on the Pāli version, individual texts in the Chinese version should be converted according to the catalog by Akanuma, Chizen: Kan-Pa shibu shiagon goshōroku. The comparative catalogue of Chinese Āgamas and Pāli Nikāyas.

Tripiṭaka (Canonical literature)
By version
Divisions not limited to a particular linguistic version
Sūtrapiṭaka
Early Buddhist suttas 1/
Khuddakanikāya - Continued

1500-1509 Apadāna
1510-1519 Buddhavaṃsa
1520-1529 Cariyāpiṭaka
1529.5 Other miscellaneous suttas, A-Z
Including non-Pāli sutras
.C55 Chih ch'an ping pi yao fa
.P34-349 Pa ta jen chüeh ching
.P35-359 Paritta

1530-1539 Avadānas
The originals are mainly in Sanskrit
1540-1549 Aśokāvadānamāla
1550-1559 Avadānaśataka
1560-1569 Divyāvadāna
1570-1579 Karmaśataka
1580-1589 Lalitavistara
1590-1599 Mahāvastu
1600 Other, A-Z

.H74-749 Hsien yü yin yüan ching
.K85-859 Kuo ch'ü hsien tsai yin kuo ching
.S94-949 Sumāgadhāvadāna
.S96-969 Suvarṇavarṇāvadāna

Poems, etc., on the life of Gautama Buddha
1603 Collections. Selections
1606 Individual. By title, A-Z

.B83-839 Buddhacarita (by Aśvaghosa)
.J53-539 Jinacaritá (by Vánaratana Mēdhamkara)

History and criticism, see BQ865

1/

The originals are mainly in Pāli. As this classification is based on the Pāli version, individual texts in the Chinese version should be converted according to the catalog by Akanuma, Chizen: Kan-Pa shibu shiagon goshōroku. The comparative catalogue of Chinese Āgamas and Pāli Nikāyas.

Tripiṭaka (Canonical literature)
By version
Divisions not limited to a particular linguistic version
Sūtrapiṭaka - Continued
1610-1619 Mahāyāna Buddhist sūtras
1620-1629 Avataṃsakasūtra. Buddhāvataṃsakamahāvaipulyasūtra
Including the 40, 60, and 80 volume Avataṃsakasūtras
1630-1639 Daśabhūmīśvara
1635 Early commentaries

e. g. Daśabhumikavibhāṣāśāstra (by Nāgārjun)
1640-1649 Gaṇḍavyūha
Including Samantabhadracaryāpraṇidhānarāja

1660-1669 Dhāraṇīs
1670 Individual dhāraṇīs, A-Z

.A63-639 Aparimitāyur dhāraṇī. Aparimitāyur jñāna nāma mahāyānasūtram

.J52-529 Jñānolka-nāma-dhāraṇī-sarvagatipariśodhani

.K85-859 Kuntīdevīdhāraṇī
.M35-359 Mahākāruṇikacittadhāraṇi

.M36-369 Mahāsannipātaratnaketu-dhāraṇī
.P37-379 Parnasabaridharani

.T35-359 Tathāgatoṣṇīṣasitātapatrāparājitamahāpratyaṅgiratparmasiddhanāmadhāraṇī

1680-1689 Fo i chiao ching
1690-1699 Fu mu ên chung ching
1700-1709 Karuṇāpuṇḍarīka

1710-1719 Kṣitigarbhapraṇidhānasūtra
1720-1729 Laṅkāvatārasūtra

1730-1739 Mahāmāyūrīvidyārājñī. Mahāmāyūrī
1740-1749 Mahāparinirvāṇasūtra

Tripiṭaka (Canonical literature)
By version
Divisions not limited to a particular linguistic version
Sūtrapiṭaka
Mahāyāna Buddhist sūtras - Continued

1750-1759	Mahāratnakūṭasūtra
1760-1769	Kāśyapaparivarta
1770-1779	Rāṣṭrāpalaparipṛcchā
1780-1789	Ratnārāśisūtra
1790-1799	Śrīmālādevīsiṃhanādasūtra (Śrīmālāsūtra)
1800	Other parts, A-Z For Sukhāvatīvyūha (Larger and Smaller), see BQ2030+
1810-1819	Mahāsaṃnipātasūtra
1820-1829	Candragarbha
1830-1839	Pratyutpannasūtra. Bhadrapāla
1840-1849	Ratnadhvaja
1850-1859	Sūryagarbha
1860	Other parts, A-Z
1870-1879	Mahāvairocanasūtra
1880-1889	Prajñapāramitās
1890-1899	Adhyardhaśatikāprajñāpāramitā
1900-1909	Aṣṭādaśasāhasrikāprajñāpāramitā
1910-1919	Aṣṭasāhasrikāprajñāpāramitā
1915	Early commentaries e. g. Prajñāparāmitāpiṇḍārtha (by Dignāga); Abhisamayālaṅkārāloka (by Haribhadra)
1920-1929	Prajñāpāramitāratnaguṇasamcayagatna
1930-1939	Jen wang po je ching
1940-1949	Mahāprajñāpāramitāsūtra
1950-1959	Pañcaviṃśatisāhasrikāprajñāpāramitā
1955	Early commentaries e. g. Abhisamayālaṅkāra (By Asaṅga); Mahāprajñapāramitāśāstra (by Nāgārjuna)
1960-1969	Prajñāpāramitāhṛdayasūtra
1970-1979	Śatasāhasrikāprajñāpāramitā
1980-1989	Suvikrāntavikrāmiparipṛcchāprajñāparāmitā
1990-1999	Vajracchedikaprajñāpāramitā

Tripiṭaka (Canonical literature)
By version
Divisions not limited to a particular linguistic version
Sūtrapiṭaka
Mahāyana Buddhist sūtras
Prajñāparamitās - Continued

2000 Other Prajñāpāramitā sūtras, A-Z

.D37-379 Daśasāhasrikā
.E53-539 Ekaviṃśatistotra

.S24-249 Sañcayagāthā
.S36-369 Saptaśatikaprajñāpāramitā

2010-2019 Pure Land sūtras
Including Ching t'u san pu ching (Jōdo sambukyō)
2020-2029 Kuan wu liang shou ching (Amitāyurdhyānasūtra)
2030-2039 Sukhāvatīvyūha (Larger)
2035 Early commentaries

e. g. Sukhāvatīvyūhopadeśa (by Vasubandhu)

2040-2049 Sukhāvatīvyūha (Smaller)
2049.5 Other Pure Land sūtras, A-Z

.A63-638 Aparamitāyurjñānadhrdaya

2050-2059 Saddharmapuṇḍarikasūtra
2060-2069 Avalokiteśvarasamantamukhaparivarta
2070-2079 Amitārthasūtra (Wu liang i ching)

2080-2089 Samādhirājasūtra
2090-2099 Saṃdhinirmocanasūtra

2100-2109 Shan o yin kuo ching
2110-2119 Ssu shih erh chang ching

2120-2129 Śūraṅgamasamādhisūtra. Sūraṅgamasūtra
2130-2139 Suvarṇaprabhāsasūtra

2140-2149 Tantras
2150-2159 Guhyasamājatantra
2160-2169 Hevajratantra
2170-2179 Kālacakramūlatantra. Kālacakratantra

Tripiṭaka (Canonical literature)
By version
Divisions not limited to a particular linguistic version
Sūtrapiṭaka
Mahāyāna Buddhist sūtras
Tantras - Continued

2180 Other individual tantras, A-Z
.C35-359 Cakrasamvaratantra
.D74-749 Dri ma med pa'i bśags rgyud
.G93-939 Guhyamūlatantra

.M34-349 Mañjuśrīmūlakalpa
.S24-249 Saṃvarodayatantra

.S26-269 Sarvadurgatipariśodhanatantra
.S94-949 Svarodaya

.T35-359 Tāratantra
.V34-349 Vajrabhairavatantra

2190-2199 Tathāgatagarbhasūtra
2200-2209 Vajraśekharasūtra
2210-2219 Vimalakīrtinirdeśa
2220-2229 Yü lan p'en ching
2230-2239 Yüan chüeh ching (Mahāvaipūrnabuddhasūtra-prasannārthasūtra?)
2240 Other individual Mahāyāna sūtras, A-Z
.A24-249 Adbhutadharmaparyāya
.A54-549 Amityatāsutra

.A77-779 Arthaviniścayasūtra
.B53-539 Bhaiṣajyaguruvaidūryaprabharājasūtra
.B83-839 Buddhapitakasuhsilanigraha
.C45-459 Ch'u fen shuo ching
.D36-369 Dasadigandhakanavidhvamsana
.D53-539 Dharmasamuccaya
.D54-549 Dharmaśarīrasūtra

.F32-329 Fa mieh chin ching

.G52-529 Ghanavyūhasūtra
.H76-769 Hsiao tzu ching

.I55-559 Insadi-sūtra
.K34-349 Kāraṇḍavyuha

.K42-429 Kha mchu nag po zi bar byed pa zes bya ba theg pa chen pa'i mdo
.K93-939 Kujō shakujōkyo

Tripiṭaka (Canonical literature)
By version
Divisions not limited to a particular linguistic version
Sūtrapiṭaka
Mahāyāna Buddhist sūtras

2240 Other individual Mahāyāna sūtras, A-Z - Continued

.M33-339 Mahāmoksasūtra
.M35-359 Mañjuśrīnāmasaṅgiti

.M84-849 Mu-lien-ching
.S33-339 Saddharmasmṛtyupasthānasūtra
.S35-359 Sālistambasūtra
.S36-369 San shih yin kuo ching

.S37-379 Saptatathāgatapūrvaprani-dhānaviśeṣavitaranāmamahāyānasūtra

.S3793-37939 Sārdūlakarnāvadāna
.S3795-37959 Sarvabuddhavisayāvatāra-jñānālokālankarasūtra

.S38-389 Sarvapuṇyasamuccayasamādhisūtra
.T313-3139 Ta fang pien Fo pao en ching

.T32-329 Ta sheng li ch'ü liu po lo mi ching
.T37-379 Tārābhattārikānāmāṣṭaśataka

.V35-359 Vajrasamadhisūtra
.V55-559 Viśeṣacintabrahmapaṛiprcchā

Vinayapiṭaka

2250-2259 Sarvāstivada School Vinaya
2255 Early commentaries

e. g. Ḥdul-baḥi mdo (by Guṇaprabha)

2260-2269 Karmavācanā
2270-2279 Prātimokṣa
2280-2289 Bhikṣuprātimokṣa
2290-2299 Bhikṣuṇīprātimokṣa

2300-2309 Skanda
2309.5 Other individual texts. By title, A-Z

.A7-79 Āryamūlasarvāstivādiśrāmaṇera-kārikā (by Nāgārjuna)

Tripiṭaka (Canonical literature)
By version
Divisions not limited to a particular linguistic version
Vinayapiṭaka - Continued

2310-2319 Theravāda School Vinaya (Pāli originals)
2315 Early commentaries

e. g. Samantapāsādikā (by Buddhaghosa); Vinayavinicca (by Buddhaghosa)

2320 Pātimokkha
2322 Bhikkhupātimokkha
2324 Bhikkhunīpātimokkha

2330-2339 Suttavibhaṅga
2340-2349 Mahāvibhaṅga
2350-2359 Bhikkhunīvibhanga

2360-2369 Khandhaka
2370-2379 Mahāvagga
2380-2389 Cullavagga

2390-2399 Parivāra
2400-2409 Dharmagupta School Vinaya
Cf. BQ8780+, Ritsu (Lü) Sect
2410 Individual texts. By title, A-Z

2420-2429 Mahāsāṁghika School Vinaya
2429.8 Individual texts. By title, A-Z

.A32-329 Abhisamācārika
.V52-529 Vinayakārikā

2430-2439 Mahīśāsaka School Vinaya
2439.8 Individual texts. By title, A-Z
2440 Vinaya of other special schools. By school, A-Z

2450-2459 Mahāyāna Bodhisattva Vinaya
For works on the discipline, see BQ7442
Bodhisattvaprātimokṣa, see BQ3060+
2460-2469 Fan wang ching

2470-2479 P'u sa ying lo pen yeh ching
2480 Other Mahāyāna Vinaya texts, A-Z

Tripiṭaka (Canonical literature)
By version
Divisions not limited to a particular linguistic version - Continued
Abhidharmapiṭaka

2490-2499 Theravāda Abhidhamma texts (Pāli originals)
2495 Early commentaries

e. g. Abhidhammattasaṅgaha (by Anuruddha)

2500-2509 Dhammasaṅgaṇi
2505 Early commentaries

e. g. Atthasālinī (by Buddhaghosa)

2510-2519 Vibhaṅga
2515 Early commentaries

e. g. Sammohavinodanī (by Buddhaghosa)

2520-2529 Dhātukathā
2525 Early commentaries

e. g. Pañcappakaraṇāṭṭhakathā (by Buddhaghosa)

2530-2539 Puggalapaññatti
2540-2549 Kathāvatthu
2545 Early commentaries

e. g. Kathāvatthuppakaraṇāṭṭhakathā (by Buddhaghosa)

2550-2559 Yamaka
2560-2569 Paṭṭhāna

Other miscellaneous Pāli texts

2570-2579 Dāṭhāvaṃsa
2580-2589 Dīpavaṃsa
2590-2599 Mahābodhivaṃsa (by Upatissa)

2600-2609 Mahāvaṃsa (by Mahānāma)
2610-2619 Milindapañhā
2620-2629 Vimuttimagga (by Upatissa)

2630-2639 Visuddhimagga (by Buddhaghosa)
2635 Early commentaries

e. g. Paramatthamañjusā (by Dhammapāla)

Tripiṭaka (Canonical literature)
By version
Divisions not limited to a particular linguistic version
Abhidharmapiṭaka
Other miscellaneous Pāli texts - Continued

2640 Other texts, A-Z

.C85-859 Cūlavaṃsa
.D37-379 Dasabodhisattuppattikathā

.D48-489 Dhammanīti
.N45-459 Nettipakaraṇa

.T45-459 Thūpavaṃsa (by Vācissara)

2650-2659 Hīnayāna Abhidharma texts (non-Pāli originals)
Including the works of the Mahāsāṅghika School, the Sarvastivāda (Vaibhāṣika) School, the Sautrāntika School, etc.
For works on the Abhidharma philosophy, see BQ4195+

2660-2669 Abhidharmadīpa
2670-2679 Abhidharmajñānaprasthānaśāstra (by Kātyāyanīputra)
2680-2689 Abhidharmakośa. Kārikā and bhāṣya (by Vasubandhu)
2685 Early commentaries

e. g. Sphuṭārthā abhidharmakośavyākhyā (by Yaśomitra)

2690-2699 Abhidharmamahāvibhāsāśāstra
2700-2709 Abhidharmanyāyānusarīśāstra
2710-2719 Samayabhedoparacanacakra (by Vasumitra)
2720-2729 Satyasiddhiśāstra (by Harivarman)
2730 Other texts, A-Z

.A35-359 Abhidharmahṛdayaśāstra (by Dharmaśreṣṭhi)
.A36-369 Abhidharmāmṛtarasaśāstra
.A3697-36979 Abhidharmaprakaraṇabhāsya

.A37-379 Abhidharmaprakaraṇapāda (by Vasumitra)
.A39-399 Abhidharmasaṃgītiparyāyapāda. Saṃgītiparyaya (by Mahākauṣṭhila)
.A44-449 Abhidharmāvatāraśāstra (by Skandhila)

Tripiṭaka (Canonical literature)
By version
Divisions not limited to a particular linguistic version
Abhidharmapiṭaka - Continued
2740-2749 Mahāyāna doctrinal texts
2750-2759 Mādhyamika School texts
Including the works of the Prāsaṅgika School and the Svātantrika School
Class here works by individual authors.
By title

2760-2769 Catuḥśatakaśāstra (by Āryadeva)
2770-2779 Dharmasaṃgraha (by Nāgārjuna)

2780-2789 Dvādaśanikāyaśāstra (by Āryadeva)
2790-2799 Madhyamakakārikā (by Nāgārjuna)

2800-2809 Akutobhaya mūlamadhyamakavṛtti (by Nāgārjuna)
2810-2819 Mādhyamikaśāstra (by Piṅgala)
2820-2829 Madhyāntānugamaśāstra (by Asaṅga)

2830-2839 Mahāyānamadhyamakaśāstravyākhyā (by Sthiramati)
2840-2849 Mūlamadhyamakavṛtti (by Buddhapalita)
2850-2859 Prajñāpradīpamūlamadhyamakavṛtti (by Bhāvaviveka)
2860-2869 Prasannapadā (by Candrakīrti)

2870-2879 Ratnāvalī (by Nāgārjuna)
2880-2889 Śataśāstra (by Āryadeva)

2890-2899 Vajrasūcī (by Aśvaghoṣa)
2900-2909 Vigrahavyāvarttanī (by Nāgārjuna)

2910 Other texts, A-Z

.C38-389 Catuḥstava (by Nāgārjuna)
.H38-389 Hastavālaprakaraṇavṛtti (by Āryadeva)

.M34-349 Madhyamakahṛdayakārikā (by Bhāvaviveka)
.M345 Early commentaries
e. g. Madhyamakahṛdayavṛtti-tarkajvālā. Tarkajvalā (by Bhāvaviveka)

Tripiṭaka (Canonical literature)
By version
Divisions not limited to a particular linguistic version
Abhidharmapiṭaka
Mahāyāna doctrinal texts
Madhyamika School texts
2910 Other texts, A-Z - Continued

.M35-359 Madhyamakaratnapradīpa (by Bhāvaviveka)
.M36-369 Madhyamakāvatāra (by Candrakīrti)

.P73-739 Pratītyasamutpādahṛdayakārikā (by Nāgārjuna)
.T35-359 Talāntāntarakaśāstra (by Bhāvaviveka)
.V34-349 Vaidalyasūtra (by Nāgārjuna)

2920-2929 Yogācāra School texts
Including the works of the Anākara School and the Sākāra School
Class here works by individual authors.
By title
2930-2939 Ālambaṇaparīksā (by Dignāga)
2940-2949 Buddhagotraśāstra (by Vasubandhu)
2950-2959 Karmasiddhiprakaraṇa (by Vasubandhu)
2960-2969 Madhyāntavibhāgasūtra (by Maitreyanātha)
2965 Early commentaries

e. g. Madhyāntavibhāgabhāṣya (by Vasubandhu); Madhyāntavibhāgaṭīkā (by Sthiramati)

2980-2989 Mahāyānasamgraha (by Asaṅga)
2990-2999 Mahāyānaśraddhotpādaśāstra (by Aśvaghoṣa?)

3000-3009 Mahāyānasūtrālaṅkāra (by Asaṅga)
3010-3019 Mahāyānottaratantrāśāstra
3020-3029 Ratnagotravibhāga

3030-3039 Triṃśikāvijñaptimātratāsiddhi (by Vasubandhu)
3035 Early commentaries

e. g. Vijñaptimātratasiddhiśāstra (by Dharmapāla); Trimśikāvijñaptimātratāsiddhibhāṣya (by Sthiramati)

Tripiṭaka (Canonical literature)
By version
Divisions not limited to a particular linguistic version
Abhidharmapiṭaka
Mahāyāna doctrinal texts
Yogācāra School texts - Continued

3040-3049 Viṁśatikāvijñaptimātratāsiddhi (by Vasubandhu)

3050-3059 Yogācārabhūmi (by Maitreyanātha?)

3060-3069 Bodhisattvabhūmi (by Maitreyanātha?)
Including Bodhisattvaprātimokṣa

3070 Other parts, A-Z

.S7-79 Śrāvakabhūmi

3080 Other texts, A-Z

.A25-259 Abhidharmasamuccaya. Mahāyānābhidharmasamuccaya (by Asaṅga)

.A255 Early commentaries
e. g. Abhidharmasamuccayavyākhyā (by Sthiramati)

.D53-539 Dharmadharmatāvibhāga (by Maitreyanātha)

.G37-379 Gāthāsaṅgraha (by Vasubandhu)

.M34-349 Maitreyapranidhāna (by Sthiramati)

.P73-739 Pratītyasamutpādavyākhyā (by Vasubandhu)

.S55-559 Śīlaparikathā (by Vasubandhu)

.S97-979 Sūtrālamkāra (by Maitreyanātha)

.T75-759 Trisvabhāvanirdeśa (by Vasubandhu)

3090-3099 Later (5th-12th century) Indian texts
Including those works of the Mādhyamika-Yogācāra School, and Buddhist logic (Hetu-vidyā, Pramāṇa, Nyāya, etc.)
Class here works by individual authors. By title. For general works on Buddhist logic, see BC25+

3100-3109 Antaryāptisamarthana (by Ratnākaraśanti)

3110-3119 Apohasiddhi (By Ratnakīrti)

Tripiṭaka (Canonical literature)
By version
Divisions not limited to a particular linguistic version
Abhidharmapiṭaka
Mahāyāna doctrinal texts
Later (5th-12 century) Indian texts - Continued

3120-3129 Avayavinirākaraṇa (by Paṇḍita Aśoka)
3130-3139 Bhāvanākrama, Parts I-III (by Kamalaśīla)
3140-3149 Bodhicaryāvatāra (by Śāntideva)

3150-3159 Hetubindu (by Dharmakīrti)
3160-3169 Hetutattvopadeśa (by Jitāri)
3170-3179 Jātinirākṛti (by Jitāri)

3180-3189 Madhyamakālaṃkāra (by Śāntarakṣita)
3190-3199 Nyāyabindu (by Dharmakīrti)
3195 Early commentaries

e. g. Nyāyabinduṭīkā (by Dharmottara); Nyāyabindutika (by Vinītadeva)

3200-3209 Nyāyapraveśa (by Śaṅkarasvāmin)
3210-3219 Pramānāntarbhāva
3220-3229 Pramānasamuccaya (by Dignāga)

3230-3239 Pramānavārttika (by Dharmakīrti)
3240-3249 Śikṣāsamuccaya (by Śāntideva)
3250-3259 Sūtrasamuccaya (by Śāntideva)

3260-3269 Tarkabhāṣā (by Mokṣākaragupta)
3270-3279 Tarkasopāna (by Vidyākaraśanti)
3280-3289 Tattvasaṃgraha (by Śāntarakṣita)

3290-3299 Vadanyāya (by Dharmakīrti)
3300 Other texts, A-Z

.G35-359 Gaṇḍīstotragāthā
.H47-479 Hetucakranirnaya (by Dignāga)
.K73-739 Kṣaṇabhangasiddhi (by Ratnakīrti)

.N93-939 Nyāyamukha (by Dignāga)
.P73-739 Pramāṇaviniścaya (by Dharmakīrti)
.S22-229 Sāmānyadūṣaṇadikprasāritā (by Pandita Aśoka)

.S24-249 Saṃbandhaparīkṣā (by Dharmakīrti)
.S26-269 Saṃtānāntarasiddhi (by Dharmakīrti)
.S74-749 Srījñānaguṇabhadra-nāmastuti (by Vajra-varman)

Tripiṭaka (Canonical literature)
By version
Divisions not limited to a particular linguistic version
Abhidharmapiṭaka
Mahāyāna doctrinal texts
Later (5th-12 century) Indian texts
3300 Other texts, A-Z - Continued

.T37-379 Tarkarahasyam

.T75-759 Trikālaparīksā (by Dignāga)

3320-3329 Tantric Buddhist texts (Sanskrit orginals only)
3340 Individual texts, A-Z

.A25-259 Acāryakriyāsmuccaya
.A34-349 Advayasiddhi (by Lakṣmīkarā)
.A55-559 Ājñāsaṃyakpramāṇa-nāma-ḍākinyupadeśa (By Ṭillopāda)

.C35-359 Caṇḍamahāroṣaṇa
.C55-559 Cittaviśuddhiprakaraṇa (by Āryadeva)
.J65-659 Jñānasiddhi (by Indrabhūti)

.K35-359 Kālacakrāvatāra (by Abhayākaragupta)
.K75-759 Kriyāsaṅgrahal (by Kuladatta)
.N57-579 Niṣpannayogāvali (by Abhayākaragupta)

.P74-749 Prajñopāyaviniścayasiddhi (by Anaṅgavajra)
.P75-759 Pratipattisāraśataka (by Āryadeva)

.S34-349 Sādhanamālā
.S35-359 Sahajasiddhi (by Dombī-heruka)
.S93-939 Subhāṣiṭaratnakaraṇḍakakathā (by Śura)

.V35-359 Vajrāvalī

Modern continuations of the canon
Modern continuations are to be developed as needed

General works
4000 Early works through 1800
4005 1801-1945
4011-4018 1946-
Divided like BQ1-8
Introductions, see BQ4021+
4020 Textbooks. Compends. Manuals, outlines, syllabi, etc.

4021-4028 Popular works. Introductions
Divided like BQ1-8
4030 Pictorial works
4032 Juvenile works

4034 General special
4036 Essence, genius, and nature
4040 Philosophy of Buddhism. Philosophy and Buddhism
Cf. B162, Buddhist philosophy

4045 Controversial works against Buddhism
Cf. BQ7001+, Special modifications, schools, sects, etc.
4050 Apologetic works
Cf. BQ7001+, Special modifications, schools, sects, etc.

4055 Addresses, essays, lectures
4060 Miscellanea. Anecdotes, etc.

Doctrinal and systematic Buddhism

4061-4068 Periodicals. Societies. Serials
Divided like BQ1-8
Collections. Collected works. Festschriften
4070 Several authors
4075 Individual authors
General works, see BQ4131+

History
Including history of doctrinal controversies
For works limited to a sect, see BQ7001+; for works limited to a particular country, see the country in BQ251+

General works
4080 Early works through 1800
4085 1801-1945
4090 1946-
4095 General special

Doctrinal and systematic Buddhism
History - Continued
By period
Early Buddhism (Primitive Buddhism)
Including Original Buddhism (Gautama Buddha era) through to the split of the Hīnayāna schools
Cf. BQ915, Sayings of Gautama Buddha

4100 Collections. Collected works
General works
4105 Early works through 1800
4110 1801-1945
4115 1946-

4120 General special
4125 Addresses, essays, lectures

Hīnayāna Sthāvira schools era, see BQ7100+
Mahāyāna Buddhism, see BQ7300+

Tantric Buddhism era (Vajrayāna Buddhism), see BQ8900+
By region or country, see BQ286+

4131-4138 Introductions
Divided like BQ1-8
Formal treatises
4140 Early works through 1800
4145 1801-1945
4150 1946-

4155 Handbooks, manuals, etc.
4160 General special
4165 Addresses, essays, lectures

4170 Creeds and catechisms. Questions and answers
Systematization of Buddhist teachings.
Methodology of classification of doctrines

4175 General works. History
For works limited to individual modifications, schools, sects, etc., see the individual modification, etc., BQ7001+

Doctrinal and systematic Buddhism - Continued
Special doctrines
4180 Buddha. Tathāgata. Threefold Buddhakāya
Including the development of the concept of Buddha

4185 Worlds of Buddhas
For Sukhāvatī, see BQ4535
Individual Buddhas, see BQ4690

4190 Dharma and dharmas
Abhidharma. Abhidhamma
4195 General works
4200 General special
4205 Special subjects, A-Z

.T5 Time

Dharmatā. Dharmadhatu. Tathatā, etc.
4210 General works
4215 General special
4220 Two realms in Tantric Buddhism (Garbhakośa and Vajrakośa)
Cf. BQ5125.M3, Maṇḍala

Four Noble Truths
4230 General works
4235 Suffering. Pain. Unsatisfactory quality of existence. Duḥkha (Dukkha)
Causes of suffering, see BQ4425
Cessation of suffering, see BQ4263
Eightfold Path, see BQ4320

Pratītyasamutpada. Causation. Relativity
4240 General works
4245 General special
4250 Special, A-Z

.D5 Dharmadhātu Origination
.S6 Six Great Origination (in Tantric Buddhism)

.T9 Twelve-linked Chain of Dependent Origination

4255 Truth. Paramārtha-satya. Saṃvṛti-satya

Doctrinal and systematic Buddhism
Special doctrines - Continued
Seal of Three Laws
4260 General works
4261 Anitya. Impermanence

4262 Anātman. Non-self
4263 Nirvāna. Vimokṣa. Cessation of suffering
Cf. BQ4398, Enlightenment
BQ4570.I5, Immortality

4270 Absolute mind
4275 Śūnyatā. Emptiness. Non-attachment
4280 Madhyamā pratipad. Middle Way

Gotra. Religious instinct
4285 General works
Śrāvaka
4287 General works
4289 Arhat
4290 Pratyekabuddha

4293 Bodhisattva
Including the development of the concept of Bodhisattva
For individual Bodhisattva, see BQ4710+
4297 Icchantika

Religious life. Religious practice. Perfection
For works limited to practice, see BQ5360+
4301-4308 General works
Divided like BQ1-8
4310 General special
4315 Awakening

4320 Eightfold Paths
4324 Four pairs of stages in Hīnayāna Buddhism
Cf. BQ4195+, Abhidharma
BQ5595+, Meditation

Ten stages in Mahāyāna Buddhism. Bodhisattva stages
4330 General works
4336 Six pāramitās
Cf. BJ1289, Buddhist ethics
For individual virtues, see BQ4420

Doctrinal and systematic Buddhism
Special doctrines
Religious life. Religious practice.
Perfection - Continued
Faith. Śraddhā. Prasāda. Adhimukti. Bhakti, etc.

4340 General works
4345 General special
4350 Threefold Refuges (Buddha, Dharma, and Saṃgha)
For confirmation of faith in Buddhism, see BQ5005; for Tri-ratna ceremony, see BQ5000; for general works on the Three Jewels, see BQ4000+; BQ4131+

4355 Praṇidhāna. Vows
4358 Reward. Blessings in the present life
For prayer for temporal benefits, rewards, blessings, etc., see BQ5633.T4

4359 Love
Cf. BQ4570.L6, Love (nondoctrinal)
4360 Karuna. Maitrī (Mettā). Compassion. Loving kindness

4363 Guṇa. Merit
4365 Parināma. Merit transference

4370 Upāya
4375 No-mind (principally in Zen Buddhism)
Wisdom. Jñāna. Prajñā. Mati
Cf. BQ4336, Six pāramitās

4380 General works
4385 General special
4394 Four types of wisdom (principally in Yogācāra Buddhism)
Including Five Wisdoms in Tantric Buddhism

Bodhi. Enlightenment
Cf. BQ4263, Nirvāṇa
BQ9288, Satori
4398 General works
4399 Thirty-seven requisites (Bodhipakkhiya-dhammas) to enlightenment

Doctrinal and systematic Buddhism
Special doctrines - Continued
Virtues and vices
Cf. BJ1289, Buddhist ethics

4401-4408 General works
Divided like BQ1-8
4410 Ten cardinal virtues and ten capital vices

Virtues
4415 General works
4420 Individual virtues, A-Z

.G6 Giving (dāna). Buddhist stewardship
Cf. BQ5136+, Temple finance
.M6 Moderation

Kleśa. Vices. Illusions, etc.
4425 General works
Ten capital vices, see BQ4410
4430 Individual vices, A-Z

4435 Karma
4440 Theory of knowledge. Buddhist epistemology
4443 Three Svabhāva theory (in Yogācāra Buddhism)

4445 Citta. Bīja. Vijñāna. Ālayavijñāna.
Vijñaptimātratā
4450 Buddhatā. Buddhahood. Tathāgatagarbha

Salvation. Other Power (principally in Pure
Land Buddhist doctrines)
4453 General works
4455 Original Vow of Dharmākara Bodhisattva. 48 Vows

4460 Nembutsu. Myōgō
For practice of Nembutsu, see BQ5630.N4
4465 Nine grades of life

Eschatology
4475 General works
4480 Saddharmavipralopa. End of the world
Transmission. Reincarnation. Rebirth, etc.
Saṃsāra

4485 General works
4487 Death
4490 Intermediate existence

Doctrinal and systematic Buddhism
Special doctrines
Eschatology
Transmigration. Reincarnation. Rebirth, etc. Saṃsāra - Continued
Ten worlds
Including the worlds of Buddhas, Bodhisattvas, Pratyekabuddhas, Śrāvakas, and Six gatis
4500 General works
Six worlds (gatis)
4506 General works
Including works dealing with two or more worlds

Individual worlds
4508 Deva-gati. Heaven. World of devas
Cf. BQ4735+, Devas
4510 Manuṣya-gati. Sahā. World of men. This world
Including the relationship with the other shore, the ideal land

4513 Asura-gati. World of Asuras
Cf. BQ4790+, Asuras
4515 Tiryañ-gati. World of animals
4520 Preta-gati. World of hungry spirits
For Ullambana ceremony, see BQ5720.U6
4525 Naraka-gati. Hell
Including the eight kinds of hells, and Yamma, the King of Hell

Future life
4530 General works
Sukhāvatī. Western Paradise. Pure Land (Amitābha Buddha's Land)
4535 General works
4540 Rebirth in Western Paradise (Pure Land)

Saṃgha
Class here works limited to doctrinal points of view only
4545 General works
Bhikṣu and Bhikṣunī
4550 General works
4555 Meaning of renunciation

Upāsaka and Upāsikā
4560 General works
4565 Lay Buddhism

Doctrinal and systematic Buddhism - Continued

4570 Special topics (nondoctrinal) and relations to special subjects, A-Z

.A35 Agriculture

Amṛta, see .I5

.A4 Amulets. Charms. Talismans, etc.

.A5 Ancestor worship

.A54 Animism

.A7 Art

.A72 The arts

Astrology, see BF1714.B7

.C3 Caste. Social classes

.C47 Children

.C58 Clairvoyance

.C6 Cosmogony. Cosmology

Including Jambu-dvīpa and Mt. Smeru

.C8 Culture. Civilization

.E25 Economics. Labor

.F3 Faith cure

.F6 Food

.F7 Freedom

.F74 Friendship

.H5 History

Class here general works on the three periods in the Buddhist doctrine; for works concerned with the end of the world or the third period (Saddharmavipralopa), see BQ4480

.H8 Humanism

.H85 Humor

.I5 Immortality. Amṛta

Cf. BQ4263, Nirvāṇa

.K5 King (Buddhist concept). Cakravartin

.L3 Language. Letters. Siddhām (a style of Sanskrit letters)

Cf. BQ5125.B5, Bījas

.L5 Life, Meaning of

Doctrinal and systematic Buddhism

4570 Special topics (nondoctrinal) and relations to special subjects, A-Z - Continued

.L6 Love
Cf. BQ4359, Love (doctrinal)
.M3 Magic

.M34 Man. Pudgala. Buddhist anthropology
For gotra (religious instinct), see BQ4285+; for manusya-gati (world of man), see BQ4510
.M37 Matter. Atoms

.M4 Medicine. Nursing. Health. Hygiene
.M45 Metaphor

.M5 Miracles
.M97 Music

.N3 Natural history. Nature
Including animals, plants, minerals, etc.
Cf. BQ4515, World of animals
.O3 Occult sciences. Spiritualism
Cf. BQ4900+, Spirits, angels, demons, etc.

.P4 Peace
Popular faith, see BQ5633.T4
.P7 Prophecies. Prophets
Cf. BQ929.P7, Gautama Buddha

.P75 Psychical research. Parapsychology
.P76 Psychology. Consciousness. Status of religious experiences, etc.
Cf. BQ4195+, Abhidharma
BQ4445, Citta, Bīja, Vijñāna, etc.

.R3 Race
.R4 Reform and renewal

.S3 Science
.S5 Shamanism

.S55 Siddhas
Social problems, see HN40.B8
.S6 Sociology

.S7 State. Politics and government
Stūpa worship, see BQ925
.S9 Superstition

.T5 Time and space
.T6 Tolerance

Doctrinal and systematic Buddhism
4570 Special topics (nondoctrinal) and relations to special subjects, A-Z - Continued

.V43 Vegetarianism
.V5 Violence and nonviolence
.V6 Votive offerings

.W3 War
.W4 Wealth

.W6 Woman
.W64 World. Buddhism and the world

Relation of Buddhism to other religious and philosophical systems
4600 General works
Including comparative studies of Buddhism and other religious and philosophical systems
For works limited to a sect, see BQ7001+
4605 General special
4610 Special, A-Z

Bon, see BQ7654
.B7 Brahmanism

.C3 Cao Daism (Vietnam)
Christianity, see BR128.B8

.C6 Confucianism
.H6 Hinduism

Islam, see BP173.B9
.J3 Jainism

.J8 Judaism
Shinto, see BL2222.23

.T3 Taoism
.Z6 Zoroastrianism

Buddhist pantheon
4620 Dictionaries
4625 Collections
4630 General works
Class here descriptive works on the natures, representations, etc., of the pantheon
4635 General special
e. g. Comparative studies with deities of other religions

Buddhist pantheon - Continued

4640 Popular works. Introductions

4645 Juvenile works

4648 Addresses, essays, lectures

4650 Doctrinal development of Buddhist deities

Cultus

4655 General works. History

4660 By region or country, A-Z

Special deities

Buddhas. Tathāgatas

For doctrinal works on Buddhas, see BQ4180+

4670 General descriptive works on various Buddhas

Cultus

4680 General works

4685 By region or country, A-Z

4690 Individual Buddhas, A-Z

Under each Buddha:

.x General works

Including nature, representation, own world, etc.

.x2 Historical development of concepts on the deity

.x3 Cultus

.x4 By region or country, A-Z

.A6-64 Akṣobhya

.A7-74 Amitābha. Amitāyus

Cf. BQ4453+, Pure Land Buddhist doctrines

.B5-54 Bhaisajya-guru

.D5-54 Dīpaṃkara

.M3-34 Maitreya (Metteyya)

.R3-34 Ratnasambhava

.S3-34 Śākyamuni

.U75-754 Uṣṇīṣavijayā

.V3-34 Vairocana

Buddhist pantheon
Special deities - Continued
Bodhisattvas
For doctrinal works on Bodhisattvas, see BQ4293

4695 Descriptive works on various Bodhisattvas

Cultus

4700 General works

4705 By region or country, A-Z

4710 Individual Bodhisattvas, A-Z

May be subdivided like BQ4690

.A8 Avalokiteśvara

Including the six types of Avalokiteśvara: Amoghapāśa, Ārya, Cintāmaṇicakra, Ekadaśamukha, Hayagrīva and Sahasrabhūja

.K7 Kṣitigarbha

.M3 Maitreya

Cf. BQ4690.M3, Maitreya as the future Buddha

.M4 Mañjuśrī

.S3 Samantabhadra

.T3 Tārā

.V34 Vajrasattva

Eight kinds of mythological beings in Hinduism who protect Buddhism

Cf. BL1216+, Special deities in Hinduism (who have become protectors in Buddhism)

4718 General works

4720 General special

Cultus

4725 General works

4730 By region or country, A-Z

Devas

4735 General works

Cultus

4740 General works

4745 By region or country, A-Z

4750 Individual Devas, A-Z

May be subdivided like BQ4690

.G35 Gaṇeśa

.I6 Indra

Cf. BL1225.I6, Indra, Hindu deity

.M35 Mahākāla

Buddhist pantheon
Eight kinds of mythological beings in Hinduism who protect Buddhism - Continued
Nāgas
4760 General works
4765 Cultus
Yakṣas
4770 General works
4775 Cultus
Gandharvas
4780 General works
4785 Cultus
Asuras
4790 General works
4795 Cultus
Garuḍas
4800 General works
4805 Cultus
Kiṃnaras
4810 General works
4815 Cultus
Mahoragas
4820 General works
4825 Cultus

Deities in other religions who protect Buddhism
4830 General works
4835 Individual deities, A-Z

Vidya-rājas
Class here works on the Tantric Buddhist guardians
4840 General works
4845 General special

Cultus
4850 General works
4855 By region or country, A-Z

4860 Individual Vidya-rājas, A-Z
May be subdivided like BQ4690

.A4 Acala
.K8 Kuṇḍalī

.R3 Railokyavijaya
.V3 Vajrayakṣa

.Y3 Yamāntaka

Buddhist pantheon - Continued
Arhats
Including principally the saints in Hīnayāna Buddhism
Cf. BQ900+, Buddhist disciples
BQ4289, Doctrinal works
4865 General works
4870 General special
Cultus
4875 General works
4880 By region or country, A-Z
4890 Others, A-Z
Under each:
.x General works
Cultus
.x2 General works
.x3 By region or country, A-Z
.x4 Local, A-Z

.D33-334 Dam-tshig-rdo-rje
.K95-954 Kun-dga'-gzon-nu
.K96-964 Kurukulla

.M56-564 Mgon-po Bse-khrab-can
.R37-374 Rdo-rje-śugs-ldan-rtsal
.V33-334 Vajrakīla
.V339-3394 Vajravārahī (Buddhist deity)
.V34-344 Vajrayoginī
.V57-574 Viśrāvaṇa
Spirits, angels, demons, etc.
4900 General works
4905 By region or country, A-Z

Practice of Buddhism. Forms of worship
For works limited to a sect, see BQ7001+
4911-4918 Periodicals. Yearbooks. Societies
Divided like BQ1-8

Collected works
4920 Several authors
4925 Individual authors

4930 Encyclopedias. Dictionaries
History
4935 General works
4940 Addresses, essays, lectures
By period, see BQ286+
General works
4945 Early works through 1800
4950 1801-
4953 General special
4955 Addresses, essays, lectures

Practice of Buddhism. Forms of worship - Continued

4960 By region or country, A-Z

Under each:

.x General works

History

.x2 General works

By period:

.x3 Early to 1200

.x4 1201-1850

.x5 1851-1945

.x6 1945-

Under countries only:

.x7 Local, A-Z

Ceremonies and rites. Ceremonial rules

For works limited to a sect, see BQ7001+

4965 Collections

4967 Dictionaries

General works

4970 Early works through 1800

4972 1801-1945

4975 1946-

4980 General special

4985 Ritualism (General)

4990 By region or country, A-Z

Under each country:

.x General works. History

.x2 Local, A-Z

4995 Service books for priests

4998 Books for laymen. "Buddhist Bible"

Special rites and ceremonies

Class here those works on rites and ceremonies which are applicable throughout Buddhism

5000 Tri-ratna Service (100th day after birth)

5005 Confirmation. Jukai

5010 Initiation of novices

e. g. Shinbyu

Practice of Buddhism. Forms of worship
Ceremonies and rites. Ceremonial rules
Special rites and ceremonies - Continued
5015 Marriage
5020 Funeral service. Wakes. Burial service. Cremation

5025 Memorial services for the dead
5030 Other, A-Z

.B63 Bodhi tree worship
.C6 Confession
Class here works principally for priests, monks, and nuns
Cf. BQ5720.U7, Uposatha
.C62 Consecration of Buddhist images
Including rites for consecration of new Buddha images, etc., for solemn enshrinement

.C64 Laying of cornerstones
.D4 Dedication
Including rites for blessing a new temple, a new house, a new family altar at home, for utensils which are no longer serviceable, and last respect rites for deceased pets, animals, fishes, etc.

.H6 Hōjöe
Class here works concerned with the ceremony for the release of captured birds, animals, or fish
.O43 Omizutori

Hymns. Chants. Recitations. Śabda-vidyā. Shōmyō. Goeika
For Buddhist music (General), see ML3197; for works limited to a sect, see BQ7001+
5035 Periodicals. Societies. Serials

Collections of hymns
5040 General
5042 By region or country, A-Z
5045 Dictionaries. Indexes. Concordances, etc.

Practice of Buddhism. Forms of worship
Hymns. Chants. Recitations. Śabda-vidyā. Shōmyō. Goeika - Continued
History and criticism
5050 General works
5055 Addresses, essays, lectures
5060 By region or country, A-Z
Under each country:

.x General works
.x2 Local, A-Z

5065 Individual texts. By author or title

Altar, liturgical objects, ornaments, memorials, etc.
Class here works limited to religious aspects
Cf. NK1676, Buddhist decoration and ornament
5070 General works
5075 Special objects, A-Z

.A6 Altars
Including both temple and home altars
.B4 Bells

.C3 Candles
.D7 Drums

.F6 Flowers
.G6 Gongs

.I6 Incense
.M4 Memorial tablets
Including Ihai, Sotōba, etc.

.P3 Pagodas
.R7 Rosaries (Jazu)

.S4 Sepulchral monuments
.S8 Stūpas
For Gautama Buddha stūpas, <u>see</u> BQ925

.W6 Wooden fish (Mokugyo)

Vestments, altar cloths, etc.
5080 General works
5085 Special, A-Z

.H3 Habit (Kesa)

Practice of Buddhism. Forms of worship - Continued

Liturgical functions

5090 General works

5095 Special functions, A-Z

Symbols and symbolism

Cf. N8193, Buddhist art (Visual art)
ND197, Buddhist paintings
NK1676, Buddhist decoration and ornament
NX676, Buddhist arts (General)

5100 General works

5105 General special

5110 Addresses, essays, lectures

5115 By region or country, A-Z

5120 Liturgical symbolism

Including colors, lights, etc.

5125 Special symbols, A-Z

.B5 Bījas (Letters)

.D4 Dharmacakra (Wheel of the Buddha's teachings)

.F6 Flags and pennants

.H4 Hensō

Principally in Pure Land Buddhism

.M3 Maṇḍala. Thang-ka

Principally in Tantric Buddhism

.M8 Mudrās (gestures of Buddhas or Bodhisattvas, etc.)

.P3 Padma (Lotus). Puṇḍarīka (White lotus)

.S8 Stūpas

Temple. Temple organization

5130 General works

5133 Membership

Temple finance

For works limited to a sect, see BQ7530+

5136 General works. History

.3 By region or country, A-Z

Under each country:

.x General works

.x2 Local, A-Z

Buddhist giving

Cf. BQ4420.G6, Buddhist virtues

.5 General works

.6 Special types of gifts (not A-Z)

.7 Fund raising

5137 Temple property

Practice of Buddhism. Forms of worship - Continued

Buddhist ministry. Priesthood. Organization

Cf. BQ6140+, Monastic life

For works limited to a sect, see BQ7001+

5140 Periodicals. Societies. Serials

5145 Collections

5150 History

5155 General works

5160 By region or country, A-Z

5165 Sermons, addresses, essays

5170 Part-time ministry

5175 Ethics and etiquette

5180 Spiritual development. Religious life

5185 Professional development

5190 Ministerial work in cities

5195 Ministerial work in rural areas

5200 Popular works, anecdotes, etc.

5210 Handbooks, manuals, etc.

5215 Election, selection, succession, appointment, etc.

5220 Ordination

5225 Hierarchical offices

Heresy trials (General)

For works limited to a sect, see BQ7001+

5230 General works

5235 History

5240 By region or country, A-Z

Under each country:

.x General works

.x2 Local, A-Z

Education and training for the ordained ministry

Including monasteries, Buddhist departments or schools in universities

For works limited to a sect, see BQ7001+

5251-5258 Periodicals, societies, etc.

Divided like BQ1-8

5260 General works

5265 Addresses, essays, lectures

5270 History of the study of Buddhism

Practice of Buddhism. Forms of worship
Buddhist ministry. Priesthood. Organization
Education and training for the ordained ministry - Continued

5275 By region or country, A-Z

Under each country:

.x General works
.x2 Local, A-Z
.x3 By institution, A-Z

Training for layworkers

5280 General works. History
5285 By region or country, A-Z

Under each country:

.x General works. History
.x2 Local, A-Z

Kinds of ministries

5290 General works. History
5295 General special

5300 By region or country, A-Z
5305 Special ministries, A-Z

.C4 Chaplains

.C6 Counselors

.P8 Public relations

Preaching

For works limited to a sect, see BQ7001+

5310 Periodicals. Societies. Serials

5315 Collected works
5320 History

5325 By region or country, A-Z
5330 General works. Treatises, etc.

5335 Addresses, essays, etc., on preaching
5336 Illustrations for sermons

Practice of Buddhism. Forms of worship
Buddhist ministry. Priesthood. Organization
Preaching - Continued
Sermons
For sermons limited to a sect, see BQ7001+
Classify sermons on a particular canonical text with the text; classify sermons on a particular subject with the subject
Collections
5340 Several authors
5345 Individual authors
5350 Sermons on and/or for special occasions, A-Z
Under each:

.x Collections. By title, A-Z
.x2 Collections and single sermons by one author. By author, A-Z

.M4 Memorial service sermons
Including funerals, wakes, etc.

5355 Other topics, A-Z

.B8 Buddhist name. Precepts-name

Religious life
Cf. BJ2019.5.B8, Buddhist etiquette
For doctrinal works, see BQ4301+; for works limited to the minister's religious life, see BQ5180; for monasticism and monastic life, see BQ6001+; for works limited to a sect, see BQ7001+

5360 Periodicals
5365 Societies
5370 Dictionaries

5375 Collections
5380 History
General works
5385 Early works through 1800
5390 1801-1945
5395 1946-

5400 General special
5405 Popular works, stories, anecdotes, etc.
Including both collections and monographs
5410 Addresses, essays, lectures, etc.

Practice of Buddhism. Forms of worship
Religious life - Continued
Religious duties
5415 General works
5420 Religious leadership
5425 Duties of lay members
5430 Religion of the family
Cf. BQ200, Religious education in the home

Religious life of special groups

Under each:

Cutter number	One number	
.xA1-19	.A1A-Z	Periodicals
.xA2-29	.A2A-Z	Collections (non-serial)
.xA3-Z	.A3-Z	General works

5435 The aged
5436 Children
5440 Parents
Including works for mothers and fathers

5445 Men
Women
5450 General works
5455 Widows
5460 Young adults. Young married couples

Youth. Students
5465 General works
5470 Young men and boys
5475 Young women and girls

5480 Other groups, A-Z

.S6 Soldiers

Precepts for laymen
Including the Five Precepts collectively
General works
5485 Early works through 1800
5490 1801-1945
5495 1946-
5500 General special

5505 Addresses, essays, lectures
5510 By region or country, A-Z

Under each country:
.x General works
.x2 Local, A-Z

Practice of Buddhism. Forms of worship
Religious life
Precepts for laymen - Continued
The Five Precepts
For works on the Five Precepts collectively, see BQ5485+

The Five Precepts individually
5521 First (Not to take life)
5522 Second (Not to take what is not given to one)
5523 Third (Not to commit adultery)
5524 Fourth (Not to tell lies)
5525 Fifth (Not to drink intoxicants)
5530 Other precepts, A-Z

Devotional literature. Meditations. Prayers
For works limited to a sect, see BQ7001+
5535 History and criticism
Collections by two or more authors
5538 Early works through 1800
5541-5548 1801-1945
Divided like BQ1-8
5551-5558 1946-
Divided like BQ1-8

Works by individual authors
5560 Early works through 1800
5561-5568 1801-1945
Divided like BQ1-8
5571-5578 1946-
Divided like BQ1-8

Selections for daily reading. Devotional calendars
5579 Several authors
5580 Individual authors

5585 Selections for special groups of readers, A-Z

.A5 Aged
.C4 Children

.F3 Families
.M3 Married people

.M4 Men
.P3 Parents
Including works for mothers and fathers

Practice of Buddhism. Forms of worship
Religious life
Devotional literature. Meditations. Prayers
5585 Selections for special groups of readers, A- Z - Continued

.P7 Prisoners
.S5 Sick

.S6 Soldiers. Armed forces. Veterans
.W6 Women

.Y5 Young adults. Young married couples
.Y6 Youth. Students

.Y7 Young men and boys
.Y8 Young women and girls

5590 Selections for special occasions and times, A-Z

.W3 Wartime

Special prayers and devotions
5592 Prayers and devotions to Buddhas, Bodhisattavas, etc., A-Z - Continued

.A44 Akṣobhya
.A45 Amitābha

.A8 Avalokiteśvara
.M3 Maitreya

.M35 Mañjuśrī
.T35 Tārā

.U75 Uṣṇīṣavijayā

5593 Prayers and devotions to Buddhist saints, A-Z

.P3 Padma Sambhava

.S55 Shōtoku Taishi

5594 Other, A-Z

.C65 Confession (Prayer)

.W4 Western Paradise (Pure Land). Rebirth in Western Paradise

Practice of Buddhism. Forms of worship
Religious life - Continued
Devotion. Meditation
For works limited to a sect, see the sect
General works
5595 Early works through 1800
5601-5608 1801-1945
Divided like BQ1-8
5611-5618 1946-
Divided like BQ1-8

5620 General special
5625 Addresses, essays, lectures
5630 Special topics, A-Z

.A6 Ānāpānasmṛti. Breathing

.D4 Contemplation on death. Maranānusmrti

.K6 Kōan

.N4 Nembutsu
Cf. BQ4460, Buddhist doctrine

.P6 Postures
.P7 Psychoanalysis of meditation

.R6 Rosary
.S16 Samadhi

.S2 Satipaṭṭhana. Smṛty-upasthāna
.V5 Vipaśyana

Prayer
5631 General works
5632 General special
5633 Special topics, A-Z

.T4 Temporal benefits, rewards, blessings, etc.

Spiritual life. Mysticism. Enlightenment. Perfection
For doctrinal works, see BQ4301+
For works limited to a sect, see the sect
5635 Collections
General works
5640 Early works through 1800

Practice of Buddhism. Forms of worship
Religious life
Spiritual life. Mysticism. Enlightenment. Perfection
General works - Continued
5650 1801-1945
5660 1946-

5670 General special
5675 Addresses, essays, lectures
5680 Other special religious practices or topics, A-Z

.C6 Copying of scriptures

Festivals. Days and seasons
For works limited to a sect, see BQ7001+
5700 General works
5705 General special
5710 History
5715 By region or country, A-Z
Under each country:

.x General works. History
.x2 Local, A-Z

5720 Special, A-Z
Including international, national and/or local celebrations; for works limited to a sect, see BQ7001+

.A8 Āsāḷha Pūjā. Dharmacakra Day
Class here those works concerned with the celebration (in July on the day of the full moon) of the Gautama Buddha's first sermon; observed principally in Sri Lanka

.B6 Birthday of Gautama Buddha. Hanamatsuri
.D5 Dhammasetkya (observed in July, principally in Burma)
.E6 Enlightenment Day of Gautama Buddha. Jodo-e

.E7 Equinox (Spring and Autumn). Higan-e
.K3 Kandy Esala Perahera
Class here those works concerned with the celebration of Gautama Buddha's Sacred Tooth Relic of the Dalada Maligawa Temple in Kandy (Sri Lanka)

Practice of Buddhism. Forms of worship
Festivals. Days and seasons
5720 Special, A- Z - Continued

.M2 Māgha Pūjā
Class here those works concerned with the celebration (in February on the day of the full moon) of the Gautama Buddha's discourse; observed principally in Sri Lanka

.N6 Nirvana Day of Gautama Buddha. Nehan-e
.P7 Poson. Dhamma Vijaya
Class here those works concerned with the celebration (in June on the day of the full moon) of the sending out of missions to foreign lands by King Asoka; observed principally in Sri Lanka

.T4 Thadingyut. Festival of Lights (observed in October at the end of the rainy season, principally in Burma)
.T5 Thingyan. Water Festival (observed in April before the rainy period, principally in Burma)

.U6 Ullambana. Ollambana. O-bon (Memorial season)
.U7 Uposatha. Full moon night confession ceremony
(Observed principally by monks and nuns in the Theravāda Buddhist countries)

.U75 Chai. Ubonei. O-toki
Class here those works concerned with the abstention from food at certain periods for purification; observed principally by the laity
.W4 Wesak. Wisakha. Vesak. Vesākhā. Vaiśākha
Class here those works concerned with the combining of festivals venerating Gautama Buddha based on the Theravāda Buddhist traditions

Folklore
Cf. GR, Folklore
For works limited to a sect, see BQ7001+
5725 Collections
5730 History and criticism
5735 By region or country, A-Z
Under each country:

.x Collections
.x2 History and criticism

Mythological tales
Cf. BQ1460+, Jātakas
BQ1530+, Avadānas
5741-5748 Collections
Divided like BQ1-8
5750 History and criticism
5755 By region or country, A-Z
Under each country:

.x Collections
.x2 History and criticism

Legends
5761-5768 Collections
Divided like BQ1-8
5770 History and criticism
5775 By region or country, A-Z
Under each country:

.x Collections
.x2 History and criticism

Parables
Cf. BQ1530+, Avadānas
5780 Collections
5785 History and criticism
5790 By region or country, A-Z
Under each country:

.x Collections
.x2 History and criticism

Proverbs
5791-5798 Collections
Divided like BQ1-8
5800 History and criticism
5805 By region or country, A-Z
Under each country:

.x Collections
.x2 History and criticism

Folklore - Continued
5810 Miscellaneous stories (Collected)
5815 Individual legends, stories, etc.

Miracle literature
5821-5828 Collections
Divided like BQ1-8
5830 General works. History and criticism
5835 By region or country, A-Z
Under each country:

.x Collections
.x2 History and criticism

5840 Addresses, essays, lectures
5845 Special texts. By title or author, A-Z

Benevolent work. Social work. Welfare work, etc.
For works limited to a sect, see BQ7001+
5851-5858 Periodicals (General)
Divided like BQ1-8
5860 Societies. Associations (International)
5865 Congresses. Conferences (International)

5868 Directories. Yearbooks
5870 Museums. Exhibitions
5880 Collections

5882 Encyclopedias. Dictionaries
5884 Study and teaching
5886 History (General)

5888 Statistics. Theory and method
5890 Biography (Collective)
General works. Treatises
5892 Early works through 1800
5894 1801-

5896 Handbooks, manuals, etc.
5897 General special
5898 Addresses, essays, lectures

5899 By region or country, A-Z
Under each country:
.x Periodicals. Societies. Collections
.x2 Congresses. Conferences
.x3 Directories. Yearbooks, etc.
.x4 History. General works. Statistics
.x5 Biography (Collective)
.x6 By province or state, A-Z
.x7 By city, etc., A-Z

Missionary work
Cf. BV2618, Christian missions to Buddhists
For works limited to a sect, see BQ7001+
5901-5908 Periodicals. Societies. Serials
Divided like BQ1-8
5910 Conferences, conventions, etc.

5912 Directories. Yearbooks
5914 Museums. Exhibitions
5916 Collections

5918 Encyclopedias. Dictionaries
5920 Study and teaching
5925 History (General)

5930 Special methods and problems, A-Z
5935 Biography (Collective)
For works limited to a sect, see BQ7001+
General works. Treatises

5938 Early works through 1800
5940 1801-1945
5942 1946-

5945 General special
5950 Addresses, essays, lectures
5960 By region or country, A-Z
Under each country:

.x General works. History
.x2 Local, A-Z

Converts to Buddhism
Cf. BV2618.3+, Converts to Christianity from Buddhism
5970 Collective
5975 Individual, A-Z

.Z9 Anonymous

Monasticism and monastic life. Saṃgha (Order)
For works limited to a sect, see BQ7001+
6001-6008 Periodicals
Divided like BQ1-8
6010 Collections
6015 Encyclopedias. Dictionaries
History
General works
6020 Early works through 1800
6025 1801-1945
6030 1946-

Monasticism and monastic life. Saṃgha (Order)
History - Continued
By period
6040 Early through 1200
6045 1201-1850
6050 1851-

General works
6065 Early works through 1800
6071-6078 1801-1945
Divided like BQ1-8
6081-6088 1946-
Divided like BQ1-8

6100 General special
6105 Addresses, essays, lectures
6110 Origins

Monastic life. Vows. Discipline.
Rules. Śīla
General works
6115 Early works through 1800
For collections or individual texts of Vinayapiṭaka, see BQ1150+; BQ2250+
6121-6128 1801-
Divided like BQ1-8

6135 General special
Monks. Priests. Bhikṣu. Bhikkhu
6140 General works
6145 Novices. Śrāmaṇera

Nuns. Bhikṣuṇī. Bhikkhunī
6150 General works
6155 Novices. Śrāmaṇerikā
6160 By region or country, A-Z
Under each country:

.x History. General works
.x2 Local, A-Z

Asceticism. Hermits. Wayfaring life
6200 History
6210 Biography (Collective)
6220 General works
6230 General special
6240 By region or country, A-Z
Under each country:

.x General works
.x2 Local, A-Z

Monasteries. Temples. Shrines. Stūpas. Sites, etc.
For works limited to a sect, see BQ7001+

6300 Collected works
6305 Directories
For directories limited to a particular country, see the country in BQ6330+

6310 History
6315 General works
6320 General special

6325 Addresses, essays, lectures

By region or country
Under each:

(1) .A2A-Z Directories
.A3-Z General works
(2) Local, A-Z, or individual A-Z, if location is unnamed
Under each locality:
.x General works
Including directories
.x2 Individual, A-Z

Asia
General works, see BQ6315
6330-6331 India
6332-6333 Sri Lanka
6334-6335 Burma

6336-6337 Thailand
6338-6339 Vietnam
6340-6341 Malaysia
Including Singapore

6342-6343 Indonesia
6344-6345 China
6346-6347 Mongolia
6348-6349 Tibet

6350-6351 Korea
6352-6353 Japan
6354 Other, A-Z
Under each:

.x General
.x2 Individual, A-Z

Monasteries. Temples. Shrines. Stūpas. Sites, etc.
By region or country - Continued
Europe
6355 General works
6356-6357 Great Britain
6358-6359 Belgium
6360-6361 France
6362-6363 Germany
6364-6365 Netherlands
6366-6367 Sweden
6368-6369 Soviet Union
6370 Other, A-Z
Divided like BQ6354

6372-6373 Africa
America
6374 General works
6376-6377 United States
6378-6379 Canada
6380-6381 Brazil
6382 Other, A-Z
Divided like BQ6354

Oceanica
6383 General works
6384-6385 Australia
6386-6387 New Zealand
6388 Other, A-Z
Divided like BQ6354

Pilgrims and pilgrimages
6400 Collections
6410 General works
6420 General special
6430 Addresses, essays, lectures
6440 History
6450 By region or country, A-Z
Under each country:

.x General works
.x2 By province or state, A-Z

Sacred shrines of Gautama Buddha in India
6460 General works
6470 Lumbinī (Rummindei, Nepal)
Birthplace of Gautama Buddha
6480 Buddhagayā (Bodh-Gayā, Bihar)
Site of Gautama Buddha's Enlightenment
6490 Isipatana (Sarnath, near Benares or Varanasi, Uttar Pradesh)
Site of Gautama Buddha's first sermon

Pilgrims and pilgrimages
Sacred shrines of Gautama Buddha in India - Cont.
6495 Kusinārā (Kusinagara, Uttar Pradesh)
Site of Gautama Buddha's death and cremation
Other individual places, see BQ6331+

Modifications, schools, etc.
For Original and Early Buddhism, see BQ4100+
7001-7008 Periodicals
Divided like BQ1-8
7010 Societies
7015 Congresses

Collections
7020 Several authors
7022 Individual authors
7025 Encyclopedias
7030 Dictionaries

7035 Directories
7040 Yearbooks
General works
7050 Early works through 1800
7055 1801-1945
7060 1946-

7070 History
7080 Miscellaneous works
Including works concerned with two or more sects, etc.
7085 General special
7090 Addresses, essays, lectures
By region or country, see BQ286+

Theravāda (Hīnayāna) Buddhism
7100 Periodicals
7110 Societies
7120 Congresses

Collections
7125 Several authors
7130 Individual authors

7135 Dictionaries
7140 Encyclopedias
7145 Terminology
7150 Study and teaching

Modifications, schools, etc.
Theravāda (Hīnayāna) Buddhism - Continued
History
Prefer classification by region or country, BQ320+
General works
7160 Early works through 1800
7165 1801-1945
7170 1946-

General works
7175 Early works through 1800
7180 1801-1945
7185 1946-

7190 General special
7200 Textbooks. Compends. Manuals
7205 Outlines, syllabi, etc.
7210 Addresses, essays, lectures

7212 Popular works
7215 Juvenile works
7220 Essence, genius, and nature
Doctrine
General works
7225 Early works through 1800
7227 1801-1945
7230 1946-

7235 General special
For Abhidharma (Abhidhamma), see BQ4195+
7240 History
7245 Introductions

Sthavira schools in India
General works
7250 Early works through 1800
7252 1801-

7255 Individual schools, A-Z
Under each:

.x General works. Doctrines
.x2 Relations to other branches of Buddhism

.M34 Mahāsāṅghika School
.S36 Sarvāstivāda (Vaibhāṣika) School

.S38 Sautrāntika School

Modifications, schools, etc.
Theravāda (Hīnayāna) Buddhism - Continued
Other schools or sects, see BQ8000+
Controversial works against Hīnayāna Buddhism
7260 Early works through 1800
7262 1801-

7265 Apologetic works
7270 Relations to other religious and philosophical systems
Relations to Mahāyāna Buddhism, see BQ7432
7273 Relations to Hinduism
7276 Other, A-Z

.C5 Christianity

7280 Meditation. Mysticism. Perfection
7285 Religious life

Mahāyāna Buddhism
7300 Periodicals. Serials
7310 Societies
7320 Congresses

Collections
7325 Several authors
7330 Individual authors

7335 Dictionaries
7340 Encyclopedias
7345 Terminology

7350 Study and teaching
History
Prefer classification by region or country, BQ286+
General works
7360 Early works through 1800
7362 1801-1945
7364 1946-

General works
7370 Early works through 1800
7372 1801-1945
7374 1946-

7380 General special
7382 Handbooks, manuals, etc.
7384 Outlines, syllabi, etc.
7386 Addresses, essays, lectures
7388 Popular works

Modifications, schools, etc.
Mahāyāna Buddhism - Continued
7390 Juvenile works
7395 Essence, genius, and nature

Doctrine
General works
7400 Early works through 1800
7402 1801-1945
7405 1946-

7410 General special
7415 History
7420 Introductions

7422 Controversial works against Mahāyāna Buddhism
7424 Apologetic works
Relations to other religious and philosophical systems
7430 General works
7432 Relations to Hīnayāna Buddhism
Including comparative studies
7434 Relations to Hinduism
7436 Other, A-Z
.C57 Christianity

7438 Meditation. Mysticism. Enlightenment
Religious life
7440 General works
7442 Bodhisattva vinaya. Mahāyāna discipline

Special schools
Including their philosophies
Mādhyamika School
7445 Periodicals
7447 Societies

7449 Congresses
Collections
7450 Several authors
7452 Individual authors

General works. History. Introductions
7454 Early works through 1800
7455 1801-1945
7457 1946-

7460 General special
7462 Addresses, essays, lectures
7464 By region or country, A-Z
7466 Controversial works against Mādhyamika School
7468 Apologetic works

Modifications, schools, etc.
Mahāyāna Buddhism
Special schools
Mādhyamika School - Continued
Relation to other religious and philosophical systems
7470 General works
7471 Relations to Yogācāra School
7472 Relations to other branches of Buddhism
7473 Relations to Hinduism
7474 Other, A-Z

7475 Meditation. Mysticism. Enlightenment. Perfection
Special branches of the Mādhyamika School
7476 General works
Including comparative studies
7477 Prāsangiḳa School
7478 Svātantrika School
7479 Mādhyamaka-yogācāra School

Yogācāra (Vijñāna) School
7480 Periodicals
7482 Societies
7484 Congresses
Collections
7486 Several authors
7488 Individual authors

General works. History. Introductions
7490 Early works through 1800
7492 1801-1945
7494 1946-

7496 General special
7498 Addresses, essays, lectures
7500 By region or country, A-Z

7502 Controversial works against the Yogācāra School
7504 Apologetic works
7506 Relations to other religious and philosophical systems
Relations to Mādhyamika School, see BQ7471
7510 Relations to other branches of Buddhism
7512 Relations to Hinduism
7514 Other, A-Z
7516 Meditation. Mysticism. Enlightenment. Perfection
Special branches of the Yogācāra School
7518 General works
Including comparative studies
7520 Anākāra School
7522 Sākāra School
Other schools or sects, see BQ8000+

Modifications, schools, etc. - Continued
Lamaism
Including Dge-lugs-pa (Dgah-ldan, Shwa-ser, Yellow Cap)
7530 Periodicals. Societies
7540 Congressess

7545 Directories. Yearbooks
7547 Dictionaries. Encyclopedias

Collections. Collected works
For sacred books, see BQ1250+, etc.
7549 General
Special
7550 Gsuṅ-hbum (Bkaḥ-ḥbum) (III)
Class individual parts of Gsuṅ-ḥbum with the person or the subject
7564 Other special, A-Z (III)

Religious education
7565 General works
7566 Methods
7567 History

7568 Of the young
7569 In the home

History
Including Buddhist history of Tibet
7570 Collections. Collected works. Sources
General works
7572 Early works through 1750
For history written by Bu-ston, see BQ262
7574 1751-1949
7576 1950

7578 Historiography
By period
7580 Early to ca. 1000 A.D. (Introduction of Mādhyamika-Tantric Buddhism to Tibet)
7582 Debate to Lhasa, 792 A.D
7584 1001-1350 (Red Cap golden era)
7586 1351-1719 (Foundation of Dalai lamas; Yellow Cap golden era)
7588 1720-1949
7590 1950- (Period of occupation by the Chinese People's Republic)

Modifications, schools, etc.
Lamaism
History - Continued
By region or country
Tibet, see BQ7572+
7592 Local, A-Z
Bhūtan, see BQ400.B5
Mongolia, see BQ580+
Sikkim, see BQ400.S5
7594 Other regions or countries, A-Z

Persecution
7596 General works. History
7598 By region or country, A-Z
Under each country:

.x General works. History
.x2 Local, A-Z

General works
Including Tibetan Buddhism in general
7600 Early works through 1750
7602 1751-1949
7604 1950-

7610 General special
7612 Addresses, essays, lectures
7614 Pictorial works
7616 Popular works

7618 Juvenile works
Lamaist literature
7620 General works
7622 History and criticism
7625 Essence, genius, nature

Doctrine
General works
7630 Early works through 1750
7632 1751-1949
7634 1950

7640 General special
7642 History
7644 Introductions
7645 Special subjects, A-Z

.L35 Lam-rim

7646 Controversial works against Lamaism
7648 Apologetic works

Modifications, schools, etc.
Lamaism - Continued
Relations to other religious and philosophical systems
7650 General works
7652 Relations to other branches of Buddhism
7654 Relations to Bonpo
7656 Other, A-Z

.H55 Hinduism

Special branches of Lamaism
7660 General works
Individual branches
Subdivide by Table VI decimally
For founders and other important leaders, see BQ7950
7662 Rñiṅ-ma-pa (Nyingmapa)
7669 Ni-guhi-ma-pa
7670 Bka'-gdams-pa (Kadampa)
For Dge-lugs-pa (Gelugpa, Dga' -ldan, Shwa-ser, Yellow Cap), see BQ7530+
7672 Sa-skya-pa (Sakyapa)
7673 Ṅor-pa (Ngorpa)
7674 Jo-naṅ-pa (Jonaṅ-pa)
7675 Nalendra-pa (Nalandapa)
7676 Źwa-lu-pa (Sect)
Bka'-rgyud-pa (Kargyudpa)
7679 General works
.9 Biography
.A2A-Z Collective
.A3-Z Founders and other important leaders, A-Z (VIII)
Including local founders
.M37 Mar-pa Chos-kyi-blo-gros, 1012-1097
7680 Śaṅs-pa (Shangpa)
7681 Dwags-po (Dakpo)
7682 Kar-ma-pa (Karma)
7683 'Brug-pa (Dukpa, Dookpa, Drukpa)
7684 'Bri-guṅ-pa (Drigungpa)
7685 Stag-luṅ-pa (Taklung)
7686 'Ba'-rom-pa (Sect)
7688 Other, A-Z (VII)
7690 Forms of worship. Religious practice
Ceremonies and rites. Ceremonial rules
7695 General works
7697 Service books
7699 Special ceremonies and rites, A-Z
.C65 Confession
.G87 Guru worship
Class here works limited to Tibetan Buddhism; for works limited to sects, see the sect

Modifications, schools, etc.
Lamaism
Forms of worship. Religious practice - Cont.
Hymns. Chants. Recitations
7700 Collections
History and criticism
7705 General works
7710 Local, A-Z
7715 Individual texts. By author or title
7720 Finance. Management

Ministry. Monkhood. Organization
7730 Collections
7735 History
General works
7740 Early works through 1750
7742 1751-1949
7744 1950-

7750 Handbooks, manuals, etc.
7752 Selection and succession of Dalai lama and Panchen lama
7754 Ordination of lamas

Education and training of lamas
7756 General works. History
7758 By region or country, A-Z
Under each country:

.x General works. History
.x2 Local, A-Z
.x3 Special institutions. By place, A-Z
Including monasteries

Sermons. Addresses. Lectures
Collections. Collected works
7760 General
Dalai lamas
7762 General
7764 Individual, A-Z

Panchen lamas
7766 General
7768 Individual, A-Z
7770 Individual, A-Z

Modifications, schools, etc.
Lamaism - Continued
Religious life
7775 General works
7780 Discipline, duties, precepts, etc.
Devotional literature
7785 Collections
General works
7790 Early works through 1750
7795 1751-

Devotion. Meditation. Prayer. Mysticism. Enlightenment. Perfection
Including Tantric yoga
7800 Early works through 1750
7805 1751-

Devotions. Meditations. Prayers (Collected)
7810 Early works through 1750
7815 1751-
Festivals. Days and seasons
7820 General works
7825 Addresses, essays, lectures, etc.
7830 Special, A-Z

Folklore of Lamaism
Cf. GR337, Folklore in Tibet
Collections
7850 Early works through 1750
7855 1751-

7860 History and criticism
7865 By region or country, A-Z
Under each country:

.x Collections
.x2 History and criticism
.x3 Local, A-Z

7890 Monastic life. Discipline. Rules
Monasteries, temples, etc.
7900 General works
By region or country, see BQ6330+

Pilgrims and pilgrimages
7910 General works. History
7915 By region or country, A-Z
Under each country:

.x General works
.x2 By province or state, A-Z

Modifications, schools, etc.
Lamaism - Continued
Biography
7920 General collections
Dalai lamas
For collections of sermons, addresses, lectures, see BQ7762+
7930 Collective
7935 Individual, A-Z (VIII)
e. g. .B77-779 Bstan-'dzin-rgya-mtsho (Dalai Lama XIV)

.N34-349 Nag-dban-blo-bzan-rgya-mtsho (Dalai Lama V)

Panchen lamas
For collections of sermons, addresses, lectures, see BQ7766+
7940 Collective
7945 Individual, A-Z (VIII)
e. g. .B75-759 Bstan-pa'i-ñi-ma, Panchen Lama IV, 1781-1854

7950 Other important leaders, A-Z (VII)

.A87 Atiśa, 982-1054
.M55 Mi-la-ras-pa, 1040-1123

.P32 Padma Sambhava, ca. 717-ca. 762
.T75 Tsoṅ-kha-pa Blo-bzan-grags-pa, 1357-1419

Other individuals, see BQ940+

Bonpo (Sect)
7960 Periodicals. Societies. Serials
.5 Congresses
.6 Directories
7961 Dictionaries. Encyclopedias
7962 General collections. Collected works
For collections of Bonpo literature, see BQ7965
7963 Religious education. Study and teaching

Modifications, schools, etc.
Bonpo (Sect) - Continued
History
7964.2 General works
By region or country
Tibet, see BQ7964.2
.3 Other regions or countries, A-Z

Bonpo literature. Bonpo authors
For sacred books (Bonpo Kanjur), see BQ7968.2+
7965 Collections. Collected works
Individual works, see the subject
7966.2 General works. History and criticism
.5 General special

Sacred books. Sources
Collections
Original
7968.2 Comprehensive
Class here collections of Kanjur alone or of Kanjur and Tenjur combined.
For collections of Tenjur alone, see BQ7976+

.5 Selections. Anthologies
Class here selections from two or more major groups of sacred books
Translations
7969.2 Comprehensive. By language, A-Z
.5 Selections. Anthologies. By language, A-Z
7970.2 General works. History and criticism
.5 General special
.7 Dictionaries
Including terminology, indexes, concordances, etc.
Special divisions and individual texts of Kanjur
7971.2-.29 Mdo (Sūtras) and other canonical texts (Table II)
.5 Individual texts, A-Z (Table III)

.B53-539 Bla med go 'phan sgrub thavs kyi mdo
.B74-749 Bskal pa bzan po'i mdo
.G94-949 Gzer mig

.G95-959 Gzi brjid
.M45-459 Mdo 'dus

.M46-469 Mdo rnam 'brel par ti ka
.S59-599 Skye sgo gcod pa'i mdo
.T48-489 Theg pa'i rim pa mnon du bśad pa'i mdo rgyud

Modifications, schools, etc.
Bonpo (Sect)
Sacred books. Sources
Special divisions and individual texts of Kanjur - Continued

7972.2-.29 'Bum (Prajnaparamitas) (Table II)
.5 Individual texts, A-Z (Table III)

.B85-859 'Bum Ñi ma dgu śar
.K53-539 Khams brgyad ston phrag brgya pa
.K54-549 Khams 'briṅ
.K58-589 Khams rtsa nes pa'i mdo

7973.2-.29 Rgyud (Tantras) (Table II)
.5 Individual texts, A-Z (Table III)

.G83-839 Gsan ba bśen thub
.M37-379 Ma rgyud sans rgyas rgyud gsum

7974.2-.29 Mdzog (Abhidharma) (Table II)
.5 Individual texts (Table III)

.M49-499 Mdzog phug

7976-7976.9 Tenjur (Table II)
For individual Tenjur texts which are commentaries of Kanjur texts, <u>see</u> the specific Kanjur text. For individual Tenjur texts and selections of subject oriented Tenjur texts, <u>see</u> the subject

7978 General works
Doctrines
7980.2 General works
.5 General special
Bonpo pantheon
7981.2 General works
.4 Individual deity, A-Z
Under each:

.x General works
Cults
.x2 General works
.x3 By region or country, A-Z

.D32 Dbal-gsas
.M37 Ma-tri

.M42 Me-ri
.S57 Sitātapatrā

.S73 Stag-lha-me-'bar

Modifications, schools, etc.
Bonpo (Sect) - Continued

7982.2 Religious life. Spiritual life
.3 Liturgy. Rituals
.4 Devotional literature. Prayers

.7 Organization. Government
.9 Benevolent work. Social work. Missionary work
7984.2 Monasticism and monastic life

Monasteries. Temples. Shrines. Sites
.5 General works
.7 By region or country, A-Z
Under each country:

.x General works
.x2 Local, A-Z or individual, A-Z if location is unnamed

Biography
7986 Collective
Individual
7987 Gsen-rab, Mi-bo (Table VIII)
For Gzer mig, Gzi brjid, and Mdo 'dus, see BQ7971.5
7989 Other individuals, A-Z (Table VIII)

Special modifications, sects, etc.
For Tables, see pp. 255-263
8000-8049 Abhayagiri-vasi (IV)
8050-8059 Sāgaliya (VI)
8060-8069 Amarapura (VI)
8080-8089 Hommon Butsuryu (VI)
Biography
8089.A2A-Z Collective
.A3-Z Founders and other important leaders, A-Z (VIII)
Including local leaders

.N34 Nagamatsu, Nissen, 1817-1890

8100-8149 Hossō (Fa hsiang) (IV)
Biography
8148 Collective
8149 Founders and other important leaders, A-Z (VIII)
Including local founders

.H78-789 Hsüan-tsang, 596 (ca.)-664

8150 Jōjitsu (Chen shih) (VI)

Modifications, schools, etc.
Special modifications, sects, etc. - Continued
8200-8249 Hua-yen Buddhism(Kegon) (IV)
Biography
8248 Collective
8249 Founders and other important leaders, A-Z (VIII)
Including local founders

.F38-389 Fa-tsang, 643-712
.G94-949 Gyōnen, 1240-1321

.M96-969 Myōe, 1173-1232
.T78-789 Tsung-mi, 780-841

8250-8259 Kusha (Chü she) (VI)
8260-8269 Mahā-vihāra (VI)
8270-8279 Mahānikāya. Tamanikāya (VI)

8300-8349 Nichiren (IV)
8319.6 Relations to other branches of Buddhism, A-Z

.S55 Shin (Sect)

Biography
8348 Collective
8349 Founders and other important leaders, A-Z (VIII)
Including local founders

.N56-569 Nichiji, b. 1250
.N57-579 Nichiren, 1222-1282

8350-8359 Bussho Gonenkai Kyōdan (VI)
8360-8369 Fuju-fuse (VI)
8370-8379 Reiyūkai (VI)
8380-8389 Risshō Kōseikai (VI)
Biography
8389.A2A-Z Collective
.A3-Z Founders and other important leaders, A-Z (VIII)
Including local founders
.N54-549 Niwano, Nichikō, 1938-
.N55-559 Niwano, Nikkyo, 1906-
8400-8449 Sōka Gakkai (Nichiren Shōshū) (IV)
Biography
8448 Collective
8449 Founders and other important leaders, A-Z (VIII)
Including local founders

.I38-389 Ikeda, Daisaku
.M35-359 Makiguchi, Tsunesaburō, 1871-1944
.T64-649 Toda, Jōsei, 1900-1958
8450-8459 Nieh p'an (VI)

Modifications, schools, etc.
Special modifications, sects, etc. - Continued
8500-8549 Pure Land Buddhism (IV)
Cf. BQ5125.H4, Hensō
For relations with Zen Buddhism, see BQ9269.6.P8
Biography
8548 Collective
8549 Founders and other important leaders, A-Z (VIII)
Including local founders

.G46-469 Genshin, Sōzu, 942-1017
.K87-879 Kūya, 903-972

.S53-539 Shan-tao, 613-681
.T36-369 T'an-luan, Shih 476-542

.T37-379 Tao-ch'o, Shih 562-645

8550-8559 Ji (VI)
Biography
8559.A2A-Z Collective
.A3-Z Founders and other important leaders, A-Z (VIII)
Including local founders

.I66-669 Ippen, 1239-1289
.S55-559 Shinkyō, 1237-1319

8600-8649 Jōdo (IV)
Biography
8648 Collective
8649 Founders and other important leaders, A-Z (VIII)
Including local founders

.H66-669 Hōnen, 1133-1212
.J57-579 Jishō, ca. 1544-1620

8650-8659 Seizan (VI)
8660-8669 Kōmyōkai (VI)
Biography
8669.A2A-Z Collective
.A3-Z Founders and other important leaders, A-Z (VIII)
Including local founders

.Y36-369 Yamazaki, Bennei, 1859-1920

8670-8679 Pai lien chiao (VI)

Modifications, schools, etc.
Special modifications, sects, etc.
Pure Land Buddhism (IV) - Continued

8700-8749 Shin (IV)
Including Hompa Honganji and Ōtani-ha Honganji
For relations with Nichiren sect, see BQ8319.6.S55
Biography
8748 Collective
8749 Founders and other important leaders, A-Z (VIII)
Including local founders

.E85-859 Eshin Ni, 1182?-1268?
.R46-469 Rennyo, 1415-1499

.S55-559 Shinran, 1173-1263

8750-8759 Kakushi Nembutsu (VI)
8760-8769 Yūzū Nembutsu (VI)
8770-8779 Rāmañña (VI)
8780-8789 Ritsu (Lü) (VI)
Biography
8789.A2A-Z Collective
.A3-Z Founders and other important leaders, A-Z (VIII)
Including local founders

.C47-479 Chien-chên, 688-763

8790-8799 San chieh (VI)
8800-8809 Sanron (San lun) (VI)
Biography
8809.A2A-Z Collective
.A3-Z Founders and other important leaders, A-Z (VIII)
Including local founders

.C55-559 Chi-ts'ang, Shih 549-623

8810-8819 She lun (VI)
8820-8829 Shugen (VI)
Including all branches
Biography
8829.A2A-Z Collective
.A3-Z Founders and other important leaders, A-Z (VIII)
Including local founders

.E55-559 En no Ozunu, 634-701

Modifications, schools, etc.
Special modifications, sects, etc. - Continued
8850-8859 Tachikawa School (VI)
8900-8949 Tantric Buddhism (Vajrayāna Buddhism) (IV)
Cf. BQ5125.M3, Maṇḍala
8919.4 Relations to other religious and philosophical systems, A-Z

.T3 Tantrism

8921 Special ceremonies and rites, A-Z

.H6 Homa (Goma)
.K34 Kālacakra (Tantric rite)
.M35 Mahāmudrā (Tantric rite)

Lamaism, see BQ7530+
8950-8999 Shingon (IV)
Including Kogi Shingon shū
Biography
8998 Collective
8999 Founders and other important leaders, A-Z (VIII)
Including local founders

.K33-339 Kakuban, 1095-1144

.K85-859 Kukai, 774-835

.S55-559 Shunjō, 1166-1227

9000-9049 Buzan (IV)
Biography
9048 Collective
9049 Founders and other important leaders, A-Z (VIII)
Including local founders
.S45-459 Sen'yo, 1530-1604
9050-9099 Chizan (IV)

9100-9149 Tendai (T'ien tai) (IV)
Biography
9148 Collective
9149 Founders and other important leaders, A-Z (VIII)
Including local founders

.C45-459 Chih-i, 538-597
.E54-549 Ennin, 793 or 4-864
Genshin, Sōzu, 942-1017, see BQ8549.G46+

.S35-359 Saichō, 767-822
.S55-559 Shinzei, Shōnin, 1443-1495

.U38-389 Uich'ŏn, 1055-1101

Modifications, schools, etc.
Special modifications, sects, etc. - Continued

9150-9199 Thammayut, Mahāyut (V)
9200-9209 Ti lun (VI)
9210-9219 Wonhyo (VI)
Biography
9219.A2A-Z Collective
.A3-Z Founders and other important leaders, A-Z (VIII)
Including local founders

.W66-669 Wŏnhyo, 617-686

9220-9229 Wŏn Pulgyo (VI)
9250-9299 Zen Buddhism (IV)
9269.6 Relations to other branches of Buddhism, A-Z

.H5 Hīnayāna Buddhism

.P8 Pure Land Buddhism

9288 Enlightenment. Satori
Biography
9298 Collective
9299 Founders and other important leaders, A-Z (VIII)
Including local founders

.B62-629 Bodhidharma, 6th cent.

.H83-839 Huai-hai, Shih, 720-814

.H85-859 Hui-nêng, 638-713

.T75-759 Ts'ung-shen, 778-861

9300-9309 Fuke (VI)
9310-9319 Ōbaku (VI)
Biography
9319.A2A-Z Collective
.A3-Z Founders and other important leaders, A-Z (Table VIII)
.I53 Ingen, 1592-1673
9350-9399 Rinzai (IV)
Biography
9398 Collective
9399 Founders and other important leaders, A-Z (VIII)
Including local founders
Bankei, 1622-1693, see .E57+
.E52-529 Eisai, 1141-1215
.E57-579 Eitaku, 1622-1693

.E59-599 Ekaku, 1686-1769
.I55-559 I-hsüan, Shih d. 867

.I56-569 Ikkyū Oshō, 1394-1481
.T33-339 Takuan Sōhō, 1573-1645

Modifications, schools, etc.
Special modifications, sects, etc.
Zen Buddhism - Continued

9400-9449 Soto (IV)
Biography
9448 Collective
9449 Founders and other important leaders, A-Z (VIII)
Including local founders

.D65-659 Dogen, 1200-1253
.E37-379 Ejō, 1198-1280
.R94-949 Ryokan, 1758-1831

.S54-549 Shokin, 1268-1325

9510-9519 Taehan Pulgyo Chogyejong (VI)
Biography
9519.A2A-Z Collective
.A3-Z Founders and other important leaders, A-Z (VIII)
Including local founders

.C45-459 Chinul, 1158-1210

9800 Other modifications, schools, sects, etc., A-Z (VII)

.G43-4392 Gedatsukai

.N35-3592 Nakayama Shingo Shōshū

.N96-9692 Nyoraikyo
Biography
.N969 Collective
.N9692 Founders and other important leaders, A-Z (Table VIII)
Including local leaders
.I77-779 Isson Nyorai Kino, 1756-1828
.P45-4592 Phật Giáo Hòa-Háo

Other beliefs and movements related to Buddhism are to be developed as needed

TABLES OF SUBDIVISIONS

TRIPITAKA AND OTHER EARLY TEXTS

Tables I	II	III	
0	0	.x	Original texts (Pāli, Sanskrit, Tibetan, Chinese, etc.) Subarranged by editor or date of imprint
1	.1	.x1	Partial editions, selections, etc. Subarranged by editor or date of imprint For selections sacred to a particular sect, see Table IV, 8, etc.
			Translations and adaptations (with or without original text) Subarranged by translator or adaptor
2.A1A-Z	.2.A1A-Z	.x2	Polyglot
.A2-Z	.2.A2-Z	.x22	Western languages, A-Z
3	.3	.x3	Oriental and other languages, A-Z
			Commentaries
5	.5	.x5	Early works to 1800
7	.7	.x7	1801- Including modern criticism, interpretation, etc.
8	.8	.x8	Sermons
9	.9	.x9	Dictionaries. Indexes. Concordances
			Bibliography, see Z7862+

TABLES OF SUBDIVISIONS

SPECIAL MODIFICATIONS, SECTS, ETC.

Tables

IV	V	
0	0	Periodicals. Yearbooks
	1	Societies, councils, associations, clubs, etc.
		For societies, associations, etc. in local areas, see 2
1		General works. History
.2		International associations, A-Z
.4		Young Buddhist associations
.6		Young men's associations
.8		Women's associations
2	2	By region or country, A-Z
		Under each country:
		.x General works. History
		.x2 Local, A-Z
		.x3 Individual, A-Z
		Financial institutions. Trusts
3	3	General works
4	4	Individual, A-Z
	5	Congresses. Conferences
5		General
.5		Special. By date
6	6	Directories
7	7	Museums. Exhibitions. By city, A-Z
8	8	Collections. Collected works
		Including selections sacred to a particular sect
9	9	Encyclopedias. Dictionaries
.5		Terminology
		Religious education
10	10	General works. History
11		By region or country, A-Z
		Under each country:
		.x General works. History
		.x2 Local, A-Z
.2	11	Religious education of the young. Sunday schools, etc.
.4		Religious education in the home

TABLES OF SUBDIVISIONS

SPECIAL MODIFICATIONS, SECTS, ETC.

Tables

IV	V	
	12	History
12		Collections. Collected works. Sources
		Chronological tables
		General works
.2		Early works through 1800
.3		1801-
.4		Historiography
		By period
.5		Early to *ca.* 1200 A.D.
.6		1201-1850
.7		1851-1945
.8		1945-
.9		By region or country, A-Z Under each country: .x General works. History .x2 Local, A-Z
	13	Persecutions
13		General works. History
.5		By region or country, A-Z Under each country: .x General works. History .x2 Local, A-Z
	14	Literature Including juvenile works
14		Collections
.2		History and criticism
.4		By region or country, A-Z Under each country: .x Collections .x2 History and criticism
	15	General works
15		Early works through 1800
.2		1801-1945
.4		1946-
.6		Popular works. Pictorial works
.7		Juvenile works
.8		General special e. g. Introduction to the sacred books of the sect, etc.

TABLES OF SUBDIVISIONS

SPECIAL MODIFICATIONS, SECTS, ETC.

Tables

IV	V	
15.9		Essence, genius, and nature
16	16	Addresses, essays, lectures, etc.
17	17	Questions and answers. Maxims
	18	Doctrine
		General works
18		Early works through 1800
.2		1801-1945
.3		1946-
.4		History
.5		Introductions
.6		General special
.7		Addresses, essays, lectures, etc.
.8		Creeds and catechism
.9		Systemization of teachings based on the sect
19	19	Controversial works against the sect. Polemics
.2		Apologetic works
.4		Relations to other religious and philosophical systems, A-Z
		.C35 Catholic Church
		.C5 Christianity
		.C65 Confucianism
		.T3 Taosim
.6		Relations to other branches of Buddhism, A-Z Prefer classification with smaller or less-known sect
20	20	Religious practice. Forms of worship
.2		Ceremonies and rites. Ceremonial rules
		Service books
.4		For priests, etc.
.6		For the laity
21	21	Special ceremonies and rites, A-Z
		.F8 Funeral service. Wakes. Burial service. Cremation
		.M4 Memorial services for the dead

TABLES OF SUBDIVISIONS

SPECIAL MODIFICATIONS, SECTS, ETC.

Tables

IV	V	
		Religious practice. Forms of worship - Continued
		Hymns. Chants. Recitations
22	22	Collections of hymns
.5		By region or country, A-Z Under each country: .x General .x2 Local, A-Z
		History and criticism
23	23	General works
.5		By region or country, A-Z Under each country: .x General works .x2 Local, A-Z
24	24	Individual texts. By author or title
.5		Liturgical objects. Vestments, etc.
25	25	Temple organization. Membership. Finance
26	26	Ministry. Organization. Government
27	27	Handbooks. Manuals
28	28	Election, selection, succession, appointment, etc. Ordination
29	29	Hierarchical offices
30	30	Heresy trials. By date
31	31	Education and training of the ordained ministry
32	32	Special ministries, A-Z Prefer classification in BQ5305, unless unique to the sect
		Preaching
33	33	General works
.5		Practical preaching
		Sermons Prefer classification with specific subject or canonical text
34	34	Several authors
35	35	Individual authors. By author and title, A-Z
		Religious life
36	36	General works
.2		Popular works, stories, etc. Including exempla
.4		Religious duties, etc. of the laity

TABLE OF SUBDIVISIONS

SPECIAL MODIFICATIONS, SECTS, ETC.

Tables

IV	V	
		Religious practice. Forms of worship
		Religious life - Continued
	37	Devotional literature
37		History and criticism
		Collections. Collected works
.2		Early works through 1800
.4		1801-
.6		Selections for daily reading. Devotional calendars
38	38	Devotion. Meditation. Prayer. Spiritual life. Mysticism. Enlightenment
	39	Devotions. Meditations. Prayers
		General works
39		Early works through 1800
.5		1801-
		Festivals. Days and seasons
40	40	General works. History
.2		By region or country, A-Z
		Under each country:
		.x General works
		.x2 Local, A-Z
.4		Special, A-Z
		Prefer classification in BQ5720, unless unique to the sect, e. g. .F6 Founder's Day
	41	Folklore
41		Collections. General works
.2		History and criticism
.4		By region or country, A-Z
		Under each:
		.x Collections
		.x2 History and criticism
	42	Benevolent work. Social work. Welfare work, etc.
42		Periodicals. Societies. Associations
.2		Directories. Yearbooks
.3		History
.4		General works
.6		Biography (Collective)
		By region or country, see BQ5899

TABLES OF SUBDIVISIONS

SPECIAL MODIFICATIONS, SECTS, ETC.

Tables

IV	V	
	43	Missionary work
43		Museums. Exhibitions
.2		History
.4		General works. Treatises
.6		By region or country, A-Z
		Under each country:
		.x General works
		.x2 Local, A-Z
	44	Monasticism and monastic life
44		History
.2		General works
.4		By region or country, A-Z
		Under each country:
		.x General works
		.x2 Local, A-Z
	45	Monastic life. Vows. Discipline. Rules
		General works
45		Early works through 1800
.5		1801-
	46	Monasteries. Temples. Shrines. Sites
46		History
.5		General works
		By region or country, see BQ6330+
		Biography
48	48	Collective
49	49	Founders and other important leaders, A-Z
		Including local founders
		Subarranged by Table VIII
		Other individuals, see BQ940+

TABLES OF SUBDIVISIONS

SPECIAL MODIFICATIONS, SECTS, ETC.

Tables

VI	VII	
0	.x	Periodicals. Societies. Congresses. Directories. Collections
1	.x1	Religious education
2	.x2	History. General works
3	.x3	Literature. Folklore, etc.
4	.x4	Doctrine. Forms of worship
5	.x5	Organization. Government
6	.x6	Religious life. Devotional literature
7	.x7	Benevolent work. Social work. Missionary work
8	.x8	Monasticism. Temples
		Biography
9.A2A-Z	.x9	Collective
.A3-Z	.x92	Founders and other important leaders, A-Z Including local founders Entries using Table VI are subarranged by Table VIII
		Other individuals, see BQ940+

TABLES OF SUBDIVISIONS

INDIVIDUAL BIOGRAPHY

Table

VIII

.x	Collected works Subarranged by date
.x2	Partial editions. Selections. Quotations, etc. Subarranged by date
.x3	Translations. By language, A-Z, and date
.x4	Individual works. By title, A-Z
.x5	Periodicals. Societies. Congresses. Exhibitions
.x6	Dictionaries. Indexes. Concordances
.x7	Biography and criticism
.x9	Sermons about the founder, etc.

TABLES OF SUBDIVISIONS

Table I

(1)	Periodicals
(3)	Societies
	Publishers and publishing, see BV2360+; Z116+
(5)	Conferences, etc.
(7)	Directories. Yearbooks, etc.
(9)	Collections. Collected works
(9.5)	Minor collections. Quotations, maxims, etc.
	Study and teaching
(11)	General works
	Individual seminaries, see BV4070
	Sunday schools (Church schools)
(12)	General works. Organization, etc.
	.A1 Societies. Conventions, etc.
(13)	Service books
(14)	Textbooks, etc.
(14.5)	Individual Sunday schools. By place, A-Z
	History
(15)	General works
	By country
(16)	United States (and Canada)
(17)	By state, A-W
(18)	By city, A-Z
	Cf. Subdivision (31), Individual churches
(18.5)	By nationality, race, ethnic group, etc., A-Z
(19)	Other countries, A-Z
(20)	By administrative unit (district, synod, etc.), A-Z
(20.5)	By subordinate administrative unit, A-Z
	e. g. Classes composing a synod
	General works. Theology. Doctrine, etc.
(21)	Early to 1950
(21.2)	1951-
(22)	Minor works. Pamphlets, etc.
(23)	Controversial works against the sect
(23.4)	Relation to other churches
(24)	Creeds and catechisms
(25)	Liturgy and ritual. Service books
	Hymns, see BV
(25.5)	Sacraments, A-Z
	Theology, liturgy, rite
	.A1 General works

TABLE OF SUBDIVISIONS

Table I - Continued

(26)	Government and discipline. Clergy and officers. Membership
	Sermons. Tracts. Addresses. Essays
	Prefer Subdivision (22) for addresses, essays, etc., on general doctrines or polity
	Cf. Subdivision (9), Collections, collected works
	Class sermons on special topics with the subject, especially biography and history
	For sermons for children, young people, etc., see BV4310+
(27.A1)	Several authors
(27.A3-Z	Individual authors
(27.3)	Benevolent work. Social work, welfare work, etc.
(29)	Individual branches, A-Z
	Camp meetings. Summer camps. Summer conferences, retreats, etc.
(30.A1)	General works
(30.A3-Z)	Individual
	Individual churches. By place
(31)	United States
(35)	Other countries
	Biography
(41)	Collective
(43)	Individual, A-Z

TABLES OF SUBDIVISIONS

II 1/ (3 nos.)	III 1/ (1 no.)	IV 1/ (Cutter no) 2/	V 1/ (Cutter no.) 2/	
(1) .A1	.A1	.x	.x	Periodicals, societies, directories, yearbooks
.A2	.A2	.x1	.x01	Official documents, governning boards, conferences .A1-5 General .A6-Z Local
				Study and teaching. Sunday schools
.A3	.A3	.x2	.x02	General works
.A32	.A32	.x22	.x022	Individual schools. By city, A-Z
.A4-Z3	.A4	.x3	.x03	History. General and United States
.Z4	.A42	.x32	.x032	By ecclesiastical jurisdiction, A-Z e. g. Dioceses
.Z5	.A43	.x33	.x033	By state, A-W
.Z6	.A44	.x34	.x034	By city, A-Z
.Z7	.A45	.x35	.x035	Other countries, A-Z
(2)	.A5-Z4	.x4	.x04	General works. Collections, collected works, dictionaries, encyclopedias .A1-5 Several authors .A6-Z Individual authors
(3) .A-Z5	.Z5	.x5	.x05	General special: Creeds, catechisms, liturgy, ritual, sacraments, government, discipline, membership
				Hymns, see BV
.Z6	.Z6	.x6	.x06	Sermons. Tracts. Addresses. Essays .A1-5 Several authors .A6-Z Individual authors. By author and title, A-Z
.Z7	.Z7	.x7	.x07	Special churches. By place, A-Z
.Z8	.Z8	.x8	.x08	Biography .A1-5 Collective .A6-Z Individual

1/
Tables II-V to be used only for churches and sects where indicated. In Table II double Cutter number is invariably used unless otherwise indicated. Table V is used in exceptional cases only. Wherever Tables II, IV, V are used, the inclusive numbers are indicated in the classification, e. g. BX7025+, Church of God (Anderson, Ind.)

2/
x= Cutter number

TABLES OF SUBDIVISIONS

TABLE VI

.x	Periodicals. Societies. Directories. Congresses
.x2	Dictionaries. Encyclopedias
.x22	General collections. Collected works
	Including selections sacred to particular sects
.x23	Religious education. Study and teaching
	History
.x3	General works
	By region or country
	General works of the country in which the sect originated, see .x3
.x32	Local of the country in which the sect originated, A-Z
.x35	Other regions or countries, A-Z
	Under each country:
	.x General works. History
	.x2 Local, A-Z
.x4	General works
.x42	General special
	Doctrines
.x45	General
.x47	General special. Special topics (not A-Z)
.x5	Relations to other religious and philosophical systems, A-Z
	Practice. Forms of worship. Religious life
.x52	General works
.x55	Liturgy. Rituals. Meditation. Devotion
.x6	Devotional literature. Prayers. Meditations. Hymns
.x7	Organization. Government. Ministry
	Monasteries. Temples. Shrines. Sacred sites
.x73	General works
.x75	Local, A-Z, or individual, A-Z, if location is unnamed
	Biography
.x9	Collective
.x92	Founders and most important leaders, A-Z
.x93	Other individual, A-Z

A

A.C. Bhaktivedanta Swami, Prabhupada: BL1285.892.A28
Aatim (Hindu deity): BL1225.A37
Abadim (Tractate): BM506.4.A15+
Abhayagiri-vasi (Buddhist sect): BQ8000+
Abhidhamma: BQ4195+
Abhidhammapiṭaka: BQ1200+
Abhidhammattasaṅgaha: BQ2495
Abhidharma: BQ4195+
Abhidharmadīpa: BQ2660+
Abhidharmahṛdayaśāstra: BQ2730.A35+
Abhidharmajñānaprasthānaśāstra: BQ2670+
Abhidharmakośa: BQ2680+
Abhidharmamahāvibhāṣāśāstra: BQ2690+
Abhidharmāmṛtarasaśāstra: BQ2730.A36+
Abhidharmanyāyānusarīśāstra: BQ2700+
Abhidharmapiṭaka
 General: BQ1160+
 Individual: BQ2490+
Abhidharmaprakaraṇabhāsya: BQ2730.A3697+
Abhidharmaprakaraṇapāda: BQ2730.A37+
Abhidharmasaṃgītiparyāyapāda: BQ2730.A39+
Abhidharmasamuccaya: BQ3080.A25+
Abhidharmasamuccayavyākhyā: BQ3080.A255
Abhidharmāvatāraśāstra: BQ2730.A44+
Abhisamācārika: BQ2429.8.A32+
Abhisamayālaṃkārāloka: BQ1915
Abhisamayālaṅkāra: BQ1955
Abidji (African people)
 Religion: BL2480.A3
Ablutions (Islam): BP184.4
Abors (Religion): BL2032.A2
Aboth de-Rabbi Nathan, see Avot de-Rabbi Nathan (Aboth de-Rabbi Nathan)
Abraham
 in
  the Midrash: BM518.A2
Abrahamites (Bohemia): BP605.A2
Absolute mind (Buddhism): BQ4270
Abū Da'ūd Sulaymān ibn al-Ash'ath al-Sijistānī: BP135.A13
Abubabaji: BP610.A32+
Acala: BQ4860.A4
Acāra: BL1312.3.A93+
Acāradaśā: BL1313.3.A83+
Acāryakriyāsmuccaya: BQ3340.A25+
Adam
 in
  the Midrash: BM518.A4
Adbhutadharmaparyāya: BQ2240.A24+
Adhimukti: BQ4340+
Adhyardhaśatikāprajñāpāramitā: BQ1890+
Adhyātmopaniṣad: BL1124.7.A45+
Ādi-Granth: BL2017.4+
Ādipurāṇa: BL1140.4.B74+
Aditi (Hindu deity): BL1225.A4
Ādityas (Hindu deity): BL1225.A443
Admonition (Judaism): BM723.5
Adonis: BL820.A25
Adults, Young, see Young adults
Advayasiddhi: BQ3340.A34+
Aeacus: BL820.A3
Aeneas: BL820.A34
Aesculapius: BL820.A4
Aesthetics
 and
  religion: BL65.A4
 Koran: BP134.A38
Afghanistan, Religions of: BL1750
African religions: BL2400+
Afro-Americans (Islamic history): BP62.B56
Āgama (Siddhānta) literature: BL1310+
Āgamas: BL1141.4+

Bible characters in the Koran:
BQ134.B5
Bible reading (Judaism): BM663
Bīja: BQ4445
Bījas (Letters)
Buddhist symbols: BQ5125.B5
Birds (Nature worship): BL442
Birifor (African people)
Religion: BL2480.B5
Birkat ha-ḥamah, see Blessing of the sun (Judaism)
Birth
Ancient Egyptian religions: BL2450.C65
Gautama Buddha: BQ932
Muḥammad, d. 632: BP77.2
Birthday of Gautama Buddha: BQ5720.B6
Bisexuality (Comparative mythology): BL325.B45
Bka′-gdams-pa (Lamaist sect): BQ7670
Bka′-rgyud-pa (Lamaist sect): BQ7679+
Bkaḥ-hgyur: BQ1260+
Bla med go ′phan sgrub thavs kyi mdo: BQ7971.5.B53+
Black Hebrew Israelite Nation: BP605.B63
Black Muslims: BP221+
Blacks (Islamic history): BP62.B56
Blasphemy (Islam): BP167.3
Blavatsky, Helene Petrovna (Hahn-Hahn): BP561
Blessing new temple, new house, etc. (Buddhism): BQ5030.D4
Blessing of the sun (Judaism): BM675.B53
Blessings in the present life (Buddhism): BQ4358
Blood
Comparative mythology: BL325.B5
Theosophy: BP573.B5
Blood accusation cases (Judaism): BM585.2
Blood as food or medicine (Islam): BP184.9.B5
Bobo (African people)
Religion: BL2480.B64
Bodhi: BQ4398
Bodhi-pūja, see Bodhi tree worship
Bodhi tree worship (Buddhism): BQ5030.B63
Bodhicaryāvatāra: BQ3140+
Bodhidharma (Buddhist leader): BQ9299.B62+
Bodhisattva: BQ4293
Bodhisattva stages: BQ4330+
Bodhisattva vinaya: BQ7442
Bodhisattvabhūmi: BQ3060+
Bodhisattvaprātimokṣa: BQ3060+
Bodhisattvas
Buddhist doctrine: BQ4293
Buddhist pantheon: BQ4695+
Body, Human: BL604.B64
Theosophy: BP573.H8
Bon (Sect), see Bonpo (Sect)
Bonpo (Sect): BQ7960+
and
Lamaism: BQ7654
Bonpo literature: BQ7965+
Book of life: BM675.M7
Borë Dēvaru (Hindu deity): BL1225.B65
Botany (Talmudic literature): BM509.B6
Boys (Buddhism)
Devotional literature: BQ5585.Y7
Religious life: BQ5470
Brahma (Hindu deity): BL1217
Brahma Samaj: BL1274.5+
Brahmajālasutta: BQ1300.B73+
Brahmakumari: BL1274.2+
Brāhmaṇas (Vedic texts): BL1116.2+
Brahmāṇḍapurāṇa: BL1140.4.B73+
Brahmanism and Buddhism: BQ4610.B7
Brahmans (Hinduism): BL1241.46
Brahmapurāṇa: BL1140.4.B74+
Brahmasaṃhitā: BL1142.8.B53+
Brahmāvaivartapurāṇa: BL1140.4.B75+
Brahmāvaivasvata: BL1140.4.B75+
Brahmo Samaj: BL1274.5+
Branches (Islam): BP191+
Bratas (Hinduism): BL1237.78
Breath (Theosophy): BP573.B7

C

Counselors and counseling
  Buddhism: BQ5305.C6
  Rabbis: BM652.5
  Shintoism: BL2224.55
Covenants (Religion): BL617
Cows (Hinduism): BL1215.C7
Creation: BL224+
  Comparative mythology: BL325.C7
  Islam: BP166.23
  Koran: BP134.C6
Creed, Thirteen articles of
  (Judaism), see Thirteen articles
  of faith (Judaism)
Creeds
  Buddhism: BQ4170
  Shintoism: BL2221.7
Cremation (Buddhism): BQ5020
  Gautama Buddha: BQ938
Crime and criminals: BL65.C7
  Greek mythology: BL795.C7
  Roman mythology: BL815.C74
Criminals, see Crime and criminals
Crocodile (Nature worship): BL440
Cross (Religious symbols): BL604.C7
Cūlamālunkyasuttanta: BQ1320.C85+
Cūlavaṃsa: BQ2640.C85+
Cūlikasuttas: BL1313.5+
Cullavagga: BQ2380+
Cults (Hinduism): BL1271.2+
Culture: BL65.C8
  Buddhism: BQ4570.C8
  Hinduism: BL1215.C76
Cultus: BL550+
  Asuras: BQ4795
  Arhats: BQ4875+
  Bodhisattvas: BQ4700+
  Buddhist pantheon: BQ4655+
  Devas: BQ4740+
  Gandharvas: BQ4785
  Garuḍas: BQ4805
  Gautama Buddha: BQ920+
  Kiṃnaras: BQ4815
  Korea: BL2236.C6
  Mahoragas: BQ4825
  Nāgas: BQ4765
  Vidya-rājas: BQ4850+
  Yakṣas: BQ4775
Cupid: BL820.C65
Curetes: BL820.C7
Customs, Religious
  Islam: BP184+
  Judaism: BM700+
Cybele: BL820.C8
Cyrene (Nymph): BL820.C85

D

Dādūdayāla: BL1285.592.D34
Dādūpanthīs (Vaishnavism):
  BL1285.5+
Daedalus: BL820.D25
ha-Daftar (Samaritans):
  BM960.3.D33
Dagari (African people)
  Religion: BL2480.D3
Daijō-sai, see Ōnie no Matsuri
Daily prayers (Judaism): BM675.D3
Daivatabrāhmaṇa: BL1121.3.D35+
Dakpo, see Dwags-po (Lamaist sect)
Dakṣiṇāmūrtyupaniṣad: BL1124.7.D35+
Dalai lamas: BQ7930+
  Sermons: BQ7762+
Dam-tshig-rdo-rje (Buddhist deity):
  BQ4890.D33+
Dana (Jainism), see Giving -
  Jainism
Danaids: BL820.D3
Dances and dancing: BL605
  Greek mythology: BL795.D35
  Judaism: BM720.D2
Darkness, see Light and darkness
Darśanopaniṣad: BL1124.7.D37+
Dāsa, Rāma Ratana: BL1279.892.D37
Daśabhūmikavibhāṣāśāstra: BQ1635
Daśabhūmīśvara: BQ1630+
Dasabodhisattuppattikathā:
  BQ2640.D37+
Daśadigandhakāravidhvaṃsana:
  BQ2240.D36+
Daśasāhasrikā: BQ2000.D37+
Daśavaikālika: BL1313.9.D38+
Dasaveāliya: BL1313.9.D38+
Daśnāmīs: BL1275.2+
Dāṭhāvaṃsa: BQ2570+

Evolution
  Islam: BP190.5.E86
  Judaism: BM538.E8
  Natural history: BL263
  Theosophy: BP573.E8
Ex-votos, see Votive offerings
Excommunication (Judaism): BM720.E9
The Exodus (Judaism): BM645.E9
Exogamy (Hinduism): BL1215.E5
Extrasensory perception (Theosophy): BP573.E9
The eye
  Comparative mythology: BL325.E93
  Religious symbol: BL619.E9

F

Fa hsiang (Buddhist sect): BQ8100+
Fa mieh chin ching: BQ2240.F32+
Fa-tsang (Buddhist leader): BQ8249.F38+
Fairies (Comparative mythology): BL325.F4
Faith
  Buddhism: BQ4340+
  Hinduism: BL1214.32.S72
  Islam: BP166.78
  Judaism: BM729.F3
Faith, Profession of, see Profession of faith
Faith, Thirteen articles of (Judaism), see Thirteen articles of faith (Judaism)
Faith cure
  Buddhism: BQ4570.F3
  Sufism: BP189.65.F35
Faith healing, see Faith cure
Fakirs (India): BL2015.F2
Falasha rite: BM672.F3
Fall of man (Comparative mythology): BL325.F3
Falsehood (Islam): BP188.14.F3
Families, Devotional literature for
  Buddhism: BQ5585.F3
  Islam: BP188.3.F3
Family
  Buddhism: BQ5430
  Gautama Buddha: BQ933
  Jainism: BL1375.F35
  Koran: BP134.F25
  Muḥammad, d. 632: BP76.8
Fan (West African people), see Fang (West African people)
Fan wang ching: BQ2460+
Fang (West African people)
  Religion: BL2480.F3
Farewell pilgrimage (Muhammad, d. 632): BP77.68
Farming, see Agriculture
Farohars, see Fravashis
Fast-breaking at the end of Ramadan: BP186.45
Fast-day prayers (Judaism): BM675.F3
Fasting
  Hinduism: BL1237.76
  Islam: BP184.5
    The five duties of a Moslem: BP179
  Judaism: BM720.F3
  Koran: BP134.F3
Fasts
  and
    feasts
      Hinduism: BL1239.82.F37
      India: BL2015.F3
  Islam: BP186+
  Judaism: BM690+
  Samaritans: BM970
  Shiites: BP194.5
Fate and fatalism: BL235
  Ancient Egyptian religions: BL2450.F3
  Germanic and Norse mythology: BL870.F3
  Islam: BP166.3
Fathers
  and
    children, Duties of (Judaism): BM725.5
  Buddhism
    Devotional literature: BQ5585.P3
    Religious life: BQ5440
  Comparative mythology: BL325.F35

Fear
  Judaism: BM645.F4
  of
    the dead: BL470
Feast of Esther: BM695.P8
Feast of Lights: BM695.H3
Feasts
  and
    fasts, see Fasts and feasts
  Islam: BP186+
  Shiites: BP194.5
Fellowship (Judaism): BM720.F4
Fellowship of Isis: BP605.F44
Female deities, see Deities - Female deities
Festival day sermons (Judaism): BM745+
Festival of Lights (Buddhism): BQ5720.T4
Festival prayers (Judaism): BM675.F45
Festivals
  Buddhism: BQ5700+
  Hinduism: BL1239.72
  Islam: BP186+
  Judaism: BM690+
  Lamaism: BQ7820+
  Samaritans: BM970
  Shiites: BP194.5
Fetishism: GN472
  Japanese religions: BL2211.F47
Field cults, see Woodland field cults
Fifth Council at Mandalay (Buddhism): BQ315
Finance (Lamaism): BQ7720
Finance, Temple (Buddhism): BQ5136+
Financial affairs (Synagogues): BM653.3
Financial institutions (Buddhism): BQ96+
Findhorn Community: BP605.F5
Finno-Ugrian mythology: BL975.F8
Fiqh: BP(140+)
Fire
  Comparative mythology: BL325.F5
  Greek mythology: BL795.F55
  Hinduism: BL1226.82.F5
  India, Religions of: BL2015.F55
Fire walking, see Timiti (Hinduism)
Fire worship: BL453
First Council at Rajagrha (Buddhism): BQ291
First sermon (Gautama Buddha): BQ937
Firstborn, Redemption of the, see Redemption of the firstborn
Fish (Ancient Egyptian religions): BL2450.F5
Fish, Wooden, see Wooden fish
The five duties of a Moslem: BP176+
Five Precepts for Buddhist laymen: BQ5485+
Five Wisdoms in Tantric Buddhism: BQ4394
Fjort (African people), see Bakongo (African people)
Flags (Buddhist symbols): BQ5125.F6
Fleeing (Comparative mythology): BL325.F6
Flowers (Buddhism): BQ5075.F6
Fo i chiao ching: BQ1680+
Folklore
  Buddhism: BQ5725+
  Lamaism: BQ7850+
Food
  Buddhism: BQ4570.F6
  Hinduism: BL1215.F66
  Koran: BP134.F58
Food offering (Hinduism): BL1236.76.F66
Foot (Greek mythology): BL795.F6
Foot worship (Hinduism): BL1226.82.F6
Footprints (Cultus of Gautama Buddha): BQ922
Forgiveness of sin (Koran): BP134.F6
Former lives (Gautama Buddha): BQ930

G

H

Islam
and - Continued
Hinduism, see Hinduism and Islam
Judaism, see Judaism and Islam
Sikhism, see Sikhism and Islam
Vaishnavism, see Vaishnavism and Islam
Islamic authors and literature: BP87+
Islamic law: BP(140+)
Islamic legends: BP137.5+
Islamic sociology: BP173.25+
Ismailites: BP195.I8+
Īśopaniṣad: BL1124.7.I76+
Isrā' (Muḥammad, d. 632): BP166.57
Israel Independence day prayers: BM675.I87
Isson Kyōdai (Buddhist sect), see Nyoraikyō (Buddhist sect)
Isson Nyorai Kīno (Buddhist leader): BQ9800.N9692I77+
Istadeva (Hinduism): BL1213.32
Itivuttaka: BQ1400+
Ittōen: BP605.I8
Itys: BL820.I8
Izumo Taisha (Sect): BL2222.I9

J

Jacob ben Asher: BM520.86
Jagannath (Hindu deity): BL1225.J3
Jahad (Holy War), see Jihad (Holy War)
al-Jahmiyah: BP195.J3+
Jaiminīyabrāhmaṇa: BL1121.3.J35+
Jaiminīyagṛhyasūtra: BL1136.3+
Jaiminīyārṣeyabrāhmaṇa: BL1121.3.J36+
Jaiminīyasaṃhitā: BL1114.3+
Jaiminīyaśrautasūtra: BL1129.6+
Jaiminīyopaniṣadbrāhmaṇa
Sāmaveda Āraṇyakas: BL1123.8+
Sāmaveda Brāhmaṇas: BL1121.3.J37+
Jain authors and literature: BL1315+
Jainism: BL1300+
and
Buddhism: BQ4610.J3
Hinduism: BL1358.2
Jambu-dvīpa: BQ4570.C6
Jambuddīvapannatti: BL1312.6.J35+
Jambūdvīpaprajñapti: BL1312.6.J35+
Janus: BL820.J2
Jason (Classical mythology): BL820.A8
Jatakarma (Hinduism): BL1215.J3
Jātakas: BQ1460+
Jātinirākṛti: BQ3170+
Jayākhyasaṃhitā: BL1141.8.J38+
Jazu (Buddhism): BQ5075.R7
Jehad (Holy War), see Jihad (Holy War)
Jen wang po je ching: BQ1930+
Jerusalem
Islam: BP190.5.P3
Judaism: BM729.P3
Midrash: BM518.J4
Jesus Christ
Anthroposophy: BP596.J4
Koran: BP134.J37
Jewish religion, Sources of: BM495+
Jewish tradition: BM529
Jewish way of life: BM723+
Jewish works against Christianity: BM590
Jewish works against Islam: BM591
Jews
Koran: BP134.J4
Talmudic literature: BM509.J48
Ji (Buddhist sect): BQ8550+
Jihad (Holy War): BP182
Hadith literature: BP135.8.J54
Jikko (Sect): BL2222.J5
Jinacarita: BQ1606.J53+
Jinja (African people), see Zinza (African people)
Jinn
Islam: BP166.89
Koran: BP134.J52
Jishō (Buddhist leader): BQ8649.J57+
Jīvābhigama: BL1312.6.J58+

Jiva (Hinduism): BL1213.56
Jñāna: BQ4380+
Jñānārṇavatantra: BL1142.6.J53+
Jñānasaṅkalinītantra: BL1142.6.J54+
Jñānasiddhi: BQ3340.J65+
Jñānolka-nāma-dhāraṇī-
  sarvagatipariśodhanī: BQ1670.J52+
Jñātādharmakathā: BL1312.3.N39+
Jo-naṅ-pa (Lamaist sect): BQ7674
Jōdo (Buddhist sect): BQ8600+
Jodo-e: BQ5720.E6
Jōdo sambukyō: BQ2010+
John, Bubba Free, see Bubba Free
  John
John, Da Free, see Bubba Free John
John the Baptist (Koran):
  BP133.7.J65
Jōjitsu (Buddhist sect): BQ8150
Jonaṅ-pa, see Jo-naṅ-pa (Lamaist
  sect)
Jones, Jim: BP605.P46
Joy (Judaism): BM645.J67
Judah, ha-Levi: BM550.J79
Judaism: BM
  Ancient Judaism: BM165+
  and
    civilization: BM537
    Buddhism: BQ4610.J8
    Islam: BP173.J8
    Zoroastrianism: BL1566.J8
  Conservative Judaism: BM197.5
  in the early centuries of the
    Christian era: BM177
  Koran: BP134.J4
Judgment
  Islam: BP166.85
  of
    the dead: BL547
Jukai (Buddhism): BQ5005
al-Jum'ah: BP186.15
Juno: BL820.J6
Jupiter: BL820.J8
Justice: BL65.J87
  Judaism: BM645.J8
Justice, Social, see Social
  justice
Jyotibā (Hindu deity): BL1225.J96

K

The Kaaba: BP187.4+
Kabirpanthis: BL2020.K3
Kadampa, see Bka'-gdams-pa (Lamaist
  sect)
Kaddish: BM670.K3
Kagen ingakyō, see Kuo ch'ü hsien
  tsai yin kuo ching
Kagura (Shinto rite): BL2224.25.K3
Kaigen, see Consecration of the
  Buddhist images
Kaisānīyah, see Kaysānīyah
Kaivalyopaniṣad: BL1124.7.K35+
Kako genzai ingakyō, see Kuo ch'ü
  hsien tsai yin kuo ching
Kakuban (Buddhist leader):
  BQ8999.K33+
Kakushi Nembutsu (Buddhist sect):
  BQ8750+
Kalabari (African people), see Ijo
  (African people)
Kālacakra (Tantric rite):
    BQ8921.K34
  Tibetan Buddhism: BQ7699.K34
Kālacakramūlatantra: BQ2170+
Kālacakratantra: BQ2170+
Kālacakrāvatāra: BQ3340.K35+
Kālakārāma Sutta: BQ1349.5.K35
Kalam: BP166+
Kālī (Hindu deity): BL1225.K3
Kālikāpurāṇa: BL1140.4.K34+
Kālītantra: BL1142.6.K34+
Kalki (Hindu deity): BL1225.K35
Kalkipurāṇa: BL1140.4.K35+
Kallah (Tractate): BM506.4.K3+
Kallah rabbati (Tractate):
  BM506.4.K35+
Kalpāvataṃsikā: BL1312.6.K36+
Kalpikā: BL1312.6.N57+
Kāma (Hinduism): BL1214.36
Kāma (Hindu deity): BL1225.K36
Kāmadhenutantra: BL1142.6.K35+
Kamagami (Japanese religions):
  BL2211.K35
Kāmākhyātantra: BL1142.6.K3592+
Kāmikāgama: BL1141.5.K35+

L

Maranānusmrti (Buddhist meditation): BQ5630.D4
Maranos: BM720.M3
Marias, see Gonds
Marīcismhitā: BL1142.3.M37+
Mārkaṇḍeyapurāṇa: BL1140.4.M37+
Marriage
  Buddhism: BQ5015
  Hinduism: BL1226.82.M3
  Judaism: BM713
Married couples, Young, see Young married couples
Married life (Gautama Buddha): BQ932
Married people
  Buddhism (Devotional literature): BQ5585.M3
  Islam (Devotional literature): BP188.16.M3
Mars: BL820.M2
Marsyas: BL820.M26
Martyrdom: BL626.5
  Islam: BP190.5.M3
  Judaiam: BM645.M34
Martyrs (Islam)
  Biography: BP72
Maruyama (Sect): BL2222.M3
Mary, Blessed Virgin, Saint (Koran): BQ133.7.M35
Maryam (Koran): BP133.7.M35
Masaharu Taniguchi: BL12228.S4
Mashona (African people)
  Religion: BL2480.M3
Mataṅgaparameśvarāgama: BL1141.5.M38+
Mathematics: BL265.M3
  Talmudic literature: BM509.M3
Mati: BQ4380+
Matriarchy (Comparative mythology): BL325.M3
Mātṛkābhedatantra: BL1142.6.M37+
Matsyapurāṇa: BL1140.4.M38+
Matsyendra: BL1278.592.M38
Matter (Buddhism): BQ4570.M37
Matuta: BL820.M3
Mawlid al-Nabī: BP186.34
Māya (Hinduism): BL1214.38
Mayas: BL2560.M3
Mazda: BL1580
Mazdaznan: BP605.M37
Mazdeism: BL1500+
Mbala (African people)
  Religion: BL2480.M33
Mbiem (African people), see Yanzi (African people)
Mdo 'dus: BP7971.5.M45+
Mdo rnam 'brel par ti ka: BQ7971.5.M46+
Mdzog (Bonpo Abhidharma): BQ7974.2+
Mdzog phug: BQ7974.5.M49+
Me-ri (Bonpo deity): BQ7981.4.M42
Meadows (Greek mythology): BL795.L3
Measuring, see Mensuration
Mecca, Period at (Muḥammad, d. 632): BP77.4+
Mecca, Pilgrimage to, see Pilgrimage to Mecca
Mecca and its pilgrimages: BP187.3+
The Meccans, Truce with (Muḥammad, d. 632): BP77.7
Medea: BL820.M37
Median religion: BL2250
Medicine: BL65.M4
  Anthroposophy: RZ409.7
  Buddhism: BQ4570.M4
  Islam: BP166.72
Medina, Flight to (Muḥammad, d. 632): BP77.5
Medina, Period at (Muḥammad, d. 632): BP77.6+
Meditation: BL627
  Buddhism: BQ5595+
  between God and man (Islam): BP166.76
  Hinduism: BL1238.32+
  India: BL2015.M4
  Lamaism: BQ7800+
  Mādhyamika School: BQ7475
  Mahāyāna Buddhism: BQ7438
  Shintoism: BL2224.3
  Theravāda Buddhism: BQ7280
  Yogācāra School: BQ7516
Meditations
  Buddhism: BQ5535+
  Judaism: BM724
  Lamaism: BQ7810+

N

O

P

Pain (Buddhism): BQ4235
Paine, Thomas: BL2735+
Paiṇṇas: BL1312.8+
Paippilāda: BL1114.7+
Palatu: BL1279.2+
Palaṭū Sāhiba: BL1279.292.P35
Palestine
  in
    the Midrash: BM518.P25
    Talmudic literature: BM509.P3
  Islam: BP190.5.P3
  Judaism: BM729.P3
Palestinian religion
  Ancient: BL1640
  Modern: BL2340+
Palestinian Talmud: BM498
Pāli version of Tripiṭaka: BQ1170+
Palms (Ancient Egyptian religions):
  BL2450.P3
Pan: BL820.P2
Panbabylonism (Assyro-Babylonian):
  BL1625.P3
Pañcappakaraṇaṭṭhakathā: BQ2525
Pāñcarātra (Vaishnavism): BL1286.8
Pañcaviṃśatisāhasrikāprajñāpāramitā:
  BQ1950+
Panchen lamas: BQ7940+
  Sermons: BQ7766+
Panegyrics (Muḥammad, d. 632):
  BP76.2
Panhāvāgarana: BL1312.3.P35+
Pannavanā: BL1312.6.P35+
Pantheism: BL220
  Bonpo: BQ7981.2+
  Hinduism: BL1213.38
  India: BL2015.P3
Panthoibi (Hindu deity): BL1225.P25
Paper (Use): BL619.P3
Papuan religions: BL2630.P3
Parables
  Buddhism: BQ5780+
  Hinduism: BL1215.P3
  in
    the Midrash: BM518.P3
    the Tripiṭaka: BQ1136.P35
  of
    Gautama Buddha: BQ915
Paradise: BL540
  Islam: BP166.87
Paramārtha-satya: BQ4255
Paramasaṃhitā: BL1141.8.P37+
Paramatthamañjusā: BQ2635
Pārameśvarasaṃhitā: BL1141.8.P38+
Parapsychology: BL65.P3
  Buddhism: BQ4570.P75
  Judaism: BM538.P2
Pāraskaragṛhyasūtra: BL1134.5+
Paraśurāma (Hindu deity):
  BL1225.P27
Pārāyanasutta: BQ1419.5.P36+
Parchment (Judaism): BM729.P35
Parent and child (Halacha):
  BM523.7.P3
Parents (Buddhism)
  Devotional literature: BQ5585.P3
  Religious life: BQ5440
Pari-nirvana (Gautama Buddha):
  BQ938
Pariṇāma: BQ4365
Paritta: BQ1529.5.P35+
Parivāra: BQ2390+
Parṇaśabarīdhāraṇī: BQ1670.P37+
Parseeism: BL1500+
Part-time ministry (Buddhism):
  BQ5170
Parvati (Hindu deity): BL1225.P3
Passover: BM695.P3+
  Prayers: BM675.P3
  Sermons: BM747.P3
Pastoral theology (Shintoism):
  BL2224.55
Pāśupatas (Saivism): BL1281.5+
Pāṭikavagga: BQ1295.5.P35+
Pātimokkha: BQ2320+
Paṭisambhidāmagga: BQ1490+
Paṭṭhāna: BQ2560+
Pattini (Hindu deity): BL1225.P34
Peace: BL65.P4
  Buddhism: BQ4570.P4
  Hinduism: BL1215.P4
  Judaism: BM538.P3; BM729.P4
  Theosophy: BP573.P3
Pegasus: BL820.P4
Pelts, see Hides and skins

Pure Land Buddhism: BQ8500+
  and
    Zen Buddhism: BQ9269.6.P8
Pure Land sūtras: BQ2010+
Pure Life Society: BP605.P8
Purification (Judaism): BM702+
Purifications (Islam): BP184.4
Purim: BM695.P8
  Prayers: BM675.P8
  Sermons: BM747.P8
Puruṣa (Hinduism): BL1213.54
Pūsan (Hindu deity): BL1225.P8
Puṣikā: BL1312.6.P87+
Puṣpacūlikā: BL1312.6.P85+
Pyrros: BL820.P9
Pyrrus: BL820.P9

Q

al-Qadirīyah: BP189.7.Q3+
Qadiyani: BP195.A5+
Qiblah: BP187.45
Qirā'āt: BP131.5
Quatrains (Islam): BP183.3
Qumran community: BM175.Q6

R

Ra (Egyptian deity): BL2450.R2
Rabbinical literature: BM495+
Rabbinical manuals: BM676
Rabbis (Judaism): BM651+
Race: BL65.R3
  Buddhism: BQ4570.R3
  Hinduism: BL1215.R34
  Islam: BP190.5.R3
  Judaism: BM645.R3
Rādhā (Hindu deity): BL1225.R24
Radha Saomi Satsang Beas, see Radhasoami Satsang
Rādhā Vallabhīs (Vaishnavism): BL1287.2+
Radhasoami Satsang: BP605.R33
The Rāgs: BL2017.427+
Railokyavijaya: BQ4860.R3
Rain, Prayers for
  Hinduism: BL1236.52.R35
  Judaism: BM720.R3
Rainbow (Comparative mythology): BL325.R2
Rainmaking rite (Japanese religions): BL2211.R34
Rāja yoga: BL1238.56.R35
Rājapraśnīya: BL1312.6.R38+
Rajneesh Foundation (International): BP605.R34
Rajputs (Religion): BL2032.R34
Rām Sanehīs
  Hinduism: BL1279.8+
  Vaishnavism: BL1287.3+
Rāma (Hindu deity): BL1225.R3
Rāmacandra (Hindu deity): BL1225.R3
Rāmacaraṇa Swami: BL1287.392.R36
Ramadan: BP186.4
  Hadith literature: BP135.8.R3
Ramakrishna: BL1280.292.R36
Ramakrishna Mission (Hinduism): BL1280.2+
Ramala Centre: BP605.R35
Ramalinga: BL1282.592.R36
Rāmananda: BL1287.592.R56
Rāmānandins (Vaishnavism): BL1287.5+
Rāmānandīs (Vaishnavism): BL1287.5+
Rāmānuja: BL1288.292.R36
Rāmañña (Buddhist sect): BQ8770+
Rāmānuja sect (Vaishnavism): BL1288.2+
Rāmatāpanīyopaniṣad: BL1124.7.R36+
Rāmavats (Vaishnavism): BL1287.5+
Rāmāyana: BL1139.2+
Rammohun Roy, Raja: BL1274.592.R36
Ramsnehi, see Rām Sanehīs
Raṇachoḍarāya (Hindu deity): BL1225.R344
Raṅganātha (Hindu deity): BL1225.R345
Rashi and his school: BM501.8
Rastafarians (Cults): BL2532.R37
Rāṣṭrapālaparipṛcchā: BQ1770+
Rationalism: BL2700+; BL2747.7

INDEX

Sūyagada: BL1312.3.S88+
Svāminārāyaṇa (Vaishnavism): BL1289.2+
Svarodaya: BQ2180.S94+
Svarog (Slavic god): BL935.S94
Svātantrika School (Mahāyāna Buddhism); BQ7478
Works of: BQ2750+
Śvetāmbara (Jainism): BL1380.S8
Śvetāśvataropaniṣad: BL1124.7.S84+
Swami Narayanis (Vaishnavism): BL1289.2+
Swami Order of America: BP605.S8+
Swami Premananda: BP605.S82+
Swastika (Religious symbols): BL604.S8
Sword (Religious symbols): BL604.S85
Symbolism of letters (Sufism): BP189.65.A47
Symbols and symbolism: BL600+
Buddhism: BQ5100+
Cultus of Gautama Buddha: BQ927
Germanic and Norse mythology: BL870.S87
Islam: BP182.5+
Judaism: BM657.2+
Koran: BP132.5
Zoroastrianism: BL1590.S95
Synagogue dedication services: BM675.S9
Synagogues: BM653+
Syrian (Semitic religion): BL1640

T

Ta fang pien Fo pao en ching: BQ2240.T313+
Ta pei chou, see Mahākāruṇikacitta-hāraṇī
Ta sheng li ch'ü liu po lo mi ching: BQ2240.T32+
Ta tsang ching (Chinese version of Tripiṭaka): BQ1210+
Taa Shōnin (Buddhist leader), see Shinkyō (Buddhist leader)
Taamidabutsu (Buddhist leader), see Shinkyō (Buddhist leader)
The tabernacle (Judaism): BM654
Tabernacle service: BM675.T2
Tablets, Memorial, see Memorial tablets
Tachikawa School (Buddhism): BQ8850+
Tadzhiks, see Tajiks
Taehan Pulgyo Chogyejong (Buddhist sect): BQ9510+
Taejonggyo: BL2240.T33
Taesun Chillihoe: BL2240.T34
Tai-Ahoms, see Ahoms
Taisei (Sect): BL2222.T2
Taisha (Sect), see Izumo Taisha (Sect)
Taita (African people)
Religion: BL2480.T27
Taittirīyabrāhmaṇa: BL1118.4+
Taittirīyaraṇyaka: BL1123.4+
Taittirīyopaniṣad: BL1124.7.T35+
Taittrīyasaṃhitā: BL1113.4+
Taiwa Kyōdan (Shinto sect): BL2222.T26
Tajiks (Religion): BL2370.T19
Tākākā (Hindu deity): BL1225.T3
Takamagahara (Japanese religions): BL2211.T3
Taklung, see Stag-luṅ-pa (Lamaist sect)
Takuan Sōhō (Buddhist leader): BQ9399.T33+
Talansi (African people), see Tallensi (African people)
Talāntāntarakaśāstra: BQ2910.T35+
Talavakārāraṇyaka: BL1123.8+
Talen (African people), see Tallensi (African people)
Talene (African people), see Tallensi (African people)
Talense (African people), see Tallensi (African people)
Talismans
Buddhism: BQ4570.A4
Islam: BP190.5.A5
Judaism: BM729.A4
Shintoism: BL2227.8.A45
Tallensi (African people)
Religion: BL2480.T3

Three Weeks (Judaism): BM695.T4
Threefold Buddhakāya: BQ4180+
Threefold Refuges (Buddhism): BQ4350
Thūpavaṃsa: BQ2640.T45+
Ti lun (Buddhist sect): BQ9200+
Tiber River: BL820.T6
Tiberinus: BL820.T6
Tibet, Buddhist history of: BQ7570+
Tibetan version of Tripitaka: BQ1250+
T'ien tai (Buddhist sect): BQ9100+
al-Tijanīyah: BP189.7.T5+
Tiḳun: BM675.R48
Tikun hatsot: BM675.T5
Tikun lel Shavu'ot, see Pentecost (Judaism)
Tikun shovavim: BM675.T52
Time
  Abhidharma: BQ4205.T5+
  Ancient Egyptian religions: BL2450.T55
Time and space (Buddhism): BQ4570.T5
Timiti (Hinduism): BL1226.82.T5
al-Tirmidhī, Muḥammad ibn 'Isā: BP135.A15
Tiryañ-gati: BQ4515
Tishri: BM693.T6
Titans: BL820.T63
Tithes (Judaism): BM720.T4
Titus, emperor of Rome
  in
    the Midrash: BM518.T5
    Talmudic literature: BM509.T5
Tivi (African people)
  Religion: BL2480.T5
Toda, Jōsei (Buddhist leader): BQ8449.T64+
Toḍalatantra: BL1142.6.T64+
Tolai religion: BL2630.T64
Tolerance (Buddhism): BQ4570.T6
Toleration (Islam): BP171.5
Tongues, Gift of, see Gift of tongues
Torah scrolls: BM657.T6
Tosafists: BM501.8
Tosefta: BM495+; BM508+
Tradition (Babylonian Talmud): BM503
Tradition, Oral, see Oral tradition
Training
  of
    Buddhist priests: BQ5251+
    lamas: BQ7756+
Translation of Tripitaka: BQ1120+
Transmigration: BL515+
  Hinduism: BL1214.74
  Judaism: BM635.7
Transmission (Buddhism): BQ4485+
Travel (Judaism): BM720.T7
Tree planting (Hinduism): BL1239.5.T74
Tree worship
  Greek mythology: BL795.T8
  India: BL2015.T7
Trees
  India, Religions of: BL2015.T7
  Nature worship: BL444
Tri-ratna Service (100th day after birth): BQ5000
Trials (Greek mythology): BL795.T85
Triangle (Religious symbols): BL604.T7
Trikālaparīksā: BQ3300.T75+
Trimśikāvijñaptimātratāsiddhi: BQ3030+
Triṃśikavijñaptimātratāsiddhibhāṣya: BQ3025
Trimurti (Hinduism): BL1213.34
Trinities: BL474
Tripiṭaka: BQ1100+
Tripurā Bhairavi (Hindu deity): BL1225.T7
Tripurasundarī (Hindu deity): BL1225.T73
Trisvabhāvanirdeśa: BQ3080.T75+
Trojan War (Greek mythology): BL793.T7
Trusts (Buddhism): BQ96+
Truth
  Buddhism: BQ4255
  Hinduism: BL1213.74
Tsoṅ-kha-pa Blo-bzan-graga-pa (Lamaist leader): BQ7950.T75
Tsung-mi (Buddhist leader): BQ8249.T78+

INDEX

Z

☆U.S. GOVERNMENT PRINTING OFFICE: 1985-456-622